MW00454419

BECOMING POETRY

# BECOMING
# POETRY

*Poets and Their Methods*

JAY ROGOFF

Louisiana State University Press

Baton Rouge

Published by Louisiana State University Press
lsupress.org

Copyright © 2023 by Jay Rogoff
All rights reserved. Except in the case of brief quotations used in articles or reviews,
no part of this publication may be reproduced or transmitted in any format or by any
means without written permission of Louisiana State University Press.

DESIGNER: Barbara Neely Bourgoyne
TYPEFACE: Adobe Text Pro

COVER IMAGE: *Orpheus,* ca. 1903–10, by Odilon Redon. Courtesy Cleveland Museum
of Art.

LIBRARY OF CONGRESS CATALOGING-IN-PUBLICATION DATA
Names: Rogoff, Jay, author.
Title: Becoming poetry : poets and their methods / Jay Rogoff.
Description: Baton Rouge : Louisiana State University Press, [2023] |
    Includes bibliographical references and index.
Identifiers: LCCN 2023007785 (print) | LCCN 2023007786 (ebook) | ISBN
    978-0-8071-8011-2 (cloth) | ISBN 978-0-8071-8090-7 (paperback) | ISBN
    978-0-8071-8096-9 (pdf) | ISBN 978-0-8071-8095-2 (epub)
Subjects: LCSH: Poetics. | Poetry—History and criticism.
Classification: LCC PN1042 .R565 2024 (print) | LCC PN1042 (ebook) | DDC
    808.1—dc23/eng/20230807
LC record available at https://lccn.loc.gov/2023007785
LC ebook record available at https://lccn.loc.gov/2023007786

*for Penny*

Out and around or even at home I wear
the work like a solitary prison cell.
It builds on itself always inward. I knock
against it and the breathing is tight but hills and woods
are there. I can lie down in it comfortably.
People see me who don't see the work
as though the work were a mirror from the other side
they can see through while inside I see the work.
They don't get in so much where I see and hear.

—WILLIAM BRONK, "CELL—APPARELLED"


For ere she reached upon the tide
The first house on the waterside,
Singing in her song she died,
          The Lady of Shalott.

—TENNYSON


There are two secrets to writing good criticism.
The first is apt quotation.
I forget the other thing.

—M. L. ROSENTHAL

# Contents

*Contents*

## III. THE EAR

# Acknowledgments

My thanks go to the editors of the publications in which these essays first appeared, sometimes in different form:

"Certain Slants: Learning from Emily Dickinson's Oblique Precision." Copyright © 2008 Johns Hopkins University Press. This article first appeared in the *Emily Dickinson Journal* 17, no. 2 (2008): 39–54. Published with permission by Johns Hopkins University Press.

"Pound-Foolishness in *Paterson.*" *Journal of Modern Literature* 14, no. 1 (1987): 35–44. Copyright © 1988 Temple University.

"Credentials." *Kenyon Review* 22, no. 3/4 (2000): 187–200.

"Heard and Unheard Melodies." *Kenyon Review* 20, no. 2 (1998): 171–76.

"The Aesthetics of Contemporary Sonnet Sequences: The Examples of Salter and Muldoon." *Literary Imagination* 12, no. 3 (2010): 335–43.

"Adding Feathers to the Learned's Wing" [as "Vendler Reads the Sonnets"]. *Salmagundi* 121/122 (1999): 256–66.

"Two Poet's Poets." *Shenandoah* 51, no. 1 (Spring 2001): 121–32.

"Andrew Hudgins's Blasphemous Imagination." *Southern Humanities Review* 32, no. 1 (Winter 1998): 25–33. Copyright © 1998 Auburn University.

"Archeological Gifts: Thomas, Hafiz, and Henry" [excerpted from "First Fruits"]. *Southern Review* 40, no. 3 (Summer 2004): 602–28.

"Better Poetry through Chemistry." *Southern Review* 43, no. 2 (Spring 2007): 451–60.

"A Formal Garden with a Real Poet in It" [excerpted from "Formal Gardens with Real Poets in Them"]. *Southern Review* 39, no. 4 (Autumn 2003): 869–90.

"Mary Oliver's Divided Mind" [excerpted from "Pushing and Pulling"]. *Southern Review* 41, no. 1 (Winter 2005): 189–209.

"New Bottles." *Southern Review* 47, no. 1 (Winter 2011): 156–71.

"Shocking, Surprising Snodgrass." *Southern Review* 42, no. 4 (Autumn 2006): 885–92.

"Why Poetry Doesn't Count as Song." *Southern Review* 48, no. 4 (Fall 2012): 684–97.

"On Writing the Sonnet Sequence *Danses Macabres:* An Interview with Stefanie Silva" [as "An Interview with Jay Rogoff"]. In *storySouth* 31 (Spring 2011). Reprinted with the kind permission of Stefanie Silva.

. . . .

"Presence," "Stonington," "Storm in a Formal Garden," "Was a Man," "After the Thresher," "Entry," "Writing It Down," and *"We used to say* Nothing's" from *Lifelines: Selected Poems 1950–1999* by Philip Booth, copyright © 1999 by Philip Booth. Used by permission of Viking

Books, an imprint of Penguin Publishing Group, a division of Penguin Random House LLC. All rights reserved.

"Cell—Apparelled" from *Our Selves* by William Bronk, copyright © 1994 by William Bronk. Used by permission of Talisman House Publishers.

Poems from *The Flashboat: Poems Collected and Reclaimed* by Jane Cooper. Copyright © 2000 by Jane Cooper. Used by permission of W. W. Norton & Company, Inc.

Robert Dana, "3:10. July. 2009.," "For Sister Mary Apolline," and "Looking for Sharks' Teeth" from *New and Selected Poems 1955 to 2010* (Anhinga Press, 2010), reprinted with the permission of the publisher.

*The Poems of Emily Dickinson: Variorum Edition,* edited by Ralph W. Franklin, Cambridge, MA: Belknap Press of Harvard University Press, copyright © 1998 by the President and Fellows of Harvard College. Copyright © 1951, 1955 by the President and Fellows of Harvard College. Copyright © renewed 1979, 1983 by the President and Fellows of Harvard College. Copyright © 1914, 1918, 1919, 1924, 1929, 1930, 1932, 1935, 1937, 1942 by Martha Dickinson Bianchi. Copyright © 1952, 1957, 1958, 1963, 1965 by Mary L. Hampson. Used by permission. All rights reserved.

Eamon Grennan, excerpts from "Facts of Life Ballymoney," "A Gentle Art," "Tower House, Ballymoney, 1978," "Lying Low," "End of Winter," "Cavalier and Smiling Girl," "Incident," "Porridge," "Lizards in Sardinia," "Kitchen Vision," "Headlines," "Firefly," "Woman with Pearl Necklace," and "Levitations" from *Relations: New and Selected Poems.* Copyright © 1998 by Eamon Grennan. Reprinted with the permission of the Permissions Company, LLC, on behalf of Graywolf Press.

Eamon Grennan, excerpts from "Facts of Life Ballymoney," "A Gentle Art," "Lying Low," "Cavalier and Smiling Girl," "Kitchen Vision," "Headlines," and "Firefly," reprinted by kind permission of the author and the Gallery Press, Loughcrew, Oldcastle, County Meath, Ireland.

Five lines from "The Peacock in the Garden," two lines from "Fleshly Answers," twenty lines from "Halfway Down the Hall," four lines from "The Fall of Troy," seven lines from "Sappho, Keats," seven lines from "Ode on His Sleep," four lines from "Two and One," eleven lines from "I Lean My Ladder," four lines from "In the Hammock," three lines from "Moments of Summer," six lines from "October," six lines from "The Last Movie," and seven lines from "The Wolf in the Bed" from *Halfway Down the Hall: New and Selected Poems,* copyright © 1998 by Rachel Hadas. Published by Wesleyan University Press. Used by permission.

Excerpts from *Hafiz of Shiraz: Thirty Poems: An Introduction to the Sufi Master* by Peter Avery and John Heath-Stubbs, copyright © 2003 by Peter Avery. Reprinted by permission of Other Press, LLC. Any third-party use of this material is prohibited.

"Early Sunday Morning," "The Beginning of Poetry," "Last Saturday," "Song against Natural Selection," "Infertility," "Omen," "My Grandfather's Poems," "The Sentence (*Inferno,* Canto Five)," and "The Asphodel Meadows" from *The Living Fire: New and Selected Poems* by Edward Hirsch, copyright © 2010 by Edward Hirsch. Used by permission of Alfred A. Knopf, an imprint of the Knopf Doubleday Publishing Group, a division of Penguin Random House LLC. All rights reserved. "For the Sleepwalkers" from *For the Sleepwalkers* by Edward Hirsch, copyright © 1981 by Edward Hirsch. Used by permission of Alfred A. Knopf, an imprint of the Knopf Doubleday Publishing Group, a division of Penguin Random House LLC. All rights reserved.

Edward Hirsch, "The Beginning of Poetry," "Early Sunday Morning," "Last Saturday," "Song Against Natural Selection," "For the Sleepwalkers," "Omen," "My Grandfather's Poems," "Infertility," "The

Sentence," "The Asphodel Meadows" from *The Living Fire: New and Selected Poems 1975–2010,* published by Carcanet Press, copyright © 2010 by Carcanet Press for the United Kingdom and the Commonwealth, excluding Canada. Used by permission of Carcanet Press.

Daniel Hoffman, "That the Pear Delights Me Now," "A Comfort," "A Special Train," "Violence," "Who Was It Came," "O Personages," "In the Beginning," "Summer," "It Cannot Come Because Desired" from *Beyond Silence: Selected Shorter Poems 1948–2003,* Louisiana State University Press, 2003. Used by permission.

Andrew Hudgins, "The Cestello Annunciation," "Dead Christ," and "Christ Carrying the Cross," from *The Never-Ending* by Andrew Hudgins. Copyright © 1991 by Andrew Hudgins. Used by permission of HarperCollins Publishers. From "The Glass Hammer," "Sit Still," "When I Was Saved," "Hunting with My Brother" from *The Glass Hammer* by Andrew Hudgins. Copyright © 1994 by Andrew Hudgins. Used by permission of HarperCollins Publishers. From "The Humor Institute," published in *Shenandoah,* vol. 46, no. 2, copyright © 1996 by Andrew Hudgins. Used by permission of the author.

Michael Jennings, excerpts from "Before Speech," "Squandered by the Hundred Millions," "Crocodile," "This, Of Course, Is What Money Won't Buy," "Hanoon," "Alexandra," and "Damaged Child, Shacktown, Elm Grove, Oklahoma, 1936," reprinted from *Bone-Songs and Sanctuaries: New and Selected Poems,* published by Sheep Meadow Press. Copyright © 2009 by Michael Jennings. Used by permission of the author and Sheep Meadow Press.

Excerpt from "This Be The Verse" from *Collected Poems* by Philip Larkin. Copyright © 1988, 1989 by the Estate of Philip Larkin. Reprinted by permission of Farrar, Straus and Giroux. All rights reserved.

Excerpt from "This Be The Verse," from *Complete Poems* by Philip Larkin. Copyright © 2014 by the Estate of Philip Larkin for the United Kingdom, the Commonwealth (excluding Canada), and Malaysia. Reprinted by permission of Faber and Faber, Ltd. All rights reserved.

Excerpts from *Horse Latitudes* by Paul Muldoon. Copyright © 2006 by Paul Muldoon. Reprinted by permission of Farrar, Straus and Giroux. All rights reserved.

Excerpts from *Horse Latitudes* by Paul Muldoon. Copyright © 2006 by Paul Muldoon for the United Kingdom, the Commonwealth (excluding Canada), and Malaysia. Reprinted by permission of Faber and Faber, Ltd. All rights reserved.

"Old Goldenrod at Field's Edge" by Mary Oliver. Reprinted by the permission of The Charlotte Sheedy Literary Agency as agent for the author. Copyright © 2004, 2005 by Mary Oliver with permission of Bill Reichblum.

"Just Lying on the Grass at Blackwater" by Mary Oliver. Reprinted by the permission of The Charlotte Sheedy Literary Agency as agent for the author. Copyright © 2004, 2005, 2017 by Mary Oliver with permission of Bill Reichblum.

Kay Ryan, "Bitter Pill" and excerpts from "The Pharaohs," "Polish and Balm," "After Xeno," "Is It Modest?" "Apology," "Osprey," "Bestiary," "Blandeur," and "Great Thoughts" from *The Best of It,* copyright © 2010 by Kay Ryan. Used by permission of Grove/Atlantic, Inc.

"Another Session" from *Open Shutters: Poems* by Mary Jo Salter, copyright © 2003 by Mary Jo Salter. Used by permission of Alfred A. Knopf, an imprint of the Knopf Doubleday Publishing Group, a division of Penguin Random House, LLC. All rights reserved.

Karl Shapiro, "The Alphabet" and excerpts from "Hospital," "The Fly," "University," "Drug Store," "Haircut," "Necropolis," "Emporium," "A Cut Flower," "Troop Train," "V-Letter," "There Was That Roman Poet," "My Father's Funeral," and "Tennyson" from *The Wild Card: Selected Poems, Early and Late*. Reprinted by permission of Harold Ober Associates. Copyright © 1998 by Karl Shapiro.

W. D. Snodgrass, excerpts from poems from *Not for Specialists: New and Selected Poems*. Copyright © 2006 by W. D. Snodgrass. Reprinted with the permission of the Permissions Company, LLC, on behalf of BOA Editions, Ltd. W. D. Snodgrass, excerpt from "Mementos I" from *After Experience: Poems and Translations* (New York: Harper & Row, 1968). Copyright © 1968 by W. D. Snodgrass. Reprinted with the permission of the Permissions Company, LLC, on behalf of Kathy Snodgrass.

"The Red Wheelbarrow" by William Carlos Williams, from *The Collected Poems: Volume I, 1909–1939,* copyright © 1951 by New Directions Publishing Corp. Reprinted by permission of New Directions Publishing Corp.

"The Red Wheelbarrow" by William Carlos Williams, from *The Collected Poems: Volume I, 1909–1939,* edited by A. Walton Litz and Christopher MacGowan, copyright © 2018 by Carcanet Press for the United Kingdom and Commonwealth, excluding Canada. Reprinted by permission of Carcanet Press.

Excerpts from the following poems: "Theremin: Solo & Command Performance," "Scrabble with Matthews," "Dithyramb and Lamentation," "Pentecost," "Dates, for Example," "Posthumous Life," "The Resurrection of the Dead, Port Glasgow," "White Lanterns," "The Shades," "God of Journeys and Secret Tidings," "The Ravenswood," and "Crayola: A Sequence" from *Interrogation Palace: New and Se-*

*lected Poems 1982–2004* by David Wojahn, copyright © 2006. Reprinted by permission of the University of Pittsburgh Press.

. . . .

I owe special thanks to several editors who showed hospitality to these essays. Marilyn Hacker first began publishing my poetry criticism in the *Kenyon Review,* back in another century, and since then I have been particularly grateful for the support of Bob Boyers at *Salmagundi;* David Mikics, whose ALSCW conference session on sonnets inspired the essay on Mary Jo Salter and Paul Muldoon, and who, with Susan J. Wolfson, subsequently chose it for a special number of *Literary Imagination;* and a remarkable line of editors at the *Southern Review*—James Olney, Bret Lott, Jeanne Leiby, and Jessica Faust—who frequently granted me space to talk about poetry, as well as other arts, and always took a gratifying interest in what I had to say.

My thanks also go to Skidmore College for granting me Research Associate status, and for an Emeritus Faculty Development Grant that assisted my work on this book.

While poetry has engaged me since I was five years old, a series of inspiring teachers enriched my understanding of it and helped nurture me into the writer I became: Hank Levy, Gerald Meyers, Michael Roman, Joel Conarroe, Roger Kaye, Daniel Hoffman, Philip Booth, W. D. Snodgrass, Paul Theiner, Richard Fallis, Jean Howard, and the extraordinary M. L. Rosenthal.

Over the years many friends and colleagues' wisdom about poetry has helped me develop my own critical confidence. I thank Bruce Bennett, April Bernard, Barbara Black, Bob Boyers, Peg Boyers, Terry Diggory, Sarah Goodwin, Maggie Greaves Ozgur, Rachel Hadas, Andrew Hudgins, Pat Keane, JoEllen Kwiatek, B. D. Love, John Menaghan, Susannah Mintz, and Bertha Rogers. Maggie, JoEllen, and Pat, as well as my wife, Penny Jolly, generously read portions of the manuscript and suggested desirable additions and necessary repairs. JoEllen also introduced me to the William Bronk poem that serves as one of this book's epigraphs. Sigrid Nunez deserves my gratitude for allowing herself to appear by name in the Introduction.

I am most grateful to James Long of LSU Press for his faith in this book, and to the manuscript's anonymous outside reader, whose suggestions led to its improvement.

Finally, I owe endless thanks to Penny Jolly for her loving and unfailing support of my pursuit of my vocation.

# BECOMING POETRY

# Becoming Poetry

AN INTRODUCTION

This book, *Becoming Poetry,* does not advance an argument for some kind of mystical transmutation of poets into the body of work they have created over their decades at the craft. Neither does it confound that work with the poet's biography, although readers have often treated poetry as a skeleton key to the lives of poets whose autobiographical poses have invited such an identification. Apparent confession in poetry did not originate in the late 1950s, but coincides with the history of lyric, from Sappho mooning over an unrequited love, to Chaucer complaining to his purse, Shakespeare bemoaning his two loves "of comfort and despair,"[1] Whitman celebrating himself and singing himself, Dickinson recalling an indescribably intense psychic state as "like a Maelstrom, with a notch,"[2] and onward through the twentieth century and into ours. The confiding intimacy poets establish with their readers creates the impression that here they are, upon the page, translated into the poetry they have given us.

That impression of presence is, of course, an illusion, and I don't mean that pejoratively. All art requires illusion, and poetry depends on the illusion of a person creating the semblance of life: a mind thinking, a body feeling, and a sensibility expressing itself through language. It is a sheerly symbolic presence that, regardless of the degree to which it shares those traits with the poet, is actually a fiction, a phantasm, granted the illusion of real existence through the reader's imaginative interpretation of markings on the page.[3] The poet of the Sonnets, who woos his young man and suffers at the hands of his lady "coloured ill," stands alongside Hamlet, Falstaff, and Rosalind as one of Shakespeare's supreme created characters, regardless of how much the sequence may autobiographically confess. Dickinson, for many readers an intensely personal poet, wrote to Thomas Wentworth Higginson in 1862, "When I state myself, as the Representative of the Verse—it does not mean—me—but a supposed person."[4] A poet's collection of imagined speakers and expressive voices does not equal or explain the biographical poet but constitutes part of what the poet becomes.

For becoming the work, becoming poetry, does not stop at the poet's becoming recognized as the set of voices and personae readers encounter in the poems. Rather, I hope that the essays in this book, published over a period of more than twenty years, make clear that the argument for the staying power of a poet's work, its likelihood to endure and enjoy a lasting identification with the poet, centers less on theme and character, and more on technique. Poetry does not present unmediated feeling, but in imagining a human presence, it creates an illusion of felt life through the devices and strategies available to the poet, an illusion that in turn creates responses in the reader. To take spontaneity as just one example, Allen Ginsberg's "I saw the best minds of my generation destroyed by madness, starving hysterical naked," carefully creates an illusion of emotional immediacy, which Ginsberg achieved partly by replacing the initial draft's "mystical" with the more kinetic "hysterical," and partly by removing the commas that originally separated the now-hurtling adjectives.[5] In the same way, Franz Kline's black-and-white paintings, exactly contemporary with Ginsberg's *Howl*, look emotionally raw in their giant gestural brushstrokes but, upon closer inspection, reveal fussy little edits in white paint, intimate articulations and corrections that Kline employed to shape his big black sweeps and swaths, perfecting the illusion of spontaneity.

Poems embody relations between form and impulse, technique and emotion, intellect and sensation. The apparently analytical methods of poetic technique, as Pound understood, ironically provide the means of communicating feeling. Technical expressiveness constantly furthers the imagined feeling of a poem, as when Shakespeare uses a single, rhythmically awkward metrical substitution to convey the realistically imperfect qualities of the woman his speaker loves:

Ĭ gránt | Ĭ név | ĕr sáw | ă gód | dĕss gó:
Mÿ mís | trĕss, whén | shĕ wálks, | *tréads ŏn* | thĕ gróund.[6]

The mistress, the technique tells us, doesn't possess a goddess's perfectly tripping iambic gait but, as I suggest in one of these essays, tends more to trip trochaically over curbs. Alternatively, the conflict between technical virtuosity and feeling can thrill, as in Donne's "A Nocturnal on St. Lucy's Day," when all the speaker's clever intellectual invention of elaborate metaphors for absence, erasure, and nothingness cannot erase the fact of his love's death, resulting in the poet's pretense of failed technique that is actually, and paradoxically, a technical triumph conveying profound sorrow. Sound can introduce similar tensions, such as the discrepancy in Keats's "Ode on a Grecian Urn" between "Heard melodies" in the "sensual ear" and the "ditties of no tone" imagined by the "spirit." His luscious-sounding, palindromic phrase "no tone," in fact, describes lifeless silence, and its sonorous tolling in *our* ears predicts the speaker's abandonment of the beautiful but lifeless, loveless world of the urn's "Cold pastoral" in favor of our realm of sensuous life.[7]

Because poetry's most vivid illusions emerge through the skilled manipulation of poetic technique, the argument for any poet becomes a technical argument. If we value Shakespeare, Donne, Keats, and Ginsberg as poets, our admiration stems from their ingenuity in controlling form, language, sound, rhythm, image, and figurative devices in order to create an imagined universe that we recognize as uniquely theirs, yet one that also, necessarily, appears to participate in the larger world we all share. In this way, a poet who has accumulated a body of work becomes recognizable as the sum of the poetry and the totality of its strategies. For that reason, I have subtitled this book

*Poets and Their Methods.* When we talk of Donne, Emily Dickinson, Edward Thomas, or William Carlos Williams, we generally do not mean the biographical person but the work that person has left us. The poet becomes the poetry.

Over half a century ago, the Shakespeare scholar Stephen Booth described *Hamlet* as "a succession of actions upon the understanding of an audience."[8] As a poet, I pay close attention to how poems work, how they operate as successions of actions upon the understanding of the reader, and how poets use the tools at their disposal to create a lyrically charged affective experience in our imagination. Those tools may range from the minutely technical, to the broadly thematic and stylistic, to the symbolic and allusive, and onward to the strategically structural quality of a single poem, a sequence of poems, or an entire book. An individual poet's work over many years shows a larger structural quality as well. As readers, we witness a poet's changing themes, obsessions, techniques, strategies, and styles as constituting a life in poetry. Many of these essays concern such lives in poetry and my subjective attempts to identify the essence and value of a number of poets who have become—or are in the process of becoming—their work.

The title section of this book, then, which contains half of its essays, examines volumes of poems selected from the author's complete oeuvre as it stood at the time I discussed it, poets who had begun that process of becoming poetry. The opening section looks intensively at how particular works of particular poets operate, ranging in time from Shakespeare to a number of my contemporaries, including Andrew Hudgins, Paul Muldoon, and Mary Jo Salter. In one of these essays, I talk about Emily Dickinson's poetic strategies next to my own, an exercise that taught me a great deal about what makes her art unique and inimitable. Since two of my essays deal with sonnet sequences, by Shakespeare and, in our time, Muldoon and Salter, I have also included an interview in which I discuss my own sequence, *Danses Macabres.*

The shorter concluding section considers just what we mean when we talk, often half-thinking, about "the music of poetry." One of its two essays attempts to clarify the distinction between the two art forms through a detailed examination of what happens to poetic texts when they become songs. The other discusses listening to recordings of poets reading their own work—yet another way of becoming the poetry—and how that experience compares to reading poems on the page. The two pieces aurally extend this book's investigation into the essential qualities of poetry and some of the poets who make it.

Unhappily, several poets I discuss are no longer with us, and their deaths have made them more purely their work. Unless we were privileged to be family or friends, the only way to know Phil Booth, Dan Hoffman, or De Snodgrass—all of whom taught me, all of whom, in different ways, played some role in helping me become the poet and the critic I became—is through reading their poetry. Poetry is who *they* became, and that is who they are. It may seem reductive, inaccurate, or inhumane to think of these gifted people, who loved, led lives, and had families, as what remains on the page. But looking at their poems, we see what they were and who they continue to be.

In 2020, when I published *Loving in Truth,* my own book of New and Selected Poems, I faced a highly subjective test of this notion. A dozen years earlier, when my collection *The Long Fault* appeared, I worried to my good friend, the novelist Sigrid Nunez, that the book, with its poems anchored in travel, historical events, photographs, works of art, and the omnipresence of death, might strike readers as impersonal. "No," said Sigrid, "I think it's a very personal book. Everything you love is here." But beyond the themes that obsessed me, the strategies through which I turned those objects of love into poetry resulted in a book through which the poet in me could be discovered. Whether poets transform their lives into art or strive to explore themes outside the self, their poetry necessarily reflects who they are, mirroring their personal obsessions and their stance toward the world through the technical choices they make and the styles they devise and accumulate. Although it covers forty years or so, much of my own life does not appear in *Loving in Truth;* yet readers opening the book enter that life nevertheless. As I look through it, even as I argue that it is not the whole truth, it reflects me back, saying, "Yet this is you."

# I.

*Formalities*

# Certain Slants

LEARNING FROM DICKINSON'S
OBLIQUE PRECISION (2008)

I'll begin with a confession. I cannot say that Emily Dickinson's practice influenced my early poetic development in any way I was conscious of, despite the critical commonplace of my youth that all twentieth-century American poets traced their ancestry from either her or Walt Whitman. Yet in the decades since my university days, when I consciously took as my models such postwar poets as Robert Lowell, John Berryman, and Randall Jarrell, and even in more recent years, when as I write I have found such diverse musics running through my head as those of Yeats, Auden, William Carlos Williams, Stevie Smith, Robert Frost, and A. R. Ammons, I have come to understand some key affinities between Dickinson's practice and mine. I have even on occasion consciously turned to Dickinson for instruction, and she has provided a glittering element in the amalgam of influences exerting pressure on my pen as it commits words to paper.

My beginnings as a poet had to do with Dickinson in only the most superficial ways. I stubbornly battled the free-verse tide of the times by working in iambics, and in quatrains, sestets, sonnets, ballad stanzas, and a variety of nonce forms, all with a kind of overheated glee. My practice didn't approach Dickinson's obsession with the ballad or hymn stanza—I was experimenting, trying anything, avoiding the pursuit of any single form as a matter of faith. At a time when apprentice poets heavily felt the influence of Whitman, mostly via Allen Ginsberg, I wanted to write poems that also contained multitudes but did not boast of doing so. I have held onto that poetic tenet—my desire for the reader to experience the sudden "superb surprise" created by "Success in Circuit." I wished to "tell it slant —" (Fr1263) and let my reader consequently realize "The Brain — is wider than the Sky —" (Fr598). Over the years, I have realized that these elements of my practice have brought me closer to Dickinson than I could have anticipated.

My essay's title, of course, alludes to one of Dickinson's most famous poems, "There's a certain Slant of light" (Fr320). I admire most the "certainty" of such slants, the paradoxical precision of her indirection. Her slant-rhymes, to take the most technically obvious example, multiply the semantic possibilities in her poems, while simultaneously focusing the intensity of each potential meaning until it burns like sunlight through a magnifying lens. My own poems often resort to slant-rhyme, the practice that brings my work closest to hers, yet I keep finding much to envy in her rhyming strategies. Dickinson's success in circuit also extends to the ambiguities of her imagery, her metaphors, and ultimately her process of using figurative language itself, so while we rationally struggle to parse what many of her lines say, we nevertheless intuit imaginatively what they do. We experience their precise creation of imaginative feeling—"internal difference — / Where the Meanings, are —." This revelatory grasping of multiple brilliant readings at once produces a sensation that strikes me often when reading her work, the feeling she prized in poetry of having "the top of my head . . . taken off."[1] I likewise aspire to having my poems appear magically to erupt into more meanings than the reader initially imagined they could have contained, and I continue to strive for a deceptively casual air in poems that wish to leave the reader breathless.

"There's a certain Slant of light" illuminates what I mean:

There's a certain Slant of light,
Winter Afternoons —
That oppresses, like the Heft
Of Cathedral Tunes —

Heavenly Hurt, it gives us —
We can find no scar,
But internal difference —
Where the Meanings, are —

None may teach it — Any —
'Tis the Seal Despair —
An imperial affliction
Sent us of the Air —

When it comes, the Landscape listens —
Shadows — hold their breath —
When it goes, 'tis like the Distance
On the look of Death —

 (Fr320)

Unlike our modern idiomatic use of "certain" as a code for its opposite—"vague" or "uncertain," as in "a certain *je ne sais quoi*"—Dickinson's "certain" conveys a specific "Slant of light," an exact time of day and season, a precise obliquity, which the poem's initial "There's" points to surely as an arrow. The line often cycles through my mind because, living in upstate New York, I *know* that slant of wintry light, but also because it so readily conflates a perceptual fact with an emotional climate. It also marks a rare occasion of a Dickinson line's prompting one of my poems.

One morning at an artists' colony in 1991, I woke, sat up, surveyed my room, and immediately thought, "There's a certain Slant of light"—more accurately, "*There's* a certain Slant of light." It was not winter but autumn, not afternoon but dawn, and my psychic weather was filled not with "the Heft / Of Cathedral Tunes —," or "the Seal Despair —," or "the look of Death —," but with the warm, golden glow of sunrise filling the room. Still in bed, I began drafting what became this sonnet:

THE LIGHT

The gold light's created in the east trees,
abrupt against trunks, lovely in the limbs

11

> looming like X-ray bones. In these rooms
> new light makes everything antique—the brass
> bed, oak dresser, last night's whisky—suffuses
> the rediscovered world like gilt combs
> combing gold hair, winnowing from my dreams
> streaks of sheer light whose falling mess of rays
> eliminates the need for clothes. White light
> at day's height batters us from far above
> the trees, wanting nothing to do with skin's
> effusions or healthy glow, but like night
> indifferent to the colors of my love,
> the gold light that dances around her bones.[2]

My sonnet, despite the form's enforced terseness, still requires thirty words more than "There's a certain Slant of light." I not only show the light source but also introduce a little origin myth for it—a source for the source, "created in the east trees"; Dickinson points "There." I lay out the physical and emotional landscape of my room's interior; she shows how "the Landscape listens —" to the psychological terrain the rest of her poem keeps implicit. I insert dark reminders of mortality— tree limbs "like X-ray bones," how the light "makes everything antique," its "falling mess of rays," and how it "dances around her bones." Dickinson, extraordinarily, also shows the effects of the light "When it goes":

> When it comes, the Landscape listens —
> Shadows — hold their breath —
> When it goes, 'tis like the Distance
> On the look of Death —

"Shadows — hold their breath" in the "Slant of light," their deathlike operations suspended, yet even they fear an ultimate darkness that will literally obliterate all shadows and, by implication, all figurative language. When Dickinson introduces "the Distance / On the look of Death —" as a disturbingly abstract simile for the passing of the light, the poem turns similitude inside out—she renders the process of figuration precisely ambiguous. Death constitutes no simile but the thing itself, from which the "certain Slant," no matter how it "oppresses," protects us. The light, however paradoxically and punningly it weighs upon us—"light" that proves hefty—feels preferable to its disappearance.

Dickinson has done everything backwards in this poem. The light grows heavy and the apparent vehicle of the simile becomes the emotional tenor of the entire poem, death emerging as the shadowy actuality lurking precisely behind it all. Further, I admire the poem's precisely oblique approach to theme: it claims insistently to be about a slant of light, yet just as certainly conveys profound feelings associated with darkness. My sonnet, while not nearly as ambitious or ambiguous, wouldn't exist without Dickinson. Her attention to "certain Slants" sensitized my perception to capture this very different—but just as certain—slant of light I found suffusing my room and place it in the peculiar sonnet sequence I found suffusing me.

"The Light" shows me using Dickinsonian slant-rhyming for expressive purposes. I typically enjamb heavily, so my slant-rhymes don't often chime—or clank—upon the ear as hers do. But I typically combine slant- with full rhyme, as Dickinson has in "There's a certain Slant of light." I have entirely slant-rhymed the octave of "The Light," suggesting perceptions a bit off, my willful interpretation of the sun-coating of the room in a golden glow eventually proving a kind of deceptive, autumnal fool's gold, something to be savored en route to the poem's harsher darknesses. My sestet introduces full rhymes as creaky as those in any Renaissance sonnet: "light" / "night" (together with the internal rhyme "height") and "above" / "love," and, though enjambed, they chime more audibly. Yet my concluding slant-rhyme, "skin's" / "bones," reasserts the difference between day and night, light and darkness, life and death, that the full rhymes attempt to confound.

In "There's a certain Slant of light," Dickinson uncharacteristically uses full rhyme, and she uses it ironically, to bring together musically the poem's antithetical feelings. Bleak "Winter Afternoons" suddenly acquire the fullness—the "Heft," though oppressive—"Of Cathedral

Tunes —." The absence of a visible sign of suffering—"no scar"—contrasts with the assertion of the presence of meanings, which simply, abstractly "are," just as the "certain Slant" is perceivably "There." The weighty "Despair" is countered by "the Air," while living "breath" finally, and perhaps too predictably, meets its end in "Death." Within the poem, as I suggested earlier, Dickinson collapses many of the distinctions between the emotional effects of these full rhymes, making "the Air," for example, feel as much like "Despair" as possible.

Yet the insistence of the poem's full rhymes can distract us from hearing the slant-rhymes Dickinson nearly buries in three of the poem's four stanzas, in lines one and three. Initially, while the "certain Slant of light" strangely resembles "Heft," the extreme slanting of the rhyme implies their contrast. In the second stanza, the Slant "gives us" not something resembling and amplifying it, but "difference," which, since it is "internal," shrinks the scale of the poem from the physical to the psychological. Finally, "the Landscape listens —" synesthetically to the "certain Slant of light" until it fades into "the Distance," leading to an altogether different silence. Each of these oppositions pinpoints a "certain Slant," a precise psychological or emotional state, and each rhyme keeps shifting the affective microclimate of both the speaker and the poem.

I also thought of Dickinson while choosing rhymes for a poem called "Cain's Gift," which likewise plays with contrasts between full and slant-rhymes:

CAIN'S GIFT

The blood cried up from the ground
and the air held its breath,
the earth's sunset-stained
face now an epitaph
for Abel's head and hands
thrust up from the grave,
that childish face profiled,
those hands clasped, a child

imagined by the sculptor
petitioning the God
who'd let the model murder
play out unimpeded.
From brother to his keeper
the singing from the sod
rose, a sunset lark
whose quavers left their mark

on Cain's consciousness,
setting him aquiver
at walking the cooling face
of earth, banished forever
from Salisbury's Chapter House,
a period put to his chapter,
and from the good book hurled
out to beget the world.[3]

The poem is in ottava rima, not in ballad stanzas, but cast, like a significant fraction of Dickinson's poems, entirely in trimeter. Like "There's a certain Slant of light," it does not use first person singular, but it feels far less personal than Dickinson's poem. I've slant-rhymed the first six lines of each stanza—the *ababab* lines—and used full rhyme for each concluding couplet, here following not so much Dickinson's prosody as Yeats's dictum that a good poem should "click shut" like a little box. Therefore, at the end, Cain's erasure from Genesis, exiled by God, ironically becomes his entry into *our* historical world, where he becomes our violent forefather. The one exception to my slant- vs. full rhyme "rule," rhyming "God" with "sod" in the second stanza, feels to me an appropriate juxtaposition of the creator with his fallible and often stupid medium ("You sod!") for making the first man, here an ambiguous "singing" substance, neither fully alive nor dead.

In "Cain's Gift," the air's horrified response to Abel's death—"the air held its breath"—resembles Dickinson's description of how, when the "certain Slant" comes, "Shadows — hold their breath." My line at first reminded me less of Dickinson than of Randall Jarrell's conclusion to "The Bird of Night": "The owl goes back and forth inside the night, / And the night holds its breath."[4] Could Jarrell have been thinking of Dickinson? Have I trafficked in goods first stolen from her?

Dickinson's oblique approach to theme has helped me address topics of political, social, and personal urgency while attempting to avoid rousing the reader's imaginative feelings through polemic, posturing, or sentimentality. Between 2002 and 2004, I wrote several poems alluding to the war in Iraq, some of them protesting our engagement there. "Folding the Flag" began out of my anger at the Bush administration's manipulation of media imagery, specifically the directive that, unlike in the Vietnam War, television news reports could not show soldiers' flag-draped coffins. Prohibited from grieving or watching others grieve, Americans would not suffer the sight of soldiers killed during the few short weeks the administration announced the war would require. Shock and awe belonged not to us, but to the enemy.

I researched the proper procedure for folding the American flag, which struck me as similar to a children's game.

FOLDING THE FLAG

With a lover or friend
stretch it out waist-height
and parallel to the ground.
Fold lengthwise so blue midnight

and its strict constellation
vanishes under pure-white
and blood-red, a frisson
along the stripes, shot

between you. Fold again
lengthwise, a lot like unmaking
a bed in which no one
is ever just sleeping.

The stars should stay outside
as in the universe.

From the stripy end, fold
it up in small triangles,

kissing when you meet.
Tuck in the end, creating
a cocked newspaper hat
from whole cloth, a thing

useful in comforting
a suddenly public wife
suddenly veiled, her gold ring
shining like eternal life,

like moist eyes, like the bright stars
in her jaunty souvenir cap,
the weight of their universe
pressing into her lap.

(*Long Fault* 13)

At the time, I sensed Dickinson's influence in the poem only in the most general, formal ways: trimeter quatrains, albeit more radically enjambed than her lines or stanzas, with a few tetrameter substitutions, plus my habitual slant-rhyme, inspired by her. I brought my slant-rhymes in the stanzas' second and fourth lines gradually closer together, arriving first at a full rhyme between a feminine and masculine ending ("creating"/"thing"), then culminating in full masculine rhymes ("wife"/"life," "cap"/"lap"). Here again, I wanted the poem to click shut—in this case, like the soldier's coffin the poem never mentions.

I also wanted the poem to accumulate hints of despair and violence before turning the flag over to the Iraq war-widow in the last two stanzas: the disappearance of the flag's stars, the "blood-red" stripes "shot // between" the two folders, and the ambiguity of the "bed in which no one / is ever just sleeping," an image suggesting a death-bed, but also whose erotic potential becomes childishly consummated in "kissing when you meet." The poem, if not the speaker, alludes to the Bush administration's deceptions by calling the folded flag "a cocked . . . hat" and something made "from whole cloth," the first idiom denoting a complete disaster, as when something gets "knocked into a cocked hat," and the second a complete fabrication. The Napoleonic "newspaper hat" of children's games, while approximating the triangular shape of the folded flag, both targets the media's complicity and implies contempt for the administration's imperialistic playing at war, toying with human lives. The final stanzas maintain a *faux naïf* cheeriness ("jaunty souvenir cap") while offering glimpses of the real toll of the war in the stoic suffering of the widow ("moist eyes," "the weight" of the stars "pressing into her lap").

After writing "Folding the Flag," I guessed it might have more affinities with Dickinson than I thought. My gesture at dark humor—the implication that any widow would welcome such a flag-hat with delight—tonally reminded me of one of Dickinson's shocking jokes: "Before I got my eye put out / I liked as well to see —" (Fr336). Here Dickinson makes a similar show of calm in service of the unspeakable, as if death in war and being blinded—which do happen every day—meant nothing special. Yet Dickinson's "got" makes this opening all the more puzzling, suggesting both helpless victimization and willful volition. The ambiguity broadens almost cosmically, just when most poets would pin down the specific event and localize the feeling.

I sought out Dickinson's most explicit Civil War poems to see how she had, in fact, addressed deaths in war, a war quite different from ours in Iraq, and was stunned when I encountered "When I was small, a Woman died":

> When I was small, a Woman died —
> Today — her Only Boy
> Went up from the Potomac —
> His face all Victory
>
> To look at her — How slowly
> The Seasons must have turned
> Till Bullets clipt an Angle
> And He passed quickly round —

If pride shall be in Paradise —
Ourself cannot decide —
Of their imperial conduct —
No person testified —

But, proud in Apparition —
That Woman and her Boy
Pass back and forth, before my Brain
As even in the sky —

I'm confident, that Bravoes —
Perpetual break abroad
For Braveries, remote as this
In Yonder Maryland —

(Fr518)

It's an amazing, deceptively casual poem. Like "Folding the Flag," it uses slant-rhymed, trimeter quatrains, with four substitutions of a tetrameter line. But whole skies open up, quite literally, in the enjambment, uncharacteristic for Dickinson, between the first and second stanzas. At first we read the dead woman's "Only Boy / Went up from the Potomac —" as if he returned home to New England from the war, "Went up" a common figure for traveling north. But the second stanza confirms that it's not a dead metaphor at all; rather, the soldier is dead: he has literally risen into "Paradise," in order "To look at her —." Dickinson's bizarrely playful account exhibits some of the same *faux naïf* qualities as my "Folding the Flag." Death becomes a children's game, a peculiar hide-and-seek in which the soldier, feeling "How slowly / The Seasons must have turned" without his mother, suddenly has his route smoothed: "Bullets clipt an Angle / And He passed quickly round —." Instead of "clipping" and killing him—and it's unclear whether Dickinson is introducing an erotic note by punning on the archaic meaning of "clip" as "kiss"—the Confederate rifles chip away the corners of the imagined obstacles keeping him from heaven. He then "passed quickly round —," a deliberate evasion of the cliché "passing away" that nevertheless calls that euphemism to mind.

The speaker's choice of "Yonder," and even the alternative reading "Scarlet," rather than, say, "Bloody," keeps its "Distance / On the look of Death —" (Fr320), pretending death lies far off, despite Dickinson's knowledge that the poem is steeped in it.

The speaker, then, imagines the soldier's journey to his mother as an entirely voluntary quest whose aim, "To look at her —," simultaneously captures the dumbstruck wonder of meeting a long-dead loved one in heaven and prevents the reunion from collapsing into hugging-and-kissing sentimentality. The austere feeling is strange and precise. The supposedly voluntary nature of his journey also resonates ironically against what surely was no intentional self-sacrifice on the battlefield. This ambiguity opens larger questions regarding the war—for example, whether these young soldiers willingly gave their last full measure of devotion, or were coerced or cajoled into laying down their lives. By refusing to confront these issues explicitly, Dickinson lets the ambivalences hang tantalizingly in the air, precisely where her speaker imagines the mother and son. The poem pretends not to commit to the idea of pride's persisting in heaven, yet simultaneously offers a vision—an "Apparition"—of its doing so. Through this certain slant, Dickinson creates a specific ambiguity about whether the Only Boy's death truly merits "Bravoes — . . . / . . . / . . . For Braveries" or despair over the waste of war that we prettify as a leap into Paradise. Unlike my partisan "Folding the Flag," Dickinson's poem, though written in abolitionist Amherst, refuses to take sides regarding the war's moral justice—its causes and issues appear nowhere—so we experience the feelings connected with the soldier's death in a larger, existential way.

The war becomes positively metaphysical—and nearly inscrutable—in Dickinson's "The Battle fought between the Soul," a poem that, like "There's a certain Slant of light," grows increasingly diffuse and abstract:

The Battle fought between the Soul
And No Man — is the One

Of all the Battles prevalent —
By far the Greater One —

No News of it is had abroad —
It's Bodiless Campaign
Establishes, and terminates —
Invisible — Unknown —

Nor History — record it —
As Legions of a Night
The Sunrise scatters — These endure —
Enact — and terminate —

    (Fr629)

Once again, what here is the tenor and what the vehicle? Does the psychological or spiritual war "between the Soul / And No Man —" allude to the Civil War, or does that historical war represent the invisible "Bodiless Campaign," whether an individual psychomachia or the ultimate, world-historical struggle between good and evil? Does the national trauma evoke nightmares, the satanic-sounding "Legions of a Night," or will the actual fighting ultimately scatter with the sunrise "and terminate" (or "dissipate," as the alternate reading suggests), like a bad dream? The reader plunges into a twilit "No Man['s]" Land, whether a psychological miasma or the confusion of a foggy or smoke-filled battlefield. Yet it's a nocturnal confusion that "The Sunrise scatters —" with its certain slants of light.

We can read the poem's journey into this strange oblivion in the progress of its rhymes, which invert the rhyming strategy I use in "Folding the Flag." Dickinson begins with an unusual resort to identical rhyme, "One" and "One," before metaphor, rhyme, and reason spin out of control. She begins with all the truth—the poem's ultimate battles collapse into "One" through the rhyme—and ends by telling it slant. First the apparently certain "Campaign" expresses its "Bodiless" nature by slant-rhyming with "Unknown"; finally the equally certain "Night" meets an abrupt end in "terminate," a slant-*rime riche* that resembles the opening stanza's "One" / "One" (*rime riche* denotes a perfect homonym; by slant-*rime riche* I mean a rhyme using identical consonants). Yet by slant-rhyming on the secondary stress of "-nate," the ending instead throws us further off balance; this poem's box clicks not shut but open, like Pandora's, allowing its spilled contents, all the wars alluded to here—historical, psychological, and cosmic—to suffuse the atmosphere of both poem and planet.

I want to conclude with a poem of mine inspired by an event I witnessed, but also partly filtered through Dickinson's sensibility. Lying on a beach, watching hordes of nearly naked people strolling between me and the waves, I saw a family of Mennonites spread their blanket, chat among themselves, and enter the water, the women wearing their long, nineteenth-century-style dresses. I suddenly found them more intriguing, even more titillating than the young women in bikinis and thongs. By the time I had finished the poem, I realized I had experienced a living enactment of Dickinson's "I started Early — Took my Dog":

I started Early — Took my Dog —
And visited the Sea —
The Mermaids in the Basement
Came out to look at me —

And Frigates — in the Upper Floor
Extended Hempen Hands —
Presuming Me to be a Mouse —
Aground — opon the Sands —

But no Man moved Me — till the Tide
Went past my simple Shoe —
And past my Apron — and my Belt
And past my Boddice — too —

And made as He would eat me up —
As wholly as a Dew
Opon a Dandelion's Sleeve —
And then — I started — too —

And He — He followed — close behind —
I felt His Silver Heel
Opon my Ancle — Then My Shoes
Would overflow with Pearl —

Until We met the Solid Town —
No One He seemed to know —
And bowing — with a Mighty look —
At me — The Sea withdrew —

    (Fr 656)

Dickinson focuses on the intimate encounter between her speaker and the sea. She first gestures at realism via the speaker's dog, who promptly disappears, then at a fantasy world with mermaids, who also depart. The speaker domesticates the sea, turning it into a house with a "Basement" and "Upper Floor," but this feminizing figurative strategy yields to the boldly masculine water that overwhelms her—the two middle stanzas' rhymes ("ooh! ooh!") suggesting her arousal—fills "My Shoes" with "Pearl," and then withdraws. Actually, it is a double withdrawal, as the sea pursues her toward "the Solid Town —," which presumably comforts the speaker but makes the sea uneasy, for "No One He seemed to know —." The pursuit is by no means one-sided, for she "felt His Silver Heel"—not his advancing toe—"Opon my Ancle —," indicating the sea's retreat from her and her human world; thus the poem enacts a back-and-forth motion, its sexuality more like a nineteenth-century dance than a rape, the sea behaving more like Darcy than Rochester. The poem's barely veiled sexuality parallels the sensuousness I aimed for in the following blank-verse poem:

MENNONITES BY THE SEA

Those nearly naked sauntering by, breasts
bikinied and buttocks thonged, rolling along
beneath white dazzle, before the turquoise sea,
their moist, sun-venomed fascination—vanished.

More than the dolphin leaping fifty yards
from shore, a group of women has swept me
off to the elemental realm of Homer:
not Nausicaa and pals tossing their beach ball,
but something homelier, the world of Winslow,
at once boldly and shyly American.
Mist rises from the sea around these barefoot
six in their brown, black, slate blue, wholesome gray
ankle-length frocks, sedately bobbling, pigeons
among the jungle flock, their tresses tucked
in tight white muslin caps with strings dangling
in the sole gesture of devil-may-care.
The youngest of them runs along the beach,
hair unbonneted, bunched in a white scrunchie.
She teases her bearded father in his homespun
trousers and suspenders, his boots redeeming
him from the burning sand, his broad-brimmed hat
staving off the classical sun. The sea
kisses the women's hems, infusing their
skirts with its brackish solution. They enter
a step, a step further, the ocean spanking
their dresses against their limbs, unexposed
and pale, until the fabric snaps like spandex
on a hip-hop siren, or Nefertiti's
splashy wrappings. How deep will they wade in?
They wear their dresses as the fish wear water,
as if no one were watching, no one lying
nearly naked and nearly unashamed.

    (*Long Fault* 57)

Dickinson's economy contrasts impressively with my expansive-
ness. I populate my poem with beachgoers (her witnesses, dog and
mermaids, instantly vanish, as does my dolphin), and I intertwine
mythic and historical contexts through allusions to two Homers,
the epic poet and the American painter. The now-exotic nature of
the women's nineteenth-century dress prompts my full description,

whereas Dickinson, describing the commonplace costume of her time, needs only "Shoe," "Apron," "Belt," and "Boddice." My ocean, kissing and infusing, but also "spanking," proves neither as virile nor as romantic as her sea, which ends its tryst with the speaker by chivalrously "bowing — with a Mighty look — / At me," as it postcoitally "withdrew —."

Through my speaker, witness and voyeur to the romance between sea and women, I have tried to achieve a sense of wonder resembling that of Dickinson's poem. My question "How deep will they wade in?" and the simile immediately following suggest that, unlike Dickinson's speaker, the Mennonite women find themselves in their element when they have allowed the sea to saturate their modest gowns: "They wear their dresses as the fish wear water." They strike the speaker as otherworldly creatures, whose home might just as well be the sea, like Dickinson's mermaids.

Yet even as the wonder lingers, I turn it into embarrassment at having spied, even on a crowded beach. The enchanted moment turns self-conscious as my passive witness doesn't quite know what to do with himself—he, not the sea, withdraws. Dickinson's speaker, fully engaged with the sea, literally immersed in its element like my Mennonite women, is honestly direct in her account—"The Sea withdrew —." This simultaneously ordinary and extraordinary experience carries no hint of moral judgment. The poem, sexual though it is, describes nothing like a fall. She stands soaked, but, despite having "met the Solid Town —," neither naked nor ashamed. The feeling is ambiguous, yet has a certain slant, like Dickinson's light, while my speaker guiltily imagines himself back to a reinvented Eden, "nearly" making it, trying to pinpoint how he feels, and "nearly" nailing it.

In a seminar many years ago, M. L. Rosenthal pointed out how often Dickinson's poems revolve around an unnamed "given"—the "it" in "'Twas like a Maelstrom, with a notch" (Fr425), or the "thing / So terrible" in "The first Day's Night had come —" (Fr423). We never learn the identity of these "its" and "things," but we learn everything about the precise psychic states they incite, and which the poems enact. We see these states in certain slants of light, illuminated by Dickinson's remarkable restraint, her slant-rhyming technique, and her uncanny conflation of figurative and literal characterizations. These qualities, in my view, make her poetry unique and ultimately inimitable. I have learned considerably from watching her certain slants cast their rays on her mysterious and veiled subjects, not always revealing the thing itself but focusing profound, attendant feelings for our imaginative understanding. I did not begin by imitating Dickinson, and despite my occasional resort to her work for its strategies or its prosody, I do not consider my poetry particularly Dickinsonian any more than, say, Yeatsian, Audenesque, or Jarrellian. Yet here I am, devoted to slant rhyme, working frequently in tetrameter and trimeter, endeavoring to startle my readers with the discovery that more happens in the poem than they initially suppose. Over time, Dickinson has given me more than I had thought to ask, and for me as both reader and poet, that marks her enduring value.

# Adding Feathers to
# the Learned's Wing (1999)

*Helen Vendler on Shakespeare's Sonnets*


An odd thing about the Shakespearean sonnet is how few great poets—and how few great poems—have exploited it since Shakespeare. Henry Howard, the Earl of Surrey, invented the form some two decades before Shakespeare's birth, most likely to make the task easier than the Italian job in rhyme-scarce English (Sir Thomas Wyatt had experimented earlier in this direction but never quite nailed it down), and since it allows the greater flexibility of seven different rhymes, as opposed to the Italian form's four or five, you would think that most poets writing in English would jump on the bandwagon.[1] But ask any poet, any reader, any critic to identify great sonneteers and sonnets in English after 1600, and the poets named will have overwhelmingly chosen the Italian over the English form. A highly informal poll I took yielded the following, listed here in order of decreasing frequency: Wordsworth, Donne, Keats, Milton, Millay, Hopkins, Frost, Yeats, Berryman, Elizabeth Barrett Browning, Robert Lowell, Cummings, Dante Gabriel Rossetti. With the exceptions of Keats, Frost, and Cummings, who all worked elegantly in both forms and introduced some signal innovations of their own, this is quite a Petrarchan group (Lowell, of course, working mostly in blank verse). Why should this be?

One possibility is that we have had it wrong all along, and that in spite of its greater generosity with rhymes, the Shakespearean form is actually more difficult to master. The juicy temptation of two new rhyme sounds for each quatrain smells too good for poets to pass up, until they confront the brevity of those quatrains and realize how much must get crammed into each—not to mention the daunting task of trying to conclude in a couplet without sounding trite. Certainly the Italian sonnet, despite the headaches of juggling a mere two rhymes for eight lines, offers in its octave and sestet more room to maneuver, to develop, to show off, giving the poet a freer hand in creating the illusion of felt life.

Another reason, of course, is the excellence with which Shakespeare manipulated the form, taking Surrey's contraption of convenience, previously adopted by no poet of genius save Sir Philip Sidney in sonnets like "Leave Me, Oh Love," and carving his powerful rhyme, a sequence varied in quality but reaching great pinnacles and profundities of poetic craft and feeling. Given Shakespeare's lyric monument, we can understand why most later poets would shy from the sonnet renamed in his honor; after all, playwrights make no attempt to improve on *Hamlet* or *Lear*.

Shakespeare's place in literary history creates even more problems for the later sonneteer because of the formal legacy of the English form. It combines, as the scholar Rosalie Colie noted, the *mel*, or honey, of love poetry with the *sal*, or salt, of epigram,[2] and that epigrammatic nature of Shakespeare's couplets gives most modern poets fits. Howard Nemerov, who wrote a number of first-rate English sonnets himself, liked to imagine Shakespeare regularly turning his three quatrains over to an apprentice: "Okay, now let's see what you can do with *that*." Ironically, the couplet, with its tight rhyme and syntactical wholeness, feels most unpoetical, most distractingly artificial to poets in our very-late-Romantic period, the part of the sonnet that refuses to hide the art. It may not be an exaggeration to say that the wit of Shakespeare's couplets ultimately inspired eighteenth-century prosody, a poetics that mined salt and a host of other spices, often to the neglect of the honeycomb. If so, the Romantic rebellion against Enlightenment practice might also have precipitated a two-hundred-year reaction against the epigrammatic and proverbial feel of the Shakespearean sonnet.

Rarely since Shakespeare, in the hands of someone like Keats, does the English form open out melodically and imagistically, instead of hemming in. The way "When I Have Fears," perhaps the greatest post-Shakespeare example, begins the couplet's thematic material early, at the end of the third quatrain, in order to achieve a moment of cosmic rapture before hauling the world back in, is both innovative and thrilling:

> then on the shore
> Of the wide world I stand alone, and think
> Till love and fame to nothingness do sink.[3]

Keats here provides something of an exception that proves the rule. Although strict construction marks both traditional sonnet forms, the larger space of the Italian sonnet's units, as well as the rhyme scheme's greater freedom in its sestet, makes the form's dictation of feeling less obvious and gives the Italian form the illusion of greater spontaneity. All the more reason, then, that Shakespeare's accomplishment fills us with awe.

Helen Vendler's new book, *The Art of Shakespeare's Sonnets,* nine years in the making, arrives as a commentary on our chief poetic god from the critic most often dubbed our god of interpretation. In fact, the book itself comically played a sort of savior when it made its stage debut at the age of three months in John Guare's *The General of Hot Desire,* far and away the best of seven commissioned short plays inspired by Shakespeare sonnets, produced under the collective title *Love's Fire.* In Guare's play, a theatrical company assigned to create a play out of the Cupid sonnets, 153 and 154 (Guare's own task, of course), encounters frustration after frustration in puzzling out the poems, until one actress arrives with a copy of Vendler's book: "Helen Vendler!" they cry, as they begin to read her commentary; "I love Helen Vendler!"[4]

*The Art of Shakespeare's Sonnets* does give us much reason to love Helen Vendler, particularly if we revere the Sonnets as living, breathing poems, rather than as skeleton keys to Shakespeare's life, sexuality, and personal attitudes, or to the secret identity of the young man, the rival poet, the dark lady, or Mr. W. H. Vendler undertakes to show the Sonnets in their considerable, if not infinite, variety, keeping in sight at all times the continual turns of thought and feeling in each poem that make it "a system in motion" and "a trajectory of changing feelings," and "trying to see the chief aesthetic 'game' being played in each sonnet" (22–23). She also argues—contrary to what I have suggested above—that Shakespeare, by "constantly inventing new permutations of internal form," proves the English sonnet "far more flexible than the two-part Italian sonnet" (32, 22). Most of all, she investigates the sonnets "from the viewpoint of the poet who wrote them," asking "what was the aesthetic challenge for Shakespeare in writing these poems?" (17). By attempting to reconstruct Shakespeare's mind in the process of composition, she tries to construct our aesthetic experience in reading them.

Vendler, then, offers a flexible kind of response theory approach to the Sonnets, and when she examines the poems' use of overlapping structures—rhetorical, syntactic, formal, affective, and so on—she is indebted to Stephen Booth, who introduced these ideas in his *Essay on Shakespeare's Sonnets* nearly thirty years before. Likewise, Vendler takes her inspiration from Booth and others in discussing how shifts of feeling in the Sonnets seldom coincide with the formal divisions of 4, 4, 4, 2; rather, in Shakespeare's hands the form more often works like an Italian sonnet, or in units of 8, 4, 2, or 4, 8, 2, or 12, 2, or 5, 7, 2, and onward almost to the limits of mathematical possibility. Vendler surpasses her predecessors in her sensitivity to Shakespeare's language, and in the astonishing thoroughness and even obsessiveness with which she considers these issues of form and feeling in *every* Shakespeare sonnet. The result feels truly encyclopedic, and readers should therefore take under advisement her caveat that "this Commentary is not intended to be read straight through" (37), lest they feel inundated by her flood of structures, diagrams, and close attention to words, puns, and even meaningful anagrams. As with an encyclopedia, the book works better as a reference—a great browse—than as a good read, a characteristic that differentiates it markedly from her books on Herbert and Keats, for example.

Vendler also departs from Booth and other response theorists in her insistence that the Sonnets finally mean something, and she thus rejects Booth's conclusion "that the critic, helpless before the plurisignification of language and overlapping of multiple structures visible in a Shakespeare sonnet, must be satisfied with irresolution with respect to its fundamental gestalt" (13). On the contrary, Vendler not only finds the individual poems comprehensible, despite the difficulties so many of them present, but she calls the richly complex, often self-contradictory, but finally coherent presentation of "Shakespeare's speaker, alone with his thoughts . . . the greatest achievement, imaginatively speaking, of the sequence" (19). Throughout her commentary, she makes good on this encouraging thesis, demonstrating that art can triumph, as Shakespeare's speaker so often brags to his young man, and that at least some major aspects of the Sonnets as a whirling virtual experience are not necessarily damned to indeterminacy.

Reviewers have complained that Vendler gives no account of the overall structure of the Sonnets (a charge justly leveled at Vendler's otherwise marvelous book on George Herbert, which never explores *The Temple*'s architecture), but in fact, *The Art of Shakespeare's Sonnets* accomplishes this somewhat—not in an individual introductory section, but in passing. We tack through the Sonnets periplum, navigating the coastline, striking strange shores and making key discoveries along the way about its overall concerns and shape, the unfolding of the speaker's personality, and the messy progress of his attachments to first the young man and then the dark lady. Thus, early in the sequence, she notes the introduction of an "I," the first address to the young man as "love," the first mention of art as a defense against death, the first identification of the speaker as a poet, the first travel sonnet, the first instance of insomnia, the first comment on the young man's flaws, and on and on, sounding a bit like MGM proclaiming, "Garbo talks!" "Garbo laughs!" Far more valuably, however, Vendler's discussion of the sonnets of disillusionment that close the young man subsequence, ending with the six-couplet "sonnet" 126, and those that round off the dark lady subsequence, create a convincing understanding of how these Sonnets plausibly operate as a whole. Unfortunately, the reader can only glean this sense of overall structure by plowing straight through, not, as I have mentioned, the most profitable way to experience the book.

To help focus the formal structure of individual sonnets, Vendler introduces the concepts of the Couplet Tie, the Key Word, and the Defective Key Word. All fruitfully remind us how Shakespeare makes a poem cohere partly by the simple device of apt repetition of important words, word roots, or even punning parts of words in its different sections. The Key Word—a word that appears in each of the three quatrains and the couplet—is a particularly welcome study aid, although Vendler succumbs to the temptation to stretch things now and then, as in Sonnet 52, where the Key Word "blessèd" masquerades as "placèd" in the second quatrain (256), or, worse, in 53, where "one" constitutes the Key Word, but only "if one is prepared to find it orthographically hiding, as well as phonetically present" in such guises as "milliONs (2), . . . AdONis (5), . . . foisON (9), . . . cONstant (14)" (260). The reconstruction of Shakespeare's thought process as he writes a sonnet surely engages a significant amount of presumed wordplay, but some readers might find Vendler's pun-and-anagram-hunting punishing. Nevertheless, one of the book's pleasures comes from learning how *Vendler's* thought process works as she reads Shakespeare—the anticipation, for example, when we reach Sonnet 100 ("Where art thou, Muse, that thou forget'st so long") that her ear and alertness to puns and transformations will lead her to identify "time" and "might" as a "possible (anagrammatic) key word" (428).

Of these three tools, perhaps the keenest insights into Shakespeare's binding together the English form come from Vendler's Defective Key Words, words appearing in all but one of a sonnet's formal units. For example, in Sonnet 85 ("My tongue-tied Muse in manners holds her still"), the Defective Key Words "words" and "thought" appear in every formal section *except* the first quatrain, where "the poet's Muse's *tongue-tied still[ness]*" suppresses them (375). Even better, in Sonnet 143 ("Lo, as a careful huswife runs to catch"), a round in which the allegorical housewife chases a chicken while her "neglected child" chases her, the word "catch" appears in each quatrain but not in the couplet, since "the mistress never catches her lover," the fowl the dark lady is here pursuing (603).

Vendler in pursuit of a sonnet's mysteries is usually a splendid thing to witness, and she brings considerable wit and intelligence to her reading. She sorts the poems into helpful categories, as when she identifies Sonnet 20 ("A woman's face with Nature's own hand painted"), the speaker's frustrated dissertation on his doting over the androgynous young man, as a "little myth of origin" (128):

> The speaker's sterile play of the master/mistress against the putative falsity of women can be explained by his anger at women for not being the young man, at the young man for not being a (sexually available) woman. . . . Though Galen thought all embryos were originally female . . . , it is Shakespeare who creates the causal myth that the change to maleness in this case arises from Nature's falling in love with the projected female, and *therefore* rendering her male. Under all the play, one is only sure that the speaker, too, has fallen a-doting; and the rather bitter wit—on *acquainted* [cunt], "*one* thing"/ "*no*-thing," and *prick* (Nature's joke on the speaker)—is the last flicker of the helplessness of one who cannot play fast and loose, as he would like to, with a physical body. (129)

Vendler here takes what she calls a *jeu d'esprit* and shows how its lascivious punning barely masks erotic despair, letting us enjoy the jokes but also making us take them seriously as entrées into complex psychological states. Her commentary, in fact, is so rich that sometimes her finest critical points arrive almost as afterthoughts, reinforcing our illusion of watching her mind work through a poem, Sonnet 71, for example ("No longer mourn for me when I am dead"): "We may

read this poem, then, in a second, and truer, way—as a defensive construct hoping to awaken in the shallow young man the very depths of
mourning that it affects to prohibit. This in fact seems to me the most
probable reading . . ." (329).

Vendler is so good at showing us things in the Sonnets that, while
she of course cannot show us everything, reading her trains us to see
more for ourselves. In Sonnet 104 ("To me, fair friend, you never can
be old"), the poem's "acceleration in the pace of transience" belies
the young man's apparent eternal youth—so much so that the sonnet
pulls off an aesthetic shock in its couplet, where the speaker addresses
"thou age unbred: / Ere you were born was beauty's summer dead."
"The stunning 'turn' by which the young man 'dies' in the space between Q₃ [the third quatrain] and C [the couplet] is in fact the major
aesthetic achievement (along with the speed-up of change which
caused it) of the poem" (442–43). Yet reading along we also notice
for ourselves the poem's insistent subjectivity regarding the young
man: "*To me* . . . you never can be old"; "Such *seems* your beauty still";
"the seasons *have I seen*"; "Since first *I saw* you fresh"; "your sweet
hue, which *methinks* still doth stand"; until finally breaking down just
before the couplet: "*mine eye* may be deceived." We augment Vendler's commentary by seeing how the poem attempts to balance the
speaker's urgent, subjective need to keep his beloved young by force
of will against the sure knowledge that such a task is impossible. The
speaker futilely tries to make the poem a safe haven, a world in which
youth and love can endure, his failure making the release of the young
man to the processes of mortality all the more poignant.

In becoming better readers, in seeing more for ourselves, we also
become better prepared to argue with Vendler's interpretations now
and again. "I have often wished, as I was reading a poem," she says in
her preface, "that I could know what another reader had noticed in
it; and I leave a record here of what one person has remarked so that
others can compare their own noticings with mine. In such a way,
we may advance our understanding of Shakespeare's procedures as

a working poet—that is, as a master of aesthetic strategy" (xiv). At times Vendler becomes so excited by her discoveries about a sonnet's strategy that key features of the poem that might further complicate our understanding fall by the wayside. In the great Sonnet 73 ("That time of year thou mayst in me behold"), she identifies the "glowing of such fire" in the third quatrain as the most vital part of the poem: "He is not the ashes of a fire, or the embers of a fire—he is no longer (as he was in the first two quatrains) a noun, but rather a verbal, an action, a *glowing* (not a dying). . . . When the speaker reads the erotic text of his emotional life, he sees a *glowing*. It is certainly easier to ask someone to love a *glowing* rather than a *ruin* or a *fad[ing]* . . ." (335–36). But while Vendler makes a strong case that the poem's quatrains successively correct each other, she ignores the psychological activity that makes the first two quatrains just as affectively—and aesthetically— active. In the opening quatrain, particularly, "When yellow leaves, or none, or few, do hang," looks perfectly straightforward until we notice the illogical progression of "leaves, none, few." The line's disorder surely enacts the speaker's resistance to aging: he depicts the leaves, then their disappearance, but immediately finds the bare branches too devastating and so restores a "few" as a momentary stay and comfort. Those few leaves express a vitality and desire to hang onto life as urgent and plaintive as the glowing of the third quatrain.

Though Vendler apologizes for "the absence, except in occasional cases below, of metrical commentary" (11), some scansions she does include feel idiosyncratic. The ninth line of Sonnet 39 ("O how thy worth with manners may I sing"), which she hears as

Ŏ ábsĕnce, | whăt ă | tórmĕnt | wŏuldst thŏu | próve,

and whose irregularity she notes, strikes me as a virtually orthodox iambic pentameter. And a line from Sonnet 108 she describes as regular, in order to reinforce the speaker's feeling of monotony,

Ĭ múst | ĕach dáy | săy o'ér | thĕ vér | ў sáme,

might more tellingly—and accurately—be scanned with four consecutive stresses on "eách dáy sáy o'ér," emphasizing the speaker's rebellion against the young man's accusation of monotony in his poems.
Her brilliant reading of Sonnet 126, the last of the young man subsequence ("O thou my lovely boy, who in thy power") is marred by her
insistence that the poem scans largely into trochees and amphibrachs.
While this peculiar scansion conveys her strong understanding of the
poem's *rhythms,* she bases it on a false prosodic premise: "I prefer the
[scansion option] which keeps words intact" (535). But scansion necessarily allows for the split word: we practice it to establish a poem's
regular metrical model so we can observe its metrical variations and
better evaluate the poet's rhythmic skill. To disdain divided words
in scanning a poem seems as absurd as disallowing notes held over a
bar line in music.

Further, some of the Sonnets move us most effectively through
their rhythmic cruxes and cry out for more prosodic attention. In
discussing Sonnet 130 ("My mistress' eyes are nothing like the sun"),
though Vendler troubles to construct an imaginary sonnet out of the
conventions Shakespeare's anti-Petrarchan gem satirizes—"My mistress' eyes are brilliant as the sun, / And coral's colour matches her
lips' red," and so on—she seems oddly uninterested in that wonderful
poem, perhaps because she doesn't focus on its simple but brilliant
prosodic climax. The third quatrain opens with three lines of perfect
iambic pentameter, confessing with completely blasé regularity, "I
grant I never saw a goddess go," in order to set up a single delicious
substitution in line twelve:

Mў mís | trĕss whén | shĕ wálks | tréads ŏn | thĕ gróund.

That trochee in the fourth position enacts precisely how the mistress
does not travel like a goddess but is more prone to tripping over curbs.

Vendler announces straight off that she has planned *The Art of
Shakespeare's Sonnets* "for those who already know the *Sonnets,* or
who have beside them the sort of lexical annotation found in the cur-

rent editions" (1). This sensible strategy allows her to dive right into some of the poems' complexities without wrangling over archaic vocabulary or paraphrasing on the most basic level. Still, in recreating Shakespeare's mind and aesthetic choices, Vendler could have more diligently historicized vocabulary, frames of reference, and especially literary usages and allusions, and for all these purposes, as Vendler recommends, an edition of the Sonnets such as Booth's provides invaluable aid in evaluating her arguments.[5] The relative absence of discussion of parallel vocabulary and language in Shakespeare's plays, especially the "lyrical" plays of the mid-1590s, his presumed sonneteering period, is especially surprising. (Her helpful invocation of language from *Love's Labour's Lost* to illuminate Sonnet 127 is the exception rather than the rule.)

Certainly our appreciation of several other sonnets would be considerably enriched by comparisons with language from the plays. For example, Sonnet 27's "jewel" simile for the beloved glimpsed in a dream—"my soul's imaginary sight / Presents thy shadow to my sightless view, / Which like a jewel (hung in ghastly night) / Makes black night beauteous"—makes this night vision, as Vendler astutely says, resemble a religious rapture, but it also reminds us of Helena in *A Midsummer Night's Dream,* who, when the lovers are re-paired, finds "Demetrius like a jewel, / Mine own and not mine own,"[6] reinforcing the Sonnet speaker's dream as dream, and underscoring his uncertain possession of his love. Sonnet 119's couplet presents a more complex example: after straying from fidelity to the young man, the speaker, thanks to "potions . . . of Siren tears," comes to his senses from "the distraction of this madding fever":

> So I return rebuked to my content,
> And gain by ills thrice more than I have spent.

Vendler reads the poem as a "post-facto description of infatuations which have led one away from true love" and sees in the couplet "no irony . . . attached, I think, to this acquiescence" (503, 506). But in

Shakespeare's plays of the mid-to-late 1590s, "content" often means grudging acceptance when faced with no alternative. In the rude mechanicals' Pyramus and Thisbe play, the divided lovers "are content / To whisper" through Wall's chink (*MND* 5. 1. 132–33). In *Henry IV, Part One,* when Hotspur rides off to plot rebellion, leaving his wife for the night, he asks, "Will this content you, Kate?" to which she sadly replies, "It must, perforce" (2. 4. 108). Perhaps most famously, in order to save his life, Shylock accepts the loss of his daughter, his wealth, and his religion with the bitter words, "I am content" (*Merchant* 4. 1. 389). Given our growing understanding throughout the Sonnets' young man subsequence of the speaker's suffering at his beloved's aloofness, hauteur, and infidelity, his professed "content" sounds ironic in this same vein, and he returns helplessly to his young man, presumably for more ill treatment, the pains of love offering no choice.

I intend all these quibbles with Vendler in the spirit in which she wrote *The Art of Shakespeare's Sonnets*—that of a reader who has found some things in the Sonnets and is curious about what others have found there. Her book adds enormously to our understanding and prods us to continue to make our own discoveries. Even the accompanying compact disc of Vendler reading sixty-five of the poems deepens her interpretations of some sonnets while raising new issues concerning others. Her subtle pauses in Sonnet 76—"Why is my verse so . . . barren of new pride? / So . . . far from variation or quick change?"—reinforce her argument that the speaker here replies to the young man's complaint of monotony in the Sonnets. On the other hand, hearing Sonnet 35 aloud ("No more be grieved at that which thou hast done") forces our attention on the uncharacteristic accumulation of four "uh" rhymes in the first quatrain—"done," "mud," "sun," "bud." The vowels surely aim to convey the speaker's disgust at both the young man's corruption and himself, but Vendler does not mention this charged handling of rhyme at all. Still, *The Art of Shakespeare's Sonnets* grafts new feathers onto the wings of our understanding, lifting us closer to Heaven's gate. By evaluating the poems as symbolic projections of imaginative experience, Vendler provides a useful, at times thrilling roadmap to the creative mind that concocted a complex and enduring self in the Sonnets, where we continually find him as poet, even if continually hiding as a man.

# The Aesthetics of
# Contemporary Sonnet Sequences

## THE EXAMPLES OF SALTER AND MULDOON (2010)

The sonnet sequence in English, even in its sixteenth-century incarnations, serves as a kind of prototype for the modern long poem. A quarter-century ago, M. L. Rosenthal and Sally M. Gall identified the structure of the modern poetic sequence as lyrical and subjective, "a grouping of mainly lyric poems and passages, rarely uniform in pattern, which tend to interact as an organic whole. It usually includes narrative and dramatic elements, and ratiocinative ones as well, but its structure is finally lyrical."[1] In "this liberated lyrical structure," the "object is neither to resolve a problem nor to conclude an action but to achieve the keenest, most open realization possible" (11). The equilibrium or sense of closure in such a work brings an aesthetic and emotional satisfaction, rather than the conclusion of a plot—the strategy of a new genre, Rosenthal and Gall argue, "which best encompasses the shift in sensibility exemplified by starting . . . 'I celebrate myself, and sing myself,' rather than 'Sing, Goddess, the wrath of Achilles'" (3).

Except for their observation that such sequences are "rarely uniform in pattern," Rosenthal and Gall have described the affective dynamics of sonnet sequences. Unfortunately, their discussion of Shakespeare's Sonnets as a precursor of modernist practice is both brief and dismissive, concluding that sonnets finally fail as a medium for long modern poems because their uniformity too strictly limits each section's expressiveness.[2] Despite Rosenthal and Gall's disdain, however, sonnet

40

sequences have helped promote the aesthetic eminence of lyric poetry for half a millennium. Progressing through Shakespeare's Sonnets, or Sidney's *Astrophil and Stella*, or Donne's Holy Sonnets, we discover new psychological possibilities continually opening up, confrontations with new and recurring erotic or sacred crises, illuminations of the expressive potential of poetry to imagine human feeling, and even technical innovations in the sonnet form itself. Though we cannot know if most early sonnet sequences appear in an order that the poet intended, even the traditional sequencing determined by either their first printers or later editors can provide a satisfying aesthetic curve.

Today's sonnet writers create sequences that embrace this tradition and push it further, in lyrical, dynamic structures that can explore all the weathers of human feeling while playing with "narrative and dramatic elements" in ways that hint at several different kinds of closure. Twenty-first-century sequences by Mary Jo Salter and Paul Muldoon show the form's enduring capacity for containing and expressing as much affective material as the poet can imagine into it.[3] In both Salter's *Another Session* (2003) and Muldoon's *Horse Latitudes* (2006), characters and situations develop, suspense builds, and actions climax. Yet in each, our chief interest remains lyrical and emotional. Salter investigates the psychology of a patient-counselor relationship after the therapist suddenly dies; Muldoon weaves a litany of historical battles together with the relationship between his speaker and a lover recently diagnosed with cancer, her body now fighting its own battles. At first glance, each sequence seems to stand as a single, integrated poem, aesthetically unexcerptable. Yet while both narrative elements and the obsessive recursiveness of both Salter's and Muldoon's poems create the feeling of an integral whole, I can imagine some future anthology reprinting *Another Session*'s opening sonnet on its own, or even the ninth, and, elliptical as they are, "Beijing" or "Burma," for example, from *Horse Latitudes*. At least some of the poems fulfill the sonnet sequence's tradition of communicating expressively on their own, as well as participating in the plan of a larger affective trajectory that strengthens their individual impact.

Each poet, while participating in the sonnet sequence tradition, experiments relentlessly with the sonnet form, devising rhyme schemes to reflect the sequence's specific affective needs. The ten sonnets in Salter's *Another Session* use ten unique schemes, often slant-rhyming heavily. Both her restless, sonnet-to-sonnet juggling of the rhyme scheme and the sometimes desperate nature of the rhymes themselves directly enlist the formal construction of her poems in the emotional quest of the entire sequence, a striving to achieve an elusive order and sense. The opening poem, which begins, "You opened with the rules," lays out the therapy sessions' guidelines, but also the sonnet rules against which the entire sequence will continually push. The tension between traditional sonnet form and Salter's experimentation enacts the tension between the speaker and the therapist:

1.

| | |
|---|---|
| You opened with the rules. Outside this room | *a* |
| nothing I said inside would be repeated | *b* |
| unless in your best judgment I posed harm | *a* |
| to myself or others. It was like being read | *b* |
| my rights in some film noir—but I was glad | *b* |
| already I'd at last turned myself in, | *c* |
| guilty of anxiety and depression. | *c* |
| | |
| And worse. Confess it: worse. Of narcissist | *d* |
| indifference to how other people felt. | *e* |
| Railing against myself, making a list | *d* |
| of everything (I thought), I'd left a fault | *e* |
| unturned: the one of needing to be praised | *d* |
| for forcing these indictments from my throat. | *f* |
| For saying them well. For speaking as I wrote. | *f*     (49) |

The therapist's regulations—"nothing I said inside would be repeated"—immediately spur the new patient's rebellious feelings. Salter's enjambment, "It was like being read / my rights in some film noir," turns his psychotherapeutic probing of her speaker's personality into a criminal prosecution (a similar enjambment in the second sonnet instantly transforms his facial expression from severe to inscrutable: "at first, a little hard / to judge" [49]). Further, the form itself rebels, dividing not into an octave and sestet, but into two septets, the second confessing to even "worse" crimes than the first—"narcissist / indifference" and "needing to be praised / for forcing these indictments from my throat." Nevertheless, the equal halves reflect a desire for emotional balance, intensified by the fact that both septets conclude with a couplet, the second employing a full rhyme to end a sonnet where the imbalances of slant-rhyme have proved the norm. The combination of an unorthodox form with a conventional ending dramatizes the speaker's struggle between her resistance to normality and her simultaneous craving for it—her wish to cease feeling "guilty," not of "dust and sin" (which would end the first septet with a perfect rhyme), as in George Herbert's "Love (III)," but of "anxiety and depression," and her consequent self-punishment, "Railing against myself, making a list," which echoes the lover "Biting my pen, beating myself for spite" in Sidney's *Astrophil and Stella*.[4]

With one exception—sonnet 6—all the sequence's remaining sonnets divide into octave and sestet, conventionally turning at line 9, although the octaves employ a series of unorthodox schemes. In sonnet 5, for example, the octave and sestet begin in parallel, with the identical word "Killed," but the octave itself begins and ends with couplets, enveloping an envelope quatrain between them:

5.

| | |
|---|---|
| *Killed instantly.* That's what a mutual friend | *a* |
| told me when I asked how it had happened. | *a* |
| *Good,* I said, *I'm glad he didn't suffer*— | *b* |
| each of us reaching (not far) for a phrase | *c* |
| from a lifetime stock of journalists' clichés | *c* |
| which, we had learned, provide a saving buffer | *b* |
| within our bifurcated selves: the one | *d* |
| that's horrified; the one that must go on. | *d* |

| | |
|---|---|
| Killed in a bicycle race. I've scrapped the Wheel | *e* |
| of Fortune, the Road of Life. No, this is real, | *e* |
| there's no script to consult: you've lost your body. | *f* |
| Still having one, I pace, I stretch, I cough, | *g* |
| I wash my face. But then I'm never ready. | *f* |
| This is the sonnet I've been putting off. | *g*   (51–52) |

The fear of inadequacy in dealing with the death permeates this sonnet. In the octave the evasion radiates from the central couplet's resort to "a phrase / from . . . journalists' clichés," backward to the italicized shock of the awful news, and forward to the stoic nostrum that "one . . . must go on." But the sestet's obsessive return to "Killed" disrupts any comfortable resolve by beginning with a couplet but not ending with one. The couplet dismisses the easy symbols—literary clichés this time— that a poet might peddle to describe death by bicycle, but unlike the octave, the sestet moves from certainty to indeterminacy. It resists ending with either the religious comfort that the therapist has merely "lost [his] body," or the speaker's personal comfort of having survived "Still having one." Instead, it concludes with a satisfying but confusing paradox: the speaker has "been putting off" the sonnet, unable to confront its facts and feelings—yet here it is, the issue of that confrontation.

Sonnet 6, which continues the syntax that seemingly brought sonnet 5 to a close, objectifies the speaker's personal confusion by marking the sequence's point of greatest formal confusion: a single, headlong sentence mimicking the chaotic death of the therapist, flying on, then off, his bicycle into "fast *oncoming traffic.*"

### 6.

| | |
|---|---|
| And also this one, in which your fancy bike | *a* |
| hits a concrete barrier and you fly | *b* |
| over it into fast *oncoming traffic*— | *a* |
| the obituary's formula for one man | *c* |
| driving a truck, who didn't even have | *d* |
| time to believe the corner of his eye, | *b* |

| | |
|---|---|
| until the thing was done, and he must live | *d* |
| always as if this nightmare were the one | *c* |
| deed he was born to do and to relive, | *d* |
| precisely the sort of person you would trust | *e* |
| in fifty-minute sessions to forgive | *d* |
| himself, to give himself at least two years | *f* |
| of post-traumatic whatsit to adjust | *e* |
| to thoughts of all those people left in tears. | *f*     (52) |

The jumbling of octave with sestet rhymes compounds the chaos, with the *d* rhymes swerving unexpectedly into the wrong lane. The constant, obsessive juggling of rhymes from sonnet to sonnet in *Another Session*—reinventing a different scheme for each—enacts the speaker's wish to keep starting over, each section's rearrangement a new, desperate attempt to hit on the secret code that would explain the doctor's death, or bring him back.

This obsessiveness extends to the way the sonnets keep talking to each other, recycling their materials to reflect, first, the speaker's neuroses, and second, her consternation at the tragedy that ironically ends up giving her more perspective on herself—the therapist's task, after all. The transition from 5 to 6 stands as the purest example— "This is the sonnet I've been putting off," "And also this one." Such self-reflexivity—the speaker thinking of herself as sonneteer, the sonnet talking about itself—would smack of precious postmodernist games, if it didn't so efficiently express as a *poetic* problem the speaker's reluctance to deal with the death. The psychological problem of confronting the doctor's death, and by extension the speaker's own mortality, becomes absorbed into the technical problem of finding a sonnet form to express feelings the speaker would prefer to evade. At this point, the speaker resists "being read" not only in the figurative, analytical sense of sonnet 1, but also in the literal sense of "putting off" the creation of the sonnet, denying readers imaginative entrée into her experience. Salter thus reinvents the sonnet sequence's tradition of self-reflexivity, descending from the Elizabethans. Sidney's "Fool, . . . look in thy heart and write," which Salter alludes to in her opening sonnet's closing words, "For speaking as I wrote," creates a miniature myth of origin for the very sonnets we have in our hands,[5] while Shakespeare's speaker continually points to one sonnet or another as a monument to his young man—"So long as men can breathe or eyes can see, / So long lives this, and this gives life to thee."[6] The Romantics experimented with this tradition by writing sonnets about the form itself—Wordsworth's "Nuns fret not" and "Scorn not the Sonnet," Keats's "If by dull rhymes our english must be chaind"—but Salter has reintegrated self-reflexivity sixteenth-century style, by having the poem's literal attention to itself function as an expression of the emotional impetus behind it. She also adds a sly new twist: because sonnets 5 and 6 almost did not get written, the imaginative feelings her speaker fights to keep secret almost remain forever unexpressed.

Sonnets 5 and 6 mark the narrative climax of *Another Session,* but not its emotional crux. After the initial session of sonnet 1, sonnets 2 and 3 detail the relaxation of the initially disturbing meetings ("This is real life. You don't live in a novel") into comfortable routine ("Gratitude. Trust. Forgiveness. Fantasies" [50]), jarred slightly by sonnet 4's emergence into "real life," a chance meeting in a restaurant ("suddenly I was nervous, my life on show" [51]). When, in sonnet 5, "real life" collides with real death, the speaker reports not so much the disaster itself as her evasive tactics in thinking and speaking of it—that "lifetime stock of journalists' clichés" and those literary clichés of "the Wheel / of Fortune, the Road of Life"; she dawdles—"I pace, I stretch, I cough, / I wash my face"—instead of getting to work. But sonnet 6 forces her task upon her when she exposes another journalists' cliché— "*oncoming traffic*"—as "one man / driving a truck," and then, in a wonderful act of sympathetic imagination, enters into the driver's feelings as he attempts to deal with his role in the accident. She puts herself in his place so thoroughly that she imagines *his* needing therapy to assuage his own guilt and depression. Yet this job well done gets revealed as a different kind of evasion in sonnet 9, the emotional climax of the sequence:

9.

| | |
|---|---|
| I'd got there early, casually saved a front | *a* |
| pew for the whole family with some flung | *b* |
| mittens and hats. (In gestures we assume | *c* |
| the shoulder-to-shoulder permanence of home.) | *c* |
| Shouldn't we come more often? "The Power of Love": | *d* |
| our sermon. A list called "Flowers in Memory of" | *d* |
| on the program's final page. I was feeling faint. | *a* |
| Your name. Your father's name? Something was wrong. | *b* |
| | |
| I knew it was you. The church was going black. | *e* |
| Head down: my first anxiety attack | *e* |
| since the bad old days. Your face at the restaurant. | *f* |
| My plate heaped up with food I didn't want. | *f* |
| Keep the head down. People would be saying | *g* |
| to themselves (and close enough) that I was praying. | *g* (54) |

Beginning cozily and festively—sonnet 8 reveals that she and her family have gathered for a Christmas Eve service—this sonnet suddenly shifts into the speaker's disorientation and dismay at seeing her therapist's name in "A list called 'Flowers in Memory of.'" The therapist has become the one "being read," and the fact of black print brings on the speaker's "first anxiety attack / since the bad old days." Her visceral response—she nearly faints—proves a catharsis, allowing Salter to end the sequence in a retrospective calm in the sestet of the final sonnet, in which the speaker instructs herself not to recall but to "Revise our last encounter":

| | |
|---|---|
| *Paris,* you said. Then, awkwardly, *Lucky you.* | *e* |
| Possessor of my secrets, not a friend, | *f* |
| colder, closer, our link unbreakable. | *g* |
| Yet we parted better than people often do. | *e* |
| We looked straight at each other. Was that a smile? | *g* |
| I thanked you for everything. You shook my hand. | *f* (55) |

The equipoise on which the poem ends, hand balancing hand, momentarily restores life to the therapist, though this rescue fools neither the reader nor the speaker. For all the poem's tragedy, the ending feels content and settled, the speaker having broken out of her self-absorption and grown intensely interested in just how to define this strange relationship with the "Possessor of my secrets." Yet the essential mystery of the therapist's personality remains, a prime example of the elusiveness of others' thoughts and feelings, as well as one's own—the kind of conundrum that necessitates imagination and sends us to therapy, and to poetry, in the first place.

Paul Muldoon's *Horse Latitudes* also experiments with the sonnet, not least by inventing a radical new form. Unlike Salter's continually revised rhyme schemes, each of Muldoon's nineteen sonnets follows a single scheme that incorporates three couplets (two of them consecutive), a six-line envelope rhyming *bcddcb* (from lines 2 through 7), and a mirroring by the final three lines of the opening three, rhyming *abc.* Here is how the internal relationships look in "Beijing," the opening poem:

BEIJING

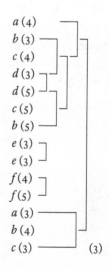

| | |
|---|---|
| I could still hear the musicians | *a* (4) |
| cajoling those thousands of clay | *b* (3) |
| horses and horsemen through the squeeze | *c* (4) |
| when I woke beside Carlotta. | *d* (3) |
| Life-size, also. Also terra-cotta. | *d* (5) |
| The sky was still a terra-cotta frieze | *c* (5) |
| over which her grandfather still held sway | *b* (5) |
| with the set square, fretsaw, stencil, | *e* (3) |
| plumb line, and carpenter's pencil | *e* (3) |
| *his* grandfather brought from Roma. | *f* (4) |
| Proud-fleshed Carlotta. Hypersarcoma. | *f* (5) |
| For now our highest ambition | *a* (3) |
| was simply to bear the light of day | *b* (4) |
| we had once been planning to seize. | *c* (3) (3) |

In addition to its rhyming innovations, the form uses lines of different lengths, ranging from three to five beats (indicated parenthetically above), with many trisyllabic feet. The sonnet form that Muldoon has crafted for *Horse Latitudes,* while ingenious, tends to feel top-heavy, with much of its structural cleverness packed into the opening seven lines—a seven-line octave, if you like, that seems ready to turn at line 8, at the introduction of the *e* rhymes.

Many of the sonnets turn later, however. The volta of "Beijing" seems to come at line 11 ("Proud-fleshed Carlotta. Hypersarcoma"); and that of "Bunker Hill," the eleventh sonnet, at either line 9 ("No looking daggers at the knife") or 10 ("She'd meet the breast-high parapet"):

BUNKER HILL

Carlotta took me in her arms
as a campfire gathers a branch
to itself, her mouth a cauter
set to my bleeding bough, heehaw.
Her grandfather sterilizing his saw
in a tub of 100-proof firewater,
a helper standing by to stanch
the bleeding in some afterlife.
No looking daggers at the knife.
She'd meet the breast-high parapet
with the nonchalance, the no fucking sweat
of a slightly skanky schoolmarm
though the surgeon was preparing to ganch
her like What's-his-face's Daughter. (13)

Muldoon's use of the form, in contrast with the structure suggested by its rhyme scheme, demonstrates the continuing sway over poets of the traditional proportions established by the top-heavy Italian sonnet, appropriate here for the sway that the fully proportioned, top-heavy Carlotta, twice admired swimming in her "close-knit wet suit" (4, 6), holds over the speaker's sexual imagination. The discrepancy,

however, between Muldoon's Petrarchan-style turns and the quite
different thematic structure suggested by his rhyme scheme creates an
expressive tension between Muldoon's form and his themes. As with
Salter's opening sonnet, the equilibrium of Muldoon's scheme might
embody a wish for balance that the materials of the sequence continually resist.

Those materials, with their overwhelming sense of personal and
global disaster, also overturn some of the smaller-scale symmetries of
Muldoon's sonnet scheme. The repetition of the opening *abc* rhymes
to conclude each sonnet, for example, might imply a nostalgia for the
way things once were, before the cancer, before the wars—a return to
a life easy as *abc*—but Muldoon's individual sonnets tend to close not
with a retrospective look, but with a springboard into the next poem,
as with the movement from "Bunker Hill" into the twelfth sonnet,
"Brandywine":

### BRANDYWINE

> I crouched in my own Little Ease
> by the pool at the Vanderbilt
> where Carlotta crouched, sputter-sput,
> just as she had in the scanner
> when the nurse, keen-sighted as a lanner,
> picked out a tumor like a rabbit scut
> on dark ground. It was as if a fine silt,
> white sand or silicate, had clogged
> her snorkel, her goggles had fogged,
> and Carlotta surfaced like flot
> to be skimmed off some great cast-iron pot
> as garble is skimmed off, or lees
> painstakingly drained by turnings and tilts
> from a man-size barrel or butt. (14)

"What's-his-face's Daughter," which ends "Bunker Hill," alludes to
"Skeffington's Daughter," mentioned by name—though not defined—
later in the sequence (17). An iron torture device that compresses

the body painfully in a fetal position, it sparks the speaker's associative thoughts at the start of "Brandywine" of "my own Little Ease," a prison cell too small to allow its inmate to stand, and then of Carlotta's crouching in the pool at a Nashville motel, "just as she had in the scanner" where her cancer was detected. The fulcrum between the two poems typifies the complex associative and punning ways in which Muldoon strings the sonnets together; "Badli-Ke-Serai," which comes next, begins by transforming "Brandywine's" "man-size barrel or butt" into "*Pork* barrels. *Pork* butts" (15).

Like much of his poetry, Muldoon's sequence is elliptical—in this case, so elliptical that he has publicly taken the trouble to explain *Horse Latitudes* as a protest against the Iraq War: "The poems have to do with a series of battles (all beginning with the letter 'B' as if to suggest a 'missing' Baghdad) in which horses or mules played a major role. Intercut with those battle-scenes are accounts of a 'battle' with cancer by a former lover, here named Carlotta, and a commentary on the agenda of what may only be described as the Bush 'regime.'"[7] While Bush and Iraq do make appearances in a number of the sonnets, most readers would hardly identify Muldoon's protest as the main thrust of either the poem's narrative content or its imaginative feeling, even though echoes of the Iraq War surface in such places as the final lines of "Blaye," the sequence's fifth sonnet: "The French, meanwhile, were still struggling to prime / their weapons of mass destruction" (7). If *Horse Latitudes* has any plot at all, it concerns the mysterious assignment of Carlotta's grandfather in World War II with the Allies in Burma, revealed in the final sonnet, the nineteenth, as "to cut / the vocal cords of each pack mule / with a single, swift excision" a practice adopted, as explained in a book on mule lore that Muldoon apparently consulted, "so their braying wouldn't give away their position."[8]

BURMA

Her grandfather's job was to cut
the vocal cords of each pack mule
with a single, swift excision,

> a helper standing by to wrench
> the mule's head fiercely to one side and drench
> it with hooch he'd kept since Prohibition.
> "Why," Carlotta wondered, "that fearsome tool?
> Was it for fear the mules might bray
> and give their position away?"
> At which I see him thumb the shade
> as if he were once more testing a blade
> and hear the two-fold snapping shut
> of his four-fold, brass-edged carpenter's rule:
> "And give *away* their *position*." (21)

The inexorable movement toward this revelation, however, does not in the least dominate our affective experience in reading *Horse Latitudes,* which triumphs mainly as a lyrical sequence. It explores and expresses a complex curve of integrated feelings, even while the speaker's tone smacks of a strange concoction of stoicism and hysterical wit. Muldoon's sequence is obsessively recursive, leading us, as does *Another Session,* through the experience of having things run through our minds again and again, transformed by the imagination each time, the kind of meditation and rumination that sonnet sequences, for all their artifice, enact so convincingly. The grandfather's "fearsome tool"—one of many instances in which sexually suggestive language turns both violent and sterile, like Carlotta's "mouth a cauter / set to my bleeding bough" in "Bunker Hill"—hearkens back to "the surgeon [who] was preparing to ganch" Carlotta at the conclusion of "Bunker Hill." In "Beijing," the speaker, dreaming of the life-size terra-cotta Chinese cavalry tomb figures, "woke beside Carlotta. / Life-size, also. Also terra-cotta," a premonition of the illness that threatens to turn her into a clay tomb figure herself. In "Brandywine," Carlotta surfacing in "the pool at the Vanderbilt" turns into "flot" (foam, or scum) "to be skimmed off some great cast-iron pot."

In weaving together all these witty and despondent parallels, the speaker, though always clear-eyed, hopes against hope even more urgently than an Elizabethan sonneteer despairing over a cruel mistress. That the sequence's one completed action—the grandfather's violent muting of the army mules—marks the despondent point at which Muldoon's sequence also falls silent does not negate our experience of the whole of *Horse Latitudes*. We emerge from its whirling wordplay and maddening allusiveness, features typical of his work, moved by the gamble that a contemporary sonnet sequence, loaded with schemes and stratagems, can still possess the imaginative power to discover secret likenesses and the formulas to transform the grim facts it confronts.

# Pound-Foolishness in
*Paterson* (1987)

William Carlos Williams's *Paterson* is both about process and itself a process. As in most modern long poems, its controlling central sensibility, the poet or Paterson, is continually in flux from section to section, page to page, strophe to strophe. M. L. Rosenthal and Sally M. Gall call it a sequence of sequences, "so that one may find, at any moment, a sudden shift of rhythmic base, or of tonal stream, or of voice or general style." They also perceive, as have many others, that "a critique of the economic interests dehumanizing our culture and stripping away the people's memories and traditions" forms one of its "great preoccupations."[1] The poem continually re-examines these economic concerns, and its progressively shifting economic discoveries form one major strain in *Paterson*'s overall lyric structure.

Williams uses Ezra Pound's voice—actually excerpts from Pound's maddeningly idiosyncratic letters—to clarify these economic discoveries, which Dr. Paterson binds together with his explorations in search of a poetic idiom and technique. The economics of *Paterson* is most useful—and most interesting—as a metaphor for these poetic concerns and as an element in the poem's lyric structure, that is, its tonal movement; Pound's markings help map out that technical territory as well. Joel Conarroe, Michael André Bernstein, and Paul Mariani have all observed how to some extent Williams wrote his own epic, *Paterson,* with Pound as his imagined cooperator and antagonist.[2] But although Pound's letters strive to convey speech patterns on the page, one of Paterson's technical aims, they move from clarity to near-lunacy, and through Books 3, 4, and 5 this degeneration disqualifies Pound as Dr. Paterson's mentor and necessitates Williams's exorcism of his friend from the poem. Through this exorcism, Williams declares his poetic and theoretical independence from Pound, and he does so by engineering responses to Pound's voice within the tonal collage of *Paterson*, in each instance placing that voice in a lyric context that will dictate approval or disgust. Since Williams obviously controls the ingredients and tonal movement of his own poem, the Ezra Pound who dwells in *Paterson* is not the biographical Pound, but a carefully selected version of Pound, though by no means a simplistic one, that Williams invents for his own purposes in order to highlight this initial dependence and ultimate rejection.

In the middle of the flood section, *Paterson* 3.3, Pound appears in a letter dated "S. Liz 13 Oct [1948]," in which he prescribes a required reading list for Dr. Paterson, only a few of the "one hundred books . . . / . . . that you need to / read fer yr / mind's sake."[3] The list juxtaposes the classics, "the Gk tragedies in / Loeb" and "Golding's Ovid . . . in / Everyman's lib.," against some of the more arcane influencers and sharers of Pound's own social and economic ideas: Leo Frobenius, a German "proponent of extreme theories of cultural diffusion"; Silvio Gesell, a Social Credit economist, also German; and Brooks Adams, who believed in "the westward movement of culture" and that "American democracy, particularly as a result of its great wealth, is . . . foreordained to degradation and decay."[4] Williams apparently accepted some of Pound's reading advice, since Gesell shows up in Williams's 1951 *Autobiography* as an economist hero, with "a plan to secure an uninterrupted exchange of the products of labor, free from bureaucratic interference, usury, and exploitation."[5]

In *Paterson* 3, however, Pound does not provide illumination but simply adds to the inundation of books, dead facts, and dead literature that Dr. Paterson encounters in the Library while searching for a vital poetic language. In fact, Pound's letter appears in the text immediately after a torrent of words and phrases torn loose from the Library in the flood and angled on the page to suggest the surging chaos, so that the letter's list of names, whether familiar or arcane, classic or crank, provides no lifeline, just more matter to wade through (137). In the middle of that torrential page appears a "*Salut à Antonin Artaud*," whose theatrical ideas Pound has mentioned to Dr. Paterson "eng / passang," but whom Pound insists "I never told you to *read.* . . . / let erlone REread. . . . I didn't / say it *wuz* ! ! *henjoyable* readin" (138). How silly, Pound implies, of Dr. Paterson, to read a book just because Pound casually mentions it. But while Paterson is at it, here are some more: "& nif you want a readin / list ask papa," says Pound the pedant, but don't presume to know what's worthwhile on your own; and as for Artaud, the letter concludes with an oddly charming bigotry: "is fraugs." After all, he's just a Frenchman.

Confronted with Pound's smug dictatorship, the poem rebels. Dr. Paterson has been digging around in the Library throughout Book 3, so Williams immediately presents a metaphor for this attempt to bore into the past, a chart documenting the unsuccessful drilling of an artesian well in Paterson in 1879–80. The report begins with red sandstone at 65 feet, proceeds through sandstone and shale, hits pyrites at 1,180 feet, but soon returns to sandstone, which it keeps encountering until 2,100 feet, when "the attempt to bore through the red sandstone was abandoned, the water being altogether unfit for ordinary use" (139). The chart not only works as metaphor, but also shows the poem literally digging into the geological past, directly confronting it and discovering nothing new. One critic has noted that the report provides "a precise image for the uselessness of 'digging' to find meaning," since "what is striking . . . is the absence of variation" among the readings.[6] Actually, Williams's visual joke is even more complex, since it illustrates how boring into the past can create the *illusion* of discovery: the pyrites, halfway down, are fool's gold, a momentary glimmer duping us into further excavation until it once more becomes simply *boring*. Even if the drill had hit real gold, though, that still would not make the ground fertile and "fit for ordinary use." When both the flood and the drilling come to a "FULL STOP" (140), and Paterson pulls up his drill, the futility of such an operation becomes clear. There, arranged on the page in an inverted pyramid, imitating visually the shape of a drill bit, are the words

> —and leave the world
>> to darkness
>>> and to
>>>> me

Archaic tools, Williams suggests, whether Thomas Gray's stiff pentameters or "*all* the Gk tragedies," make cultural archaeology doubly desperate. An American epic needs not Greek and Latin but "a *reply* to Greek and Latin with the bare hands" (2) [my italics]. The poem rebuts Pound's letter in a manner characteristically Williams's in its invention, its fully implicit handling of theme, and its visual use of the page. However, it shakes Pound off somewhat petulantly, fully capable of denying his influence but still not having discovered a working alternative to his advice. Book 3 soon ends immersed in the attempt to "comb out the language" from the deafening waterfall and with the bold yet somewhat hysterical assertion that "this rhetoric / is real!" (145).

Pound's annoyed, humorous response to this use of his letter in *Paterson* 3 appears in *Paterson* 4.2, where he picks up on the drill chart and continues the argument over Williams's insistence on locality in *Paterson*: ". . . just because they ain't no water fit to drink in that spot (or you ain't found none) don't mean there ain't no fresh water to be had NOWHERE . . . (182) But despite Pound's blast at Williams's apparent provincialism ("in that spot"), this section of the poem works toward a hard-earned harmony between the poets. *Paterson* 4.2 celebrates both Marie Curie's discovery of radium and the liberating potential of an economy based on credit rather than on money. Both the scientific discovery of "the radiant gist" (185) and the economic discovery of credit emerge as implicit metaphors for the poem's grails, the linguistic gist and the vision of beauty in the commonplace. They also become metaphors for each other, in equations that Williams arranges on the page as if chalking up lecture notes: "Money : Joke," "credit : the gist," "Uranium : basic thought—leadward" (184). And Williams, now playing the pedagogue himself, also injects bits of pseudo-Socratic catechism:

| What is credit? | the Parthenon |
| What is money? | the gold entrusted to Phideas for the statue of Pallas Athena, that he "put aside" for private purposes (183) |

The equations, the aggressive tone, the peculiar muckraking, and the pedantry of the section all reverberate with Pound's voice, as several readers have noted[7] and as others have mourned. Randall Jarrell's heart sank as he discussed Williams's use of "Credit and Usury, those enemies of man, God, and contemporary long poems. Dr. Williams has always put up a sturdy resistance to Pound . . . yet he takes Credit and Usury over from Pound and gives them a good home . . .—his motto seems to be, *I'll adopt your child if only he's ugly enough*."[8] Paul Mariani, though, suggests that Williams's equations are "really, one[s] that he'd promised his [readers] in the prologue to the poem years before," uniting the poem's search for native cultural fertility with Curie's healing "radiant seed" in the "womb-shaped alembic" and with the economic fecundity of credit.[9]

It is not at all clear how or even if Williams's equations here hold up logically: Mariani treats them with seductive, festive language in a critical tour de force that creates the illusion of coherence, but the equivalence of "money" with "joke" or "credit" with "the gist" still resists rational analysis. The important technical feature, however, is the poem's tone of triumph at this point, regardless of logic. The poem convinces us that the equations constitute a great discovery because it believes so, and we are swept along—rightly—on this liberating, even patriotic, tide of emotion. The exuberance of the equations also marks an achievement of equilibrium with Pound, who returns to applaud the poem's ingenuity:

IN

venshun.

O.KAY

In venshun (184)

Williams uses these pronouncements of Pound to echo *Paterson*'s own celebration of "invention" in 2.1: "Without invention nothing is well spaced, / unless the mind change" (50), a section which itself seems deliberately to echo Pound's forty-fifth Canto, "With *Usura*." The economic and poetic symbiosis of the two poets appears complete.

Yet among all this harmonious fertility, Williams has sown discordant seeds. In 4.2, not content with simply complimenting *Paterson*, Pound has to push on and assign Williams additional homework: "and seeinz az how yu hv/started. Will you consider/ a remedy of a lot : / i.e. LOCAL control of local purchasing / power . / ? ?" (185). And although Dr. Paterson appears to agree with that sentiment throughout the poem's festive extolling of "Credit. Credit. Credit," the poem dissonantly counters Pound at the same time as it appears to harmonize with him. "You can't steal credit : the Parthenon," the poem lectures, but then it immediately suggests how much we do have to be ashamed of: "—let's skip any reference, at this time, to the Elgin marbles" (183). In other words, any culture's theft of another culture's monuments for its own enrichment is fruitless and criminal, as are Pound's endless cultural appropriations in *The Cantos* and, perhaps, his admiration at the end of *Paterson* 4.2 of "splendour of renaissance cities" (185). And Williams certainly puns on his friend's name—as Pound himself often did—when, in offering his economic equations, he writes,

Money : Joke
could be wiped out
at stroke
of pen
and was when
gold and pound were
devalued (184)

The stroke of the pen can offer credit, relieving the public from the cruel practical joke of monetarism,[10] but the stroke can also assert Williams's control over his own epic, devaluing Pound whenever necessary to maintain the poem's unique vision or technique. The passage amounts to a declaration of poetic independence at the same time as *Paterson* seems most Poundian in its themes and techniques, the poem subtly rebelling just as it appears to knuckle under to Poundian pressure. And the poem immediately reminds itself—and its author— that its economic discoveries are metaphors and do not necessarily yield poetic discoveries: regardless of Dr. Paterson's joy in credit, his ecstasy has distracted him, as the opening of 4.3 will immediately chastise, from his "virgin purpose, / the language" (186).

Further, this devaluation of "pound"/ Pound prepares for the more profound economic and poetic break between Pound and Williams in *Paterson* 5.2, where Williams lets Pound devalue himself in a stagnant, excessive letter, "a page of economic junk," as John Berryman politely called it in a review.[11] Yet the letter opens endearingly and affectionately:

13 Nv   OkeHay    my BilBill    The Bull Bull, ameer. (215)

The tone is confident and confidential: All right, my William Williams, here's the straight poop, chief. Pound's playful punning on Williams's name, from "BilBill" to "Bull Bull," seems also designed to praise his friend, since "bulbul" is the Persian term for both nightingale and poet, and "Ameer Bulbul" a Persian honorific meaning "prince of Poets." Pound's salutation also free-associates to a popular song that both he and Williams would doubtless have known as children, "Abdul, the Bulbul Ameer," about an absurd duel between a reckless Persian prince and a bold Russian warrior.[12] The fond playfulness of a man unashamed to sound warm and silly to his old friend provides the salutation's dominant tone.

But just when Pound seems finally and unselfishly to give Williams his long-awaited due, and just when his tone seems to lighten into conviviality, the letter itself erupts into such shocking excess that it is unclear whether "Bul Bull" really means "double bullshit," "the bullshit about bullion," Pound's own "papal bull on bullion," or any combination of the above. Its clearest parts are Pound's rantings against Roosevelt and American economic policy:

> Wars are made to make debt, and the late one started by the ambulating dunghill FDR has been amply successful.
>
>                     and the stink that elevated
>
> him still emits a smell.
>
> Also the ten vols/ treasury reports . . . show that . . . you suckers had paid ten billion for gold that cd/ have been bought for SIX billion. (216)

Wendy Stallard Flory considers Pound's vitriol towards Roosevelt in the context of widespread hostility toward the president and shows that some of Pound's views on the government's betrayal of the Constitution in fiscal matters apparently stem from ideas long held by Pound's immediate family.[13] But the letter's self-righteous extremism distances him finally from the reader as well as from the poem, especially because Pound still plays the pedant, asking Dr. Paterson, "Is this clear or do you still want DEEtails?" and "If there is anything here that is OBskewer , say so" (216). Further, this OBskewerity and this lack of DEEtail suggest Pound's lack of sympathy with particular cases, a penny-wisdom that could restore his missing sense of proportion and that does provide *Paterson* with its greatest triumphs. Williams devotes much of Book 5 to developing these sympathetic particulars, and through the remainder of the poem they continue to repudiate Pound tacitly.

    The immediate poetic context of Pound's letter sandwiches it between two particular presentations of the beautiful, both of which bring the ancient past vitally into the present. Dr. Paterson agrees with the end of Pound's letter that "offering da shittahd aaabull instead of history is undesirable," but unlike the letter, he attempts to present that world-historical sense through these particular visions that underscore the poem's refusal to acknowledge or assimilate Pound's voice. Preceding Pound comes Williams's translation of Sappho's fragment 31, which he begins, "Peer of the gods is that man." While the version is overheavily influenced by Symonds's translation in its opening,[14] with its archaic syntactic inversion, it successfully conveys the poem's love-terror in a contemporary idiom: "my eyes / are blinded and my ears / thunder. // Sweat pours out . . . / 1 grow paler / than dry grass" (215). Williams then follows Pound with the lyric "There is a woman in our town," who, with her "Grey eyes" and "male attire, / as much as to say to hell // with you," becomes *Paterson*'s modern-day Athena as well as the poet's muse: "have you read anything that I have written? / It is all for you" (217–18). In these lovely, unsentimental passages, Williams reminds the reader—and himself—of what Pound has apparently forgotten: that in conjunction with the living language, "Rigor of beauty is the quest" (3), not to be subordinated to economic concerns.

The notion that the imaginative quest for beauty redeems the artist dominates *Paterson 5*, but in that quest the poem's final book demonstrates several times how far *Paterson* has moved beyond Pound's foolish iconoclasm. For example, the poem implicitly attacks Pound's antisemitism when a collage of those who pursued and realized visions of beauty, including Dürer, Leonardo, Freud, Picasso, and Beethoven, ends with the poem presenting, in Williams's newly devised poetic medium, the triadic-lined variable foot, its own vision,

> recalling the Jew
>         in the pit
>                 among his fellows
> when the indifferent chap
>         with the machine gun
>                 was spraying the heap   .
> he had not yet been hit
>         but smiled

comforting his companions    .
    comforting
        his companions (221)

Williams's sympathy here offers a completely opposing vision to Pound's world of kikes and fraugs and an implicit condemnation of the disastrous fascist sympathies into which Pound's overzealous economic obsessions led him.

Williams, however, has not in the least abandoned his own economic imperatives. Later, in 5.3, the poem's strange improvisation on Bruegel's *Adoration of the Kings* does not insist overtly on the macroeconomic concerns of Pound's letter, but embeds the larger economic needs in a highly particular, highly democratic vision. The Nativity "is a scene, authentic / enough, to be witnessed frequently / among the poor." The family's humble station and "the soldiers' ragged clothes" contrast with "the rich robes" of the Magi, whom the poem casts as "highwaymen" who have "stolen" the gifts they offer to the child (223–25), a peculiar Marxist reading of the painting that persists in the later poem devoted to it in the "Pictures from Breughel" sequence. The economic views to some extent still compare with Pound's, and *Paterson* proceeds to attack "this featureless tribe that has the money now— staring into the atom, completely blind—without grace or pity," as well as "the age of shoddy" produced by the decline of craftsmanship (225). But just as in the immediately following letter from Edward Dahlberg, about an impoverished but "highly intelligent" Danish woman writer (226), Williams integrates the economic argument through particularity and sympathy, making economics—as well as the atheism of his reading of the Nativity—a recurring tonal note within the larger structural chord, that of "the / imagination," which, as the poem insists Bruegel knew, "must be served / . . . / dispassionately" (225).

Finally, Williams had to decide that Pound's presence in *Paterson* was no longer desirable, that Pound's foolishness and extravagant spleen would hinder more than help the poetic usefulness of *Paterson*'s economic strain. And it is characteristic of Williams's honesty and fidelity that in creating his Ezra Pound he decided neither to sentimentalize the sick man in St. Elizabeth's nor to turn him into an easily exorable fascist monster. Pound's letters are very much *in* the poem, and *Paterson*'s continuing dialogue with them provides those sections with much of their humor and tension, but ultimately the letters are not *of* the poem. In creating its circuitous lyric structure, *Paterson* had continually insisted with terrible sadness that visions of beauty exact a terrible price. "I love the locust tree," Book 3 began. "How much? / How much does it cost / to love the locust tree / in bloom? // A fortune . . . // [a] heavy cost" (95). And both Dr. Paterson and the young black woman who has been gang-raped in Book 3's "Beautiful Thing" lyric learn of the envious rage that would destroy the beautiful (127–28). It is a lesser sadness but by no means a small one that in order to preserve *Paterson*'s pursuit of beauty, Williams, despite all his innate and hard-won sympathy with Pound, had to pay the price of finally eliminating from the poem his friend's voice, grown dissonant and stagnant in a way that no longer yielded discovery, and to make such a point of doing so.

# Andrew Hudgins's Blasphemous Imagination (1998)

What distinguishes the painting poems of Andrew Hudgins from most others is their obsession with religious themes, especially problems of belief, an obsession that grows directly out of Hudgins's Southern upbringing. Hudgins's work has always explored the fringe religious element, simultaneously sympathetic with and horrified by those in the grip of mysteries they don't understand and which won't let them live in peace. In the title sequence of his first book, *Saints and Strangers* (1985), a young woman recounts surviving her upbringing as the daughter of a fundamentalist tent preacher in eight dramatic monologues that range, often in the same poem, from the hilarious to the harrowing. Hudgins's second book, *After the Lost War* (1988), is a book-length sequence of lyrical monologues in which the poet Sidney Lanier confronts, in the wreckage of the Confederacy, the deterioration of his own mental and physical health and the consequent challenges to his faith. Subsequently, in Hudgins's autobiographical *The Glass Hammer: A Southern Childhood* (1994), what passes for religion, in its alternating boredom and horror, continually assaults the sensibilities and intelligence of young Hudgins, enough to give readers the blue flusions and send them screaming to the nearest Atheists' Pub. Through those first two books, a major affective tension arises from the conflict between traditional Christian faith and the evolving agnosticism of many of his personae, understandably tempted away from belief.

Throughout Hudgins's third book, *The Never-Ending* (1991), this tension emerges in wonderfully effective ways, most energetically through a series of half a dozen poems inspired by Renaissance paintings, woven as a leitmotif throughout the book. These poems affect an analytical air: they want to understand mysteries of faith, but they also weigh the evidence of the paintings' physical and psychological human situations. They therefore seem to echo Randall Jarrell's famous rejoinder to Auden—"About suffering, about adoration, the old masters / Disagree"[1]—but they go further than Jarrell's or Auden's take on Renaissance art, producing deliberately blasphemous readings of the paintings' religious events. These willful misinterpretations—sometimes *faux naïf,* sometimes scurrilous—paradoxically heighten our affective response to the participants' human dilemmas, so successfully that when we return to the paintings—two by Botticelli, one each by Mantegna, Bosch, Bruegel, and Fra Angelico—we have the illusion that Hudgins has read the artists' minds. I want to look closely at three of these strange and beautiful improvisations—"The Cestello Annunciation" (Botticelli), "Dead Christ" (Mantegna), and "Christ Carrying the Cross" (Bruegel)—to demonstrate how Hudgins's blasphemous poses evoke in us humanitarian sympathy and humanistic revelation.[2]

"The Cestello Annunciation," by sympathizing with Mary's human situation as a frightened, flesh-and-blood young woman, reads the painting as Botticelli's protest against God's unconscionable exercise of power upon her as a vessel through which to work his will.

### THE CESTELLO ANNUNCIATION

The angel has already said, *Be not afraid.*
He's said, *The power of the Most High*
*will darken you.* Her eyes are downcast and half closed.
And there's a long pause—a pause here of forever—
as the angel crowds her. She backs away,
her left side pressed against the picture frame.

He kneels. He's come in all unearthly innocence
to tell her of glory—not knowing, not remembering

how terrible it is. And Botticelli
gives her eternity to turn, look out the doorway, where
on a far hill floats a castle, and halfway across
the river toward it juts a bridge, not completed—

and neither is the touch, angel to virgin,
both her hands held up, both elegant, one raised
as if to say *stop,* while the other hand, the right one,
reaches toward his; and, as it does, it parts her blue robe
and reveals the concealed red of her inner garment
to the red tiles of the floor and the red folds

of the angel's robe. But her whole body pulls away.
Only her head, already haloed, bows,
acquiescing. And though she will, she's not yet said,
*Behold, I am the handmaid of the Lord,*
as Botticelli, in his great pity,

lets her refuse, accept, refuse, and think again. (4)

The poem plays an elaborate game with time. It begins in time, with
the angel having "already said, *Be not afraid,*" but then it stops time—
"there's a long pause"—and immediately proceeds to obliterate time:
"a pause here of forever." Hudgins counters the eternity of God's glory,
"how terrible it is," with the eternity artists create out of human sympathy: "Botticelli / gives her eternity to turn." The painter's compassion
suspends all action: the castle "floats," the bridge "juts" "halfway across
the river . . , not completed," and Mary and the angel have not touched.
In the poem the different gestures of her two hands express her ambivalence, her feeling caught, as the poem's last line tells us, between
refusal—as if she really could refuse—and acceptance. But although
Botticelli stops time in his artifice of eternity, the pressure of God's
quite different eternity still operates on Mary, and ironically, it forces
on her the confining urgency of time and space, so that "her whole
body pulls away," "her left side pressed against the picture frame." Ultimately even the "pause . . . of forever" must end, because "she will,"
although "she's not yet said, / *Behold, I am the handmaid of the Lord.*"

But in addition to this play with time and eternity, the poem's persistent images of incompleteness also build into metaphors of desire, culminating in Hudgins's treatment of Mary's clothing: her right hand

> parts her blue robe
> and reveals the concealed red of her inner garment
> to the red tiles of the floor and the red folds
> of the angel's robe.

Iconographically, of course, the red of Mary's "inner garment"— her kirtle, worn under her blue robe—connotes the Passion, and the consequent suffering she will undergo as Christ's mother. But the poem, in inviting us to consider Mary as a young woman whose role in the world's salvation evokes pity, also invites us to look upon her gesture as a confession of desire, of sexual passion, even of exhibitionism, Mary's human secret revealed only to the sympathetically colored floor tiles and robe of the angel. Hudgins's speaker refrains from observing the painting's startling expression of both Mary's sexuality and her selection as God's vessel, namely, how the vertical pleats of her red kirtle over her womb create a visual pun on vaginal labia.

The angel himself, however, is not sympathetic but inhuman. He is merely the messenger, "unearthly" and ignorant, "not knowing, not remembering / how terrible" glory and eternity are. The "great pity" of Botticelli, famous painter of extraordinarily beautiful women, derives at least in part from the fact that Mary's only consummation will not be sexual, but rather one of terrible knowledge, since she will be filled with God's Word, which "*will darken you*" and result in unimaginable suffering.

A different temptation permeates "Dead Christ," which examines the Mantegna painting, famous for its radically foreshortened perspective, with the viewer placed at Christ's feet. The speaker's pose in this poem is one of utter skepticism: a skepticism so thorough, in fact, that it becomes oxymoronic, as we follow the poem's meditation from incredulity at Christ's death, through a vivid confrontation with death's visual evidence, to an ultimate denial of this Christ's ability to triumph over mortality.

### DEAD CHRIST

There seems no reason he should've died. His hands
are pierced by holes too tidy to have held,
untorn, hard muscles as they writhed on spikes.
And on the pink, scrubbed bottom of each foot
a bee-stung lip pouts daintily.
No reason he should die—and yet, and yet
Christ's eyes are swollen with it, his mouth
hangs slack with it, his belly taut with it,
his long hair lank with it, and damp;
and underneath the clinging funeral cloth
his manhood's huge and useless with it: Death.

One blood-drop trickles toward his wrist. Somehow
the grieving women missed it when they bathed,
today, the empty corpse. Most Christs return.
But this one's flesh. He isn't coming back. (7)

The opening line sounds naive, with no understanding of a "reason" behind Christ's death, the poem feigning ignorance of the larger "reason" for his sacrifice. Yet the line also acknowledges first of all, in the word "seems," that the lack of a reason or purpose for his death might be illusory, and second, that the significance of Christ's death takes us beyond issues of reason into the realm of faith. But the fussy complaints about the irrationality of his death persist: the nail holes in Christ's hands look "too tidy to have held / . . . hard muscles as they writhed on spikes," and the hole in each foot recalls "a bee-stung lip." Decrying this apparent prettification, a startling but precise description of the grim Mantegna painting, the poem finds, emphatically, "No reason he should die."

"And yet, and yet" this close visual attention suddenly places the poem in direct confrontation with all the evidence of death, rummaging over Christ's eyes, mouth, belly, hair, and finding them pervaded by death, culminating in the discovery that "underneath the clinging funeral cloth / his manhood's huge and useless with it." This emphasis on Christ's sexuality corresponds with Renaissance painters' determination to emphasize Christ's humanity by not shrinking from his sexual nature. However, the poem reads Christ's erection not as an emblem of the triumph of the Resurrection, as iconographers like Leo Steinberg would have it,[3] but as one of ultimate futility: like the rest of his body, Christ's genitals are engorged with death. His manhood, though huge, is paradoxically useless, and its uselessness carries the suggestion that his manhood in a larger sense—the miracle of the Incarnation itself—has proven a futile venture. The fullness with which death fills his body renders it an "empty corpse."

The affective movement of "Dead Christ" resembles the meditative structure of seventeenth-century metaphysical lyrics, and the poem "imagines," with Mantegna's assistance, the ruin of Christ's body, its wounds, its writhing on spikes, with the vividness of, say, Donne's imagining of the Crucifixion in "Good Friday, 1613." But the poem's progression of paradoxes culminates not in resolution and prayer but in denial. How are we to read "Most Christs return. / But this one's flesh. He isn't coming back"? Has the poem simply got it wrong, even to the point of mistaking the painted illusion of flesh for flesh itself? Has Hudgins ironically set up a *faux naif* persona as a fall guy, so to speak, who constructs an interpretation of the painting that misses the point, as "the grieving women" miss the "one blood-drop [that] trickles toward his wrist," the one drop that would, as Marlowe's Faustus recognizes, save his soul? Or do the painting's horrific realism and the poem's emotions present a legitimate humanist challenge to faith and to our received wisdom concerning "most Christs"? Hudgins's poem here appears deliberately ambivalent, as paradoxical and mysterious as the events it considers.

In "Christ Carrying the Cross," Hudgins improvises on Bruegel's *Procession to Calvary,* constructing the dramatic situation using a strategy and tone reminiscent of a standup joke.

CHRIST CARRYING THE CROSS

Two crosses on a hill await a third.
A crowd stands in a circle as other townsfolk
swarm slowly up the hill to join them. Where's Christ?
They frolic, gossip, rear their horses, laugh.
Even the soldiers celebrate. They sport
red jackets as they keep some order here.
Not too much. It's an execution, after all.
Where's Christ? There are the thieves. In a horse cart,
one prays, one stares into the sky and howls.
Where's Christ? There's a small town, there's a crag
with a black windmill, rickety, on top.
And there's Christ, hard to see, right in the center.
He's fallen beneath his huge cross. Can he rise?
The revelers kick and taunt him. At church we sing,
*Were you there when they crucified my Lord?*
A crow perched on a torture-wheel looks off
into the distance. Christ staggers, falls, stays down.
Eternity's a long walk, Lord. Get up! (36)

Until nearly the end, the poem sounds dispassionate, almost flippant, its comedy-routine rhythm like some of Stephen Dobyns's seriocomic poems that begin, "A man comes home to find his wife in bed / with the milkman," or "Two angels meet on a fleecy white cloud."[4] In Hudgins's hands this strategy creates tension between the tone and the solemn, world-historical nature of the poem's events, obvious, for example, in the affective twist created at the comma in "It's an execution, after all." Further, the playfully repeated "Where's Christ?" pretends to turn the entire poem into a children's game, a Christian humanist version of "Where's Waldo?" with Bruegel's intensively populated canvas as the game board. The poem therefore plays the same kind of trick with space that "The Cestello Annunciation" plays with time, searching all around the painting until it finds Christ, "hard to see, right in the center."

Paradoxically, the poem has trouble finding Christ at the exact point it should have known to look, but even when it seeks him there, he is literally "hard to see," not to mention difficult to understand, or virtually impossible to follow or emulate. The poem's hunt for Christ naively dramatizes the Christian's hunt for the true path, a path lined ironically with much festivity—people who "frolic, gossip, rear their horses, laugh," and soldiers who "celebrate" and "sport / red jackets." The poem describes the holiday air characteristic of much of Bruegel, and of course it *is* a holiday, not only the holy day of Good Friday, but the Hebrew festival of Passover. The soldiers' attempt to "keep some order here" recalls that holiday's emphasis on order, since the Last Supper was probably a Passover Seder, the symbolic meal whose name literally means "order." But the holiday atmosphere, like the poem's standup-comedy rhythm, so clashes with the events leading up to the Crucifixion that it contributes to the discordant tension.

Once the poem succeeds in identifying Christ, the repeated, childlike "Where's Christ?" yields to a new *faux naïf* question: "Can he rise?" Initially it looks like a simple question of whether Christ is capable of standing and taking up his burden once more, but of course the poem simultaneously is asking, skeptically, about Christ's ability to be resurrected, to transcend his mortal trappings and the human degradation surrounding him. And then, as "the revelers kick and taunt him," the poem drops its pretense of objectivity, and "we" enter for the first time: "At church we sing, / *Were you there when they crucified my Lord?*" Assisted by the painter, the poem suddenly reaches far into the future, with the same kind of transcendent power attributed to Botticelli in "The Cestello Annunciation," to drag us into the scene, where we now search for ourselves—were we there?—just as we have previously looked for Christ. No longer mere observers of the painting or the poem, we become implicated in its action. We not only watch as "Christ staggers, falls, stays down"; we deliver the poem's punch line: "Eternity's a long walk, Lord. Get up!"

On the one hand, this is the punch line of a standup joke, with its echo of Frank O'Hara's "oh Lana Turner we love you get up."[5]

It's a cruel joke, however, unlike O'Hara's social satire, and we have become part of the cruel mob, the revelers kicking and taunting, the soldiers insisting Christ get to his feet and finish the arduous journey to his execution. But as with the ending of "Dead Christ," the poem's apparent blasphemy opens up several theological ambiguities: we may be Christ's persecutors forcing him to his death, but we may also be his petitioners, urging him with astonishing bluntness to rise beneath the cross, so that he might rise *upon* the cross, and thereby rise to heaven, enabling us to rise with him.

None of these issues becomes easily resolved in Hudgins's poetry. With clear, direct language his poems convey affective and theological complexities, and the emotional and linguistic paradoxes of his poems represent metaphorically the paradoxes inherent in Christian myth. The painters who have inspired Hudgins, while probably not anticipating the willfully wrongheaded catechizing performed in these poems, certainly meant their work to generate religious meditations in their audience and so had these paradoxes at heart. Faith is difficult, perhaps impossible, and Hudgins's work does not exhort us to come down on any one side. His improvisations on Renaissance art do, however, communicate the complexities of the human suffering at the core of Christian events, creating in us a sympathy that lets us "refuse, accept, refuse, and think again."

Subsequently, in *The Glass Hammer: A Southern Childhood*, Hudgins movingly updated his work's religious ambivalence by drawing more extensively than ever upon his Baptist upbringing and illuminating how in our daily lives we continue to refuse, accept, refuse, and think again—and yet again. Immanence enters these poems more often not as a religious but as a perceptual or emotional event, sometimes illusory, as in the glorified moment in the book's title poem, when, peering through a crystal knickknack, the infant Hudgins sees "the living room / shift, waver, and go shimmery—haloed // with hidden fire."[6] The poems that communicate transcendence often do so in defiance of biblical texts: when "Hunting with My Brother" (a poem slightly revised from *The Never-Ending*) ends with joyful laughter "at

Cain and Abel coming home / no meat, no beans, and both alive," the poem has escaped from the authoritarianism of Genesis and moved beyond it to a secular but spiritual vision of love and redemption (95).

The liberation of the spiritual impulse in Hudgins requires escaping not Christianity so much as the dogmatic attempts of the Church to govern its flock with terror and ignorance, attempts that cannot purge young Hudgins of his desire in "Gospel" to spend Sunday not in devotion but watching football (42), or, in "When I Was Saved," of his ravening adolescent sexual drive that maintains the demon in his heart "and someplace lower too" (56). In "Sit Still," Brother Vernon's tautological insistence that "God's word is true . . . // because the Bible says it's true. . . . // God says it's true. / And, brother, that's good enough for me," arouses such religious fervor in the congregation that Hudgins mourns, "I sincerely wished that I were stupid" (50). He watches himself trapped in situations that, while certainly not as dire as those of the biblical characters in his painting poems, leave him momentarily as bereft of any human feeling but suffering, and searching for any alternate path in a world that appears fully and miserably determined.

Hudgins's especial distrust of institutions that preach dogmatically rather than ministering to the fragility of humans and their feelings permeates a later poem called "The Humor Institute."[7] In this poem "Officials at the Humor Institute want you / to know they've got work to do" and are tired of prank calls asking for "Anita Dick" and "Fonda Peters," or "another burning sack of dog shit on the porch." "Officials at the Humor Institute," the poem ends, "do not care to speculate / why an elephant is like a quart of milk. / They don't believe you're really seeking knowledge." Hudgins loves jokes. They pervade *The Glass Hammer,* and, as we have seen, he also uses a joke structure in "Christ Carrying the Cross," his poem about the most solemn of religious events. For him, jokes are serious business, but his parodistic Humor Institute kills their joy by treating them the way the Church treats religious belief. "The Humor Institute" protests the way institutions can stifle the human quest for knowledge, the kind of ultimate knowledge about the human heart his poems on Renaissance paintings desire. Into such mysteries Hudgins aims to push us just a little deeper.

# On Writing the Sonnet Sequence
## *Danses Macabres* (2010)

AN INTERVIEW WITH STEFANIE SILVA

**Stefanie Silva:** Why did you choose the sonnet form for this series?

**Jay Rogoff:** I began intending to write a single poem concerning the Dance of Death for a related sequence about dance and saw immediately that it would grow into a sequence of its own. I had recently finished a sonnet sequence called *Venera,* a set of love poems very different in their emotional terrain and trajectory from the *Danses Macabres,* so I was still in "sonnet mode," if you like. Writing sonnets is a pleasure and it can become an obsession; just look at the extended sonnet sequences of the Elizabethans, of the nineteenth century, and even of today (a friend has just told me he has written three hundred sonnets in the past year). Many things make the sonnet attractive as a form: you know many facts about it in advance—how long your poem will be, what much of its rhyme scheme will entail, and, if you're following the Italian form, that it will consist of two major movements climaxing about sixty percent of the way through, with a turn at or around line 9 (or "volta," as it has become fashionable to say). You can then start thinking as you write about how you want to handle those two major motions and what kind of torque you want to give your turn, and as you write your way into the sonnet, language and ideas will accumulate about how it needs to end. I often write in sequences of all kinds, not just sonnets, in which the poems talk to one another, allow you to deal with some thematic and technical obsessions extensively, and relieve you somewhat of having to reinvent a new micro-universe for each new poem. I also like having a sequence that lets me participate in a major literary tradition. No one is likely to better Shakespeare's sonnets (and that's just one reason why I almost always write Italian sonnets, others being that the English form's quatrains seem too compressed to allow a fully developed movement, and that its concluding couplet can chime archaically), but it's nice to get in the game. For a series of specific takes on a larger general theme, the Dance of Death in my case, the sonnet is hard to beat. It allows you to show off, too, in the best way of a poet's showing off: attempting to achieve a satisfying integration of form and expressiveness.

**SS:** I noticed that while the poems don't necessarily have perfect rhyme, very clever sound patterns are used throughout. Can you talk a little about your process in writing these poems? Were you always paying particular attention to alliteration, assonance, and consonance, or were you more concerned about content first over form?

**JR:** The poems follow strict rhyme schemes, but those schemes might sometimes be disguised by the fact that I often slant-rhyme: I will change vowels and occasionally consonants, and sometimes match a masculine with a feminine rhyme. They are all Italian sonnets, with octaves rhyming *abbaabba* and sestets using any combination of two or three rhymes. As for the other sonic devices, I am a very aural poet, which is why rhyme (though usually slant) often enters my work, even many of my poems in free verse. Clusters of language come to me as much for their "music" as for their sense, and internal rhyme, assonance, consonance, alliteration all tend to contribute to my poems' sonic texture. I put "music" in quotes because I'm leery of parallels with actual music; when Eliot says the problems of poetical composition are largely "quasi musical," the qualification "quasi" is significant, and we shouldn't mistake one art for the other. But the frequency and intensity of sonic devices mark one important distinction between poetry and prose, which also means between poetry and speech. Wordsworth said poetry should use "a selection of the language really spoken by men," but sometimes poets forget the importance of selecting. The appeal to my ear is one major criterion I use in selection, and often sound will help me discover either what my poem wants to express or how to get my poem to embody what I intend it to express.

SS: In the first half of the series, the speaker is very knowledgeable about Death, but is removed or distanced from the situations described. Later on, however, starting with "Death's Love," a distinct "I" comes out of the rest of the poems that was absent before—an "I" that seems more emotionally attached. Who did you imagine the speaker to be? Is the speaker the same throughout the series?

JR: The earlier poems in the sequence do create the illusion of objectivity, describing what they see, though often with an attitude. Some of the poems are sarcastic, some of them elegiac, some hysterical, some a mixture of these and other tonalities. But by the end of the sequence—the last seven sonnets, say—the poems create a different kind of illusion, one of personal feeling, as they start to witness and suffer more, responding to someone ill with AIDS, talking about the death of a mother, a wife, a child, a lover. Is this all the same "I"? I think so— I think much of the grim comedy of the sequence starts taking on greater seriousness as Death begins to infect the life of the speaker who has been watching its operations with shocked but amused detachment, and he learns that when it comes to death you don't know nothing, as Yogi Berra said. I hope the sequence accumulates greater poignancy and a touch of horror as it moves towards the end and the speaker understands, loss by loss, that no one is immune, that no one gets out alive.

SS: In these poems, Death is sometimes sexual and lewd, sometimes funny, sometimes gruesome. Why did you want to present so many facets of Death?

**JR:** Well, death does come to us in many forms, but that probably wasn't my motivation. The traditional Dance of Death, dating from medieval times and represented in a series of sixteenth-century woodcuts by Holbein (and maybe most vividly for us in Bergman's film *The Seventh Seal*) shows people from all walks of life being led away by Death in person, from kings and popes down through nobles, gentry, merchants, housewives, farmers, to peasants. I wanted to capture some of that sense of universality in a contemporary guise. Since we live in a democracy, I ignored the strict social stratification of the original models, but I tried to bring in all kinds of modern people who encounter death: little girls, dancers, soldiers, newspaper readers, stylish women, movie audiences, lovers straight and gay, and family members (the mother, bride, baby son)—how would Death make his appearance to each? How would he come for each of these people? That and the imagery of many of my visual sources led into the variety of roles Death plays in the sequence. And having him accompany Adam and Eve—who, after all, did bring death into the world—I hope helps universalize their predicament so we see it as ours as well.

**SS:** In some poems, such as "Death Makes the Man" and "Death's Love," Death seems to take on qualities of an all-powerful maker. "Death Makes the Man" has Death "creating" a creature like Frankenstein's and in "Death's Love," the last line reads, "how Death loves us and molds us in his image," which makes the reader think of God. Again, why did you choose to portray Death that way? What assumptions were you hoping to change about Death?

**JR:** Death as creator—or "Creator," as you suggest—certainly is ironic casting, since death is of course our destroyer. His creations in the poems—the monstrous "man," his molded "image," the (presumably poisonous) "fruit" he prepares at the end of "Death in the Woods," the dances he makes for the ballet student and, in "Curtain Call," the lover, are all intended to further his destructive purposes. They're all weapons of mass destruction (in the sense that they will lay all of us low), so his role really is revealed to be that of an "unmaker," not a "maker." As to Death's—or death's—power, well, death really does intervene in every life in a way God does not. I realize some readers may disagree, but I say this as someone who believes God exists solely in the human imagination, a plausible theory that no one could believe about death.

SS: "Death's Sentence" describes how people "adored / his extremities' probing, his profound love- / play stopping ears, mouths, throats, and orifices. . . ." Does the Death you created love us or are we all fooled?

JR: We are all time's fools, and death's as well, and I hope that comes through in the poems. Death's "love" for us is like the lion's "love" for the zebra, the pederast's "love" for the child (as "Death's Sentence" and especially "Death and the 7-Year-Old Pilot" suggest), and as alluded to a number of times in the sequence, the rapist's "love" for his victim—in other words, cruelty disguised as love (and Death, as you noted, wears many disguises in the sequence). I happen to be teaching *King Lear* right now, and it occurs to me that Goneril, Regan, and Edmund all offer the same kind of masquerade: they're like Death, dolled up hypocritically as loving daughters and a loving son.

SS: Dancing is very important in these poems; dancing, of course, is supposed to be fun, lively, playful, possibly glamorous and sophisticated—everything death is not. What made you decide to present Death as a dead Fred Astaire? How did you come up with such a twist of logic?

JR: Well he's sometimes Dead Astaire, I suppose, though he takes on many roles in addition to ideal dance partner: comforter, lover, ballet master, guide, nurse, poet, inventor, salesman, inmate, adulterer, and so on. Some of these roles are sophisticated, some of them pretty mundane, and just about all of them ironic. I do intend him to be master of all situations—because our mortality does master us all, finally. But I also want readers to perceive his hypocrisy, the holes in his arguments, the ways in which his seductiveness is finally a betrayal of everything that makes us human. Like most modern people, I really have no conception of a personified Death, just as (possibly unlike most modern people) I have no belief in a personified God. But I wanted the sequence to entertain in a gallows humor way. I wanted the poems to be as much fun as possible, but still be about our mortality and still have a morbid creepiness about them. That's why I use so many puns (a device I resort to in much of my poetry, humorous or serious), and also why Death is so lively—an antimatter *bon vivant.* The opening poem, in fact, in which "Death Goes to a Party," takes its title from the old *Life* magazine, which used to talk about itself in third person. When a photo spread of some big social event appeared, it would carry the heading "*Life* Goes to a Party."

**SS:** Did your experience as dance critic influence your poems in *Twenty Danses Macabres?*

**JR:** No, for the simple reason that I drafted most of the sonnets in the 1990s, before I started writing dance criticism. However, I was also working at the time on a long series of poems inspired by dance, and that certainly gave me the idea to extend that theme into the Dance of Death motif. At first, as I said, I was going to write a single sonnet on the Dance of Death, but writing sonnets is addictive, and I ended up drafting a sonnet a day for about a month during a stay at Yaddo.

For what it's worth, I started writing dance criticism in 1999, when I did a piece for *Kenyon Review* about books and exhibitions about the New York City Ballet, which had just marked its fiftieth birthday. Over the next few years I wrote more review-essays on dance books (for *Southern Review* and *Georgia Review*), and in 2007 I became summer dance critic for my local paper, *The Saratogian,* reviewing the annual Saratoga season of NYCB, as well as occasional modern dance performances. Since 2009 I have also been writing about dance four times a year for the *Hopkins Review,* and I have recently begun contributing to *Ballet Review.*[1] My own dance going dates back to my high school days, but I have never taken ballet or modern dance.

**SS:** Humans also are very important to these poems: some of them seem to be fooled by Death, for they seem to think that Death can provide a better "life." In "Death the Dietician," for example, the "she" in the poem has put life on pause, "slamming the brakes" on growth because of anorexia. Did you intend to make some commentary about how humans take life for granted, or humans' fear of mortality?

**JR:** Certainly our fear of mortality is in there, but I don't intend any commentary as much as an exploration of that fear as a human response that can range from the stoical and accepting to the hysterical and extreme. As with traditional Dance of Death imagery, parts of the sequence are satirical (when Death comes for the miser in a famous Bosch painting, he reaches not for his Bible but for his moneybags), and one thing I play with is the romanticizing of death, the sometimes seductive illusion that somehow death is better than living, that Death is beautiful, that Death is the only one who really cares about us, that Death brings the cure for illness, the solution for all the problems of our lives. As a living, more or less functioning person, I find that glamorous kind of despair thoroughly unseductive; as a poet, I find it useful and fascinating. This conflict, which I often find in myself as a poet (for example, I have often played with Christian imagery though I was not raised in Christianity and believe that religious faith is an imaginary delusion), I think accounts for the multiple ironies of Death's many roles, which I mentioned earlier. He often appears eager to assist and comfort but it's all a very well-rehearsed act.

**SS:** Poems like "Death's Deal" take a very informal tone (Death is described as a "shyster"), seemingly stripping away the formality of Death. Why did you choose to write some of these poems in an informal way?

**JR:** For me one of the pleasures of writing poetry is playing with diction, and I love mixing levels of language within a series of poems, and even in the same poem. I'm not sure any single sonnet is wholly elevated or wholly casual in its diction: I think in almost every one you'll find both something Poetic with a capital P alongside something demotic. You're right in saying that "Death's Deal" is mostly informal; it's dominated by slang and a comic collection of clichés (some of which come, if I'm remembering correctly, from the dialogue of a telephoning skeleton in an old Betty Boop cartoon). Yet it also goes Elizabethan, pulling in "mazzard" from *Hamlet,* even though I use the word for comic effect (as does Hamlet). More typically in the sequence you'll see a combination of high and low: "Death in Disguise" contains the word "*ka-boing*" but also "twining himself round any alphabet / as subtly as snaking through a tree"; "Death Sings Lieder" pulls in the Yiddish expression of dismay, "*Oy vey iz mir,*" alongside Death "Singing her delicate and beautiful."

**SS:** Who was your inspiration for these poems? Were you reading some specific poets at the time you were writing these poems?

**JR:** Many factors inspired me, many of them visual. My wife is an art historian who works on late medieval and early Renaissance art, and some of the sonnets have specific visual sources—most obviously the opening sonnet, "Death Goes to a Party," which imaginatively enters the 1493 woodcut of dancing skeletons that appears on the chapbook's cover and frontispiece. A few sonnets are inspired by images of Death in the very strange paintings of the German artist Hans Baldung Grien. The Renaissance imagery felt appropriate for a sonnet sequence, but I also wanted to bring the material down through history into the present, and not to limit the sources to what we think of as "fine art" (though woodcuts were mass-produced images). "Death Sings Lieder" rings some changes on the lyrics of Schubert's chilling song "Death and the Maiden," translated for me by my musicologist friend Tom Denny; "Death at Midnight" brings together visual imagery from Daniel Chodowiecki's Dance of Death prints (1792) with lines (mischievously altered) from Coleridge's "Frost at Midnight" (1798), a poem that has long obsessed me; "Sweet Decorum" (a title that I hope will remind readers of Horace but especially Wilfred Owen) was inspired by a monograph another friend, the Romanticism scholar Sarah Goodwin, shared with me, on personifications of Death in World War I medals; two of the sonnets, "Death's Deal" and especially "Death's Animation," use imagery and language from 1930s Betty Boop cartoons. "La Valse" takes off from the George Balanchine ballet of the same name, set to Ravel's astonishing and disturbing waltzes. This is not to say that all my sources are other works of art. "Death's Love" records an actual experience I had walking down a New York City street and initially mistaking a young man with AIDS for someone elderly; many lines in "Horoscope" came verbatim—or nearly verbatim—from one day's set of horoscopes in the *Saratogian,* my local newspaper ("Paranormal abilities may surface"—you can't improve on that!); the seven-year-old pilot's death was a big news story in 1996; "Death's Sentence" derives from my years of teaching and advising in Skidmore College's now-defunct bachelor's degree program for prison inmates—I witnessed both the guard whistling *Für Elise* and officers running their nightsticks along the bars to irritate inmates; some of the imagery in "Death in the Woods" came during a stay at Yaddo as I watched a woodchuck through a wavery old window; "Breathless" was inspired not by a dream of my own, but by one a friend related to me about a dead boyfriend.

As far as literary sources and other poets, I've already mentioned Coleridge and Owen with regard to particular sonnets; "Death's Sympathy," of course, is a rewriting of the ending of *Paradise Lost,* with Death taking the place of Providence leading Adam and Eve, and it plays with some of Milton's language; "Death's Sentence" uses a line from Donne's "The Extasie"; "Death in Disguise" begins as a travesty of Wallace Stevens. There was no one poet in particular behind the sequence, though in my twenties I was obsessed with Berryman, and something of his strange mixture of diction (though not his grammatical wackiness) has permanently become part of my style; that mixture is often highly allusive, and sometimes my poems will import phrases from Shakespeare ("mazzard" in "Death's Deal" comes from Hamlet's conversation with the gravedigger), Keats, Wordsworth, Lowell, and others, often wrenched woefully out of context and put to my own devices—whatever seems to work. At the time I was writing the *Danses Macabres,* Anthony Hecht was working on his Death poems, gathered in *The Flight among the Tombs,* but I had not yet read any of them so they weren't an influence. I also love Christian Morgenstern's *Gallows Songs,* but I wasn't specifically looking at them, either. I *have* in the past consciously stolen things I found in other poets: at one time I was deliberately trying to emulate some of A. R. Ammons's syntactic tricks, and I have always loved the illusion of candor and rawness of feeling in Randall Jarrell's late work. One sequence I have written tries to marry Auden and Stevie Smith, with rather strange results. But there's no one poet or group of poets lurking behind the *Danses Macabres.*

Of course another inspiration was the fact that I had come midway through my life's journey and entered my forties. But as far as meditations on death, I think some of the poems in my book *The Long Fault* [2] come closer to my personal sense of my own mortality. The *DMs,* I hope, breathe a darkly jaunty carnival/Days of the Dead atmosphere, with dread underlying the whole.

SS: How is the process of writing a chapbook different from writing an entire poetry book? Did you intend for these poems to become a chapbook? Are you hoping for the chapbook to become part of your next book?

JR: You've actually guessed correctly: *Twenty Danses Macabres* is a selection from a longer sequence, simply called *Danses Macabres.* The full sequence has thirty-four poems, giving it greater variety, including a few sonnets even nastier than those in the chapbook (a poem called "Matter of Death" ends with the sentence "Death's shit is shit"). It will be the second half of my next book, *The Art of Gravity,* which LSU Press will publish in fall 2011. The first half, a sequence called *The Code of Terpsichore,* is a set of poems that uses dance in a variety of ways. Some are near-ekphrastic poems that deal with specific ballets and modern dances, some take dance as an occasion for metaphysical meditation or romantic fantasy, some are homages to specific dancers, some reflect the personal experience of dancing, and some use dance as symbol or metaphor.

As far as assembling the chapbook, I made a selection from the complete thirty-four of twenty poems I thought would work together well and still give a sense of the full sequence's emotional and thematic range as well as its affective trajectory. I always thought that some of the sonnets would make a strong chapbook, but since I had so many of them (the thirty-four were themselves selected from about fifty that I had drafted), making the chapbook became a matter of editing down. The poems in *Twenty Danses Macabres* appear in more or less the same order as in the full sequence, which has more poems interspersed among them. There's also a final poem, "Come Away, Death," that I append after the chapbook's last sonnet, "Curtain Call," as an Envoy. It's a thirteen-line sonnet in first person—I liked the idea of the speaker having his work cut short. The book opens with a poem called "Invocation" and ends with that Envoy, giving it a kind of symmetry.

I hope the full sequence will appeal to those who like the chapbook and, equally important, that it balances *The Art of Gravity*'s opening section about dance, which so often aspires to the air, with the reminder that gravity insists on pulling us back down.

# II.

*Becoming Poetry*

# Credentials (2000)

*On Rachel Hadas, Eamon Grennan, and Karl Shapiro*

We experience poets' selected works far differently from the way we read books of their new poems. Beyond our evaluation of its individual poems, a book of new work provokes questions of thematic and technical unity, of organic wholeness. But when we read a selected, we usually suspend that category of our aesthetic judgment in favor of larger considerations that make such a volume, in spite of the fact that most of its contents have seen the light of day, a riskier undertaking for the poet. We embark on a more variegated enterprise, and while we can't expect a book made of poems plucked from, say, half a dozen well-shaped books to offer a satisfying affective trajectory of its own, we do ask such a collection to provide new explanations and satisfactions, and to answer more rigorous questions about the poet's development and importance.

If a single book of poems resembles a painter's exhibition of new work, a selected volume is the retrospective. Most, like most retrospective art shows, employ chronology as their organizing principle, enabling us to chart the poet's career and watch the work's themes and obsessions bud, blossom, and ripen. A poet who disregards chronology in arranging such a selection only intensifies our desire to know what came when, a desire frustrated by, for example, Randall Jarrell's thematic sorting for his 1955 *Selected Poems* (all the more frustrating because Farrar retained it for the *Complete Poems*). We don't really need an organization by topic, since we can readily *see* what subjects obsess poets again and again; in a picture gallery, we may trip over ourselves running from room to room to compare Degas's successive handlings of musicians or horses, but we can easily flip back and forth to lay an early poem about fathers and children against a later: what we want to *know* is the biography of the poetry, the journey of the poet's imaginative evocations of parents or birds or illness or Greece.

A chronologically arranged selected poems, then, invites us to evaluate the progressive search for themes and struggle with style that define a considerable segment of the poet's career. In such an evaluation, we look less for the satisfying unity of the book as a work of art, and more for the literary-historical unity of the poet—not the biographical poet, but the artistic construct created by the accumulation of years of poems—as a force to be reckoned with. We start to judge the poetry not as something produced *by* the poet, but as a set of credentials that *is* the poet, and which will permanently identify the poet as having some claim in the kingdom. In such a book, the poet begins the process of becoming the work.

With a selected poems, then, the poet hazards his or her reputation, and two poets discussed here, Rachel Hadas and Eamon Grennan, both well-established and midway in their careers, both keenly attuned to how the dailiness of human existence helps us confront and accommodate our world's disturbances, roll out some impressive credentials. The third poet, Karl Shapiro, has given us memorable poems for over six decades, and, at a time when almost all his poetry is out of print, this new selection assembled by Stanley Kunitz and the late David Ignatow should ensure that the best of his work remain before us.

I almost wish that Rachel Hadas's *Halfway Down the Hall* didn't begin with her thirty-three new poems, because the best of them would make a sumptuous dessert. For starters, we should sample the poems written in her twenties, from her 1975 chapbook *Starting from Troy*, with their savor of technical mastery:

Sing now the heavy furniture of the fall,
the journey's ending. Strong Aeneas bears
deep on his shoulders all the dark wood chairs
and tables of destruction.

    ("The Fall of Troy" [67])

The girls in Lesbos have dark eyes
and scorn to play their natural role.
Flowers don't photosynthesize
on beach and field there, blooming damp
and rich in moonlight. Mushroom-pale
they must have been, but Sappho saw
what flowers blossomed at her feet.

    ("Sappho, Keats" [68])

Neither of these two poems ends as confidently as it begins, but through
clever reimagining, both beginnings playfully lighten what could have
become heavy literary self-importance. In "The Fall of Troy," Hadas's
*faux naïf* literal rendering of the mythological "endings of houses," furniture and all, punningly turns the historical record into a mahogany
"table of destruction," domesticating the *Aeneid* as a rainy-day game
she might have invented with her classicist father (the subject of several other poems), in a household where the classics *were* the furniture.
The witty tetrameters of "Sappho, Keats" create a sophisticated Eliot-
like distance, while at the same time dreamily imagining Lesbos as a
mysterious realm of night-creatures and night-flowers.

    This combination of neoclassical wit and Romantic sensibility, es-
tablished so early here, continues to drive Hadas's best work throughout her career. The early poems also show how Hadas's own classical
training has engaged her in literary tradition so sympathetically that
nothing seems self-consciously dressed up: the past is her comfortable
habit, and it's therefore no surprise that she translates superbly for a
modern audience, as shown by her recent version of Euripides' *Helen*.
(One section of *Halfway Down the Hall,* from Hadas's 1994 book of

translations, *Other Worlds Than This,* contains a chorus from *Helen,* as well as versions from Tibullus, Victor Hugo, Baudelaire, Valéry, and the modern Greek poet Kostas Karyotakis, and is marred only by its lack of notes.)

Far from settling into a career as a confirmed formalist, Hadas has always experimented with a wide variety of forms and with free verse. In her early books, however, she doesn't always find the right balance of form and subject, especially in the exuberance of some of her poems from *A Son from Sleep* (1983), which overindulge in a kind of Victorian baby worship, neither fully creating the illusion of complex personal emotion nor bursting free of the forms that contain them. "Two and One," for example, in spite of its skillful Blake-like dimeter ("mother, father, / baby, lie / close together / under the sky" [99]), doesn't push beyond the sentimental nursery form to a psychological revelation about the newly nuclear family.

But Hadas's obsessive exploration of her subject—the new baby— leads her to poetic resources that yield profounder feeling. "Ode on His Sleep" considers our entry into a world of mortality and flux by beginning with a Donne-like conceit of the baby as the earth—"you have once again / done your nocturnal spin," . . . "two / points of a compass that points everywhere" (95)—and then makes good on its intellectual frame through a Romantic vision in which our death masquerades as a return to childhood sleep, an entry into the crib-like grave where we all become that earth:

> Tired, we are glad to see the cozy pen,
> its tidy lines dividing time and space again.
> We climb back in and sleep a lifetime off. (96)

Hadas turns increasingly to these more complex songs of experience as her poems chronicle the child's growth. Several poems involve the act of mother and son reading together, "Starting with fairy tales, / . . . from heroes' feats / down to the intricate workings of a blood cell" ("In the Hammock" [135]), an activity "where space and time curl up together," collapsing the distance between the mother and her dead father, so "Disparate gravities of our two ages / dissolve as we lie back and let the pages / take us, float us, sail us out to sea" ("Moments of Summer" [136]). Hadas's poems more urgently acquire life from the entrance of death, and her formal organizations acquire more power in their symbolic enactment of the creative force necessary to sustain life. When her speaker responds to her son's demand to "Fix it!" the task of mending a toy is nothing less than repairing the Fall:

> I lean my ladder on
> the beautiful, the flawed
> handiwork of God
> and turn to spy my son
>
> busy way down there
> patching a balloon,
> filling in the moon.
> The whole world needs repair.
>
> ("I Lean My Ladder" [105])

The mother "climb[s] up to mend the blue / disasters in the sky," but Hadas's poems begin to encounter with greater frequency things unmendable except in the imagination.

As her poems move further out into the fragile world, Hadas's key elegiac subjects include AIDS victims—several poems emerge from a poetry workshop she taught for patients with the disease—and her mother, who dies of cancer. Her speaker sees her workshop students as a

> Circle of pale men
> living their lives ahead of the unknown
> allotted season, day, or afternoon,
>
> hour, minute. (Achilles to Lykaon:
> "Morning or midday, friend, my time will come.")
> A waxy light pervades this basement room. . . . ("October" [150])

The ring of shades and the tercets gesturing at terza rima give us a glimpse of pain like that of Dante's Hell. The poem chiefly alludes, though, to the fates of the *Iliad*'s warriors: the fact that AIDS patients, like Achilles, live with terrible knowledge of their doom and, also like Achilles, quite literally struggle against themselves, renders them heroic and the poem stoically unsentimental.

Hadas also sings such heroism in individual cases, as in "The Last Movie," which ends by offering the speaker's dying friend, now blind, the choice of raging like Lear or retreating to bed—as we all do at the end of "Ode on His Sleep"—but not deigning to privilege either option. Rather, she ends on a heartbreaking note of sympathy:

> from this extremity you can attempt
> to rise to rage and grief. Or you can yield
>
> to the cozy quicksand of the bed.
> You wave your hand at walls of books:
>
> "What do I do? Do I throw all these away?"
> Their anecdotes, their comforts—now black glass. (210–11)

The AIDS elegies join with the mother poems in an extraordinary poem, "The Wolf in the Bed," in which the speaker visiting her dying friend imagines her dying mother joining them, and all three snuggling down with Red Riding Hood's wolf, a perfect emblem of the ravages of both bodies:

> Now I arrive and climb in with you both
> (the wolf makes room for me a little while)
> and gingerly, so as not
> to jar your various lifelines,
> cradle you in my arms, my friend, my mother,
> and read you stories of children
> walking unattended through dark woods. (212)

As confronting mortality broadens the world of Hadas's poems, her dealings with AIDS give them a more urgent, always subtle moral and political edge. Yet the power of her new poems—enough first-rate new work to have merited a book all its own—emanates from the strength of feeling they create. In "The Peacock in the Garden," all these fresh deaths suddenly come to her via the gorgeous bird in an annunciation, at first dreaded like that in "Leda and the Swan": "I imagined the thump of a landing, the unwieldy weight." But the speaker makes her peace with the peacock, by seeing in him emblems of those she mourns: "My silent dead looked out at me from him. / Oceans were coded on his brilliant back; / a deep green forest and a galaxy / were doubly folded in the starry tail" (12).

In these new poems, Hadas works vigorously and confidently in a variety of forms: blank verse, quatrains, heroic couplets, sonnets, a villanelle, Sapphics, dactylic tetrameter, a kind of Spenserian stanza, and more. The poem "Halfway Down the Hall" uses highly conversational triplets with carefully enjambed rhymes:

> Bruno Bettelheim observes somewhere
> that autistic children in his care
> reduce domestic articles to their
>
> lowest denominator. Thus (he wrote)
> butter became *grease,* sugar *sand.* I quote
> this sketchily remembered anecdote
>
> from one of the Anchor Books that would arrive
> in our apartment on Riverside Drive
> back when both my parents were alive. (56)

Hadas purposefully exploits this matter-of-fact expository tone to unleash a prodigious flood of memory, primarily of "crouching in the nook" at the bookcase "halfway down the hall," absorbing the host of authors that have, to a very real extent, created her speaker. And then the poem tells us her grasp on language and the world it creates has begun to slip as strangely as if she were one of Bettelheim's autistics:

> Because Alzheimer's—yes, senility—
> or midlife intimations anyway
> make it hard to process what I see.

> Grown strange through too much familiarity,
> everything specific falls away.
> I have to grope for what I want to say;
>
> it still emerges alien. (57)

After a slew of new poems that exhibit exquisite detail and clarity but seem to stop short of overt visionary experience, "Halfway" comes like a slap. We suddenly realize that in Hadas's work the quotidian *is* visionary, and the ability to see, hear, articulate—the dailiness of life—is in fact miraculous. As "the normal nourishment of brain and eye / flickers toward invisibility" (58), *Halfway Down the Hall* movingly enacts how, as "Fleshly Answers" puts it, "We are passing through the world. / This is some of what it does to us" (13).

The earliest work in *Relations: New and Selected Poems* shows that Eamon Grennan has always had a superb ear:

> Three sounds to measure
> My hour here at the window:
> The slow swish of the sea
> The squeak of hungry birds
> The quick ticking of rain. ("Facts of Life, Ballymoney" [5])

Grennan has learned a great deal from his Irish masters Seamus Heaney and Derek Mahon, and in another early poem, "A Gentle Art," the speaker imagines his mother teaching him anew how to light a fire (though a coal fire, not turf), placing us smack in the midst of Irish domestic myth. In a Yeatsian fashion, though without Yeatsian grandeur, Grennan's care with language enlarges the craft of firemaking so that it truly becomes a gentle, not a peasant art:

> At a certain moment you may be sure (she'd say)
> It's caught. Then simply leave it be:
> It's on its own now, leading its mysterious
> Hungry life, becoming more itself by the minute,
> Like a child grown up, growing strange. (7)

The final two lines end the poem wonderfully through the simile, a subtle reminder of how we are all consumed with that which we were nourished by. Further, the final "strangeness" of the child and fire recalls Coleridge's abstruser musings upon the fluttering fireplace "stranger" in "Frost at Midnight," another meditation upon the tentativity of the parent-child connection as both grow inexorably apart. The allusion forecasts things to come, for Grennan's poetry has become increasingly Romantic, and his virtues, strategies, and some of his shortcomings often resemble Wordsworth's. Further, having lived in America now for the bulk of his career, he has acquired something of the colloquial voice and occasional quirkiness of Frost.

As good as Grennan's early poems can be, however, they are sometimes plagued by a couple of young-poet flaws. One of these is a sentimentality that substitutes Poetry for psychological plausibility, emerging most frequently in his poems about animals. He imagines a dead rabbit "tranquil, / As if he's dreaming / the mesmerised love of strangers // Who inhabit the red tent / Of his ribs, the radiant / Open house of his heart" ("Lying Low" [22]), a dream I'm certain no rabbit ever dreamt, dead or alive; and when, after boiling lobsters, his speaker dumps the shells and "that last / knowing spasm eels up my arm again / and off, like a flash, across the rueful stars" ("Incident" [37]), it hardly seems an occasion made for cosmic atonement—they're *lobsters.* Similarly, some allegorical moments have little to do with realistic human activity: it's symbolic but improbable that "I spent the morning my father died / Catching flies" ("End of Winter" [23]). Another odd mannerism of his early poems is their casting of tautologies in terms of simile: thus "the cat, nimble as a cat" ("Tower House, Ballymoney, 1978" [14]), "the milk shone white as milk" ("Porridge" [43]), and a lizard that moves "quick as a lizard" ("Lizards in Sardinia" [50]) don't reveal much about cat, milk, or reptile.

I like Grennan best when he's looking hard at a fixed subject and using language fruitfully, as in the punning ending of "Cavalier and Smiling Girl," his poem on a Vermeer painting:

No grief in this luminous
Mortal minute, this little room
Where her indigenous smile
Fixes something between them—
Making light of her life. (24)

That last line divulges the seriousness of Dutch frivolity when captured by the painter's miraculous technique. Such attention, far from
making Grennan a miniaturist, compresses enormous feeling into
the microcosm. A later poem, "Kitchen Vision," describes "my own
view of things / come to light at last: I loom, huge / freckled hands, in
the electric kettle's / aluminum belly" (79). The funhouse reflection
sucks the entire world in, even a print that shows "the tiny mourning face / of Botticelli's Venus, hung / above a Lilliputian door," and
the speaker's careful observations of this distorted world admit the
equally careful deflation of the playful ending, which literally lets the
steam out:

and you—a mile away at the stove
turning the eggs—turn round

to look at me gazing
at my own
sharply seen misshapen self
in the kettle
that's just starting to sing,
its hot breath steaming. (79–80)

Grennan's poetry is careful, decorous, and often cast in stanzas of
equal length, so his work feels very formal, even though almost all
of it is in free verse. He thereby visually restrains his Romantic sensibility, but despite this care, his speakers can succumb to the kind
of egotistical indulgence that sometimes mars Wordsworth, as if the
world were created expressly for them. "Kitchen Vision" winningly
parodies the kind of self-absorption all too prevalent in other Grennan
poems, "Firefly," for instance, in which the insect shows

> a brilliance beyond description
> which filled my eyes as if responding to
> the bare encouragement of breath I'd offered,
> this kiss of life in a lighter dispensation,
> as if I'd been part of its other world
> for a minute, almost an element of air
> and speaking some common tongue to it,
> a body language rarefied beyond the vast
> difference between our two bodies. . . . (162)

And so on. When Grennan gets on his metaphysical high horse, or when he overdoes his descriptions, I mentally bluepencil words, phrases, even groups of lines. But when a great subject focuses him, as in "Head-lines," the speaker's memory of his mother set in the context of the Irish Troubles, he carves language with shimmering intensity:

> I knock on the tree. It opens
> into my mother's grave: a beech tree
> coming into leaf. Wan green
> springlight: one wind-up wren
> clicking for cover, making her bed
> in a tenement of dead wood. (149)

The poem brilliantly and brutally flashes images of "a girl's head, a man's hand / holding the gun against it: she feels / the small round point of it for a second," all set against a sensuous riot of spring, "lacy / sprays of laurel, cherry blossom's / pink boudoir."

Happily, this kind of attention and intensity marks most of Grennan's twenty-eight new poems, which, like Rachel Hadas's, also show a more urgent obsession with mortality. A new Vermeer poem, "Woman with Pearl Necklace," trickily exploits a momentary confusion of grammatical tense, using future instead of past perfect to intimate how art will outlast us all:

> Since he painted her, she will always be putting this pearl necklace on
> in her own ordinary room of light. . . . (191)

And "Levitations" uses long lines and rolling rhythms to provide another moving meditation on mutability, with echoes of Hopkins's "The Windhover":

> the ground we think is steady under us
> isn't, but spins its heartless wheel, while those savvy
> whitebreasted swallows or sandmartins standing on the wind
> like idle things, are all the time working their hearts out
> to stay in the one place, still as we are, and go on holding. (217)

Grennan seems to have succeeded at paring away much of his excess, and if he keeps cutting and shaping as he has in these new poems, he will offer us jewels.

Karl Shapiro burst upon the scene in his twenties, won the Pulitzer at thirty-one, and in the 1940s and '50s was at least as widely read as Jarrell, Lowell, or Berryman. As such, he presents a somewhat different case from that of Hadas or Grennan, and it's criminal that Random House let all his books go out of print, including the *Collected Poems*. Therefore it's gratifying to have *The Wild Card*, a new, large selection of his work, a book nearly twice the size of his 1986 *New and Selected Poems*.

In his famous early poems, from *Person, Place and Thing* (1942), Shapiro focuses like a sociological surgeon on the American scene, anatomizing our cultural institutions in "Hospital" ("Inside or out, the key is pain" [9]), "University" ("To hurt the Negro and avoid the Jew / Is the curriculum" [13]), "Drug Store" ("It baffles the foreigner like an idiom, / And he is right to adopt it as a form / Less serious than the living-room or bar" [15]), "Haircut" ("In mirrors of marble and silver I see us forever / Increasing" [16]), "Emporium" ("Not Faust, who longed for Hell, would sell his light / For moving stairs and mirrors set in miles / Where wives might wander with their sex in sight" [25]), and "Necropolis" ("Even in death they prosper; even in the death / Where lust lies senseless and pride fallow" [21]). But Shapiro is no mere satirist. Though he could famously apostrophize "The Fly" in a mock-Romantic swoon—"Oh hideous little bat, the size of snot, / With polyhedral eye and shabby clothes" (11)—he could also animate "A Cut Flower" with such tenderness as to obliterate the divisions among person, place, and thing, and focus the essential pathos of life, just when young men were being cut down in Europe and Asia:

> Yesterday I was well, and then the gleam,
> The thing sharper than frost cut me in half.
> I fainted and was lifted high. I feel
> Waist-deep in rain. My face is dry and drawn.
> My beauty leaks into the glass like rain.
> When first I opened to the sun I thought
> My colors would be parched. Where are my bees?
> Must I die now? Is this a part of life? (44)

The war poems of Shapiro's Pulitzer book, *V-Letter and Other Poems* (1944), carry on the tradition of Wilfred Owen and others by refusing to let even a "good" war disguise the fact of human suffering, showing—in a reversal of the personification of "A Cut Flower"—how soldiers are reduced to cargo, and by highlighting the ambiguous feelings they attach to their country in wartime:

> Trains lead to ships and ships to death or trains,
> And trains to death or trucks, and trucks to death,
> Or trucks lead to the march, the march to death,
> Or that survival which is all our hope;
> And death leads back to trucks and trains and ships,
> But life leads to the march, O flag! at last
> The place of life found after trains and death—
> Nightfall of nations brilliant after war. ("Troop Train" [48])

And "V-Letter," conversely, personalizes the war by showing its impact on human love: "I love you first because your years / Lead to my matter-of-fact and simple death / Or to our open marriage, / And I pray nothing for my safety back" (72).

Beyond his postwar poetry, including the wonderfully eccentric and unexcerptable *Essay on Rime* (1945), the book that led William

Carlos Williams to declare, "Shapiro Is All Right,"[1] the war continued
to obsess Shapiro well into the 1950s. His selected volume *Poems of a
Jew* (1958) carries on a personal resistance to the horrors of the Holocaust and the indignities of American bigotry. The handful of new poems Shapiro produced for that book rank among his best—"Messias,"
"The Confirmation," "The Murder of Moses," and especially "The Alphabet," which I quote in full:

> The letters of the Jews as strict as flames
> Or little terrible flowers lean
> Stubbornly upwards through the perfect ages,
> Singing through solid stone the sacred names.
> The letters of the Jews are black and clean
> And lie in chain-line over Christian pages.
> The chosen letters bristle like barbed wire
> That hedge the flesh of man,
> Twisting and tightening the book that warns.
> These words, this burning bush, this flickering pyre
> Unsacrifices the bled son of man
> Yet plaits his crown of thorns.
>
> Where go the tipsy idols of the Roman
> Past synagogues of patient time,
> Where go the sisters of the Gothic rose,
> Where go the blue eyes of the Polish women
> Past the almost natural crime,
> Past the still speaking embers of ghettos,
> There rise the tinder flowers of the Jews.
> The letters of the Jews are dancing knives
> That carve the heart of darkness seven ways.
> These are the letters that all men refuse
> And will refuse until the king arrives
> And will refuse until the death of time
> And all is rolled back in the book of days. (115)

This great poem, perhaps the greatest Shapiro has written, takes on all
of history with an uncanny fervor. The Hebrew alphabet, flames that

purge and flowers that endure, represents both the Jews' strength and the tortures heaped upon them: the Nazi pyre becomes the burning bush, and at the end of time, when "all is rolled back in the book of days," the final conflagration will be the light of Creation that begins Genesis. It is a brilliant myth of history that confronts every antisemitic tradition with the declaration that the Hebrew scriptures behave cyclically and have both the first and last Word.

Some believe Shapiro's work has grown increasingly slack after the 1950s, when he began to abandon strict forms and produced his notorious prose-poem sequence, *The Bourgeois Poet* (1964), generously excerpted in *The Wild Card*. But the sequence is great fun in the way it meshes Shapiro's impulse towards social satire with the confessional imperative driving such contemporary works as Lowell's *Life Studies* and Berryman's *Dream Songs*. As Shapiro himself has pointed out, the pieces aren't prose and in fact his sentences frequently scan into iambics. *The Bourgeois Poet* has a fascinating associative eccentricity that feels more casual than the earlier work, and it also greatly enlarges Shapiro's humorous attention to the erotic life.

*The Wild Card*, however, overly scants Shapiro's later work, including only one poem from his sometimes silly, sometimes charming sequence *White-Haired Lover* (1968), six from *Adult Bookstore* (1976), and five from *The Old Horsefly* (1992). The *White-Haired Lover* poem, a proem to that book, shows Shapiro's use of an increasingly colloquial style to create the illusion of spontaneity:

> There was that Roman poet who fell in love at fifty-odd.
> My God, *Venus,* goddess of love, he cried,
> Venus, for Christsake, for the love of God,
> Don't do that to me!
> Don't let me fall in love, a man of my age.
> I beg you on my knobby knees, lay off. ("There Was That Roman Poet"
>      [171])

Shapiro's late poetry combines this disarmingly casual feeling (his poem "Tennyson" begins, "Like many of us he was rather disgusting"

[188]) with poems so elegantly formal and moving as to convince us he is still a proud disciple of Auden (who receives three moving elegies) and Yeats. But Shapiro long ago passed beyond discipleship to become an original, someone who helps explain to us what it has meant to be American—and an American Jew—in the twentieth century. "My Father's Funeral" mixes elegy for a parent who "made us learn Hebrew and shorthand" with elegy for a city and a way of life, ending with the peace that passeth understanding:

> In the old forgotten purlieus of the city
> A Jewish ghetto in its day, there lie
> My father's father, mother and the rest,
> Now only a ghetto lost to time,
> Ungreen, unwhite, unterraced like the new
> Cemetery to which my father goes.
> Abaddon, the old place of destruction;
> Sheol, a new-made garden of the dead
> Under the snow. Shalom be to his life,
> Shalom be to his death. (179)

I wish the book had more: the brilliant "Adam and Eve," the brutal "Rape of Philomel," even his deliberately outrageous bad-taste catalog poem, "Fucking." But *The Wild Card* has most of the best of this fine, cantankerous poet, and even given its editors' omissions, its pages present Shapiro's credentials in all their variety and plenty.

# Archeological Gifts

THOMAS, HAFIZ, AND HENRY (2004)

Handsel Books began publication early this century with a mission of specializing "in contemporary essays, novels, and poetry," as well as reviving "from time to time . . . works by nineteenth- and twentieth-century writers who have been unduly overlooked or whose books have regrettably gone out of print." The majority of Handsel's first fruits, however, better fit the supposedly "from time to time" mission of publishing the overlooked and out of print, and the press's early handsels to readers include three great gifts in earnest: the reappearance of the complete poems of Great War poet Edward Thomas, a revival of Peter Avery and John Heath-Stubbs 1952 translations from the medieval Persian poet Hafiz of Shiraz, and the reanimation of a forgotten Victorian poet named James Henry.[1]

Edward Thomas, a friend of Robert Frost, came to poetry late, just two and a half years before a shell killed him at Arras on April 9, 1917; *The Poems of Edward Thomas* returns to print Thomas's 142 poems, plus revised versions of three. Safe from conscription at thirty-eight, he nevertheless volunteered for action. When asked why, according to Peter Sacks's introduction, he "bent down, scooped up a handful of dirt, and said, 'Literally, for this'" (xiv). The anecdote reflects the way the literal in Thomas's poetry acquires a symbolic power pulsing out from his often humble imagery, as in "Adlestrop," when a blackbird's song heard "Close by" at a train station ripples into the surrounding countryside, until the speaker imagines hearing "round him, mistier, / Farther and farther, all the birds / Of Oxfordshire and Gloucestershire" (35). Thomas's handful of "this," collected literally from the war-threatened ground he lived on, of course also represents England and a whole English way of existence—or Britain and British existence, since Thomas was Welsh. But to a man whose mind so often found the mythic Fall in the living countryside, the handful of dust also must have summed up his own essential humanity.

It would be easy to dwell on the irony of Thomas's personal commitment to a war now generally viewed as the sacrifice of millions of young men to imperialist and economic greed, but Thomas is no Rupert Brooke, sentimentally dreaming himself into a continental grave in "some corner of a foreign field / That is for ever England."[2] Though Christopher Ricks, in *Reviewery*, his Handsel collection of book reviews, calls him "the friend of Frost and the heir of Hardy,"[3] irony does not form a significant part of Thomas's inheritance, and his poetry generally avoids it. As a war poet, he has neither the weightily graceful irony of Siegfried Sassoon, the manic bitterness of Isaac Rosenberg, nor the acid pity of Wilfred Owen. In fact, Thomas is barely a war poet at all, but when he does write about soldiers, he displays an intense sympathy for their predicament, very different from Owen's tragic perspective or Sassoon's satire. His earliest poem connected with the war exhibits this tone:

A PRIVATE

This ploughman dead in battle slept out of doors
Many a frozen night, and merrily
Answered staid drinkers, good bedmen, and all bores:
"At Mrs. Greenland's Hawthorn Bush," said he,
"I slept." None knew which bush. Above the town,
Beyond "The Drover," a hundred spot the down
In Wiltshire. And where now at last he sleeps
More sound in France—that, too, he secret keeps. (33)

Unlike Hardy's "Drummer Hodge," in which the rural Englishman's "Northern breast and brain," bewildered by the wilderness and night sky of South Africa during the Boer War, ironically "Grow to some Southern tree,"[4] Thomas's ploughman/soldier is thoroughly knowledgeable, not ignorant, but keeps his counsel, and any carnal knowledge suggested by "Mrs. Greenland's Hawthorn Bush," punningly "private." He deliberately befuddles those prying into his nocturnal habits, as his soldier's death now puzzles any wishing to identify his grave. Thomas's poem interests us in this interesting, unschooled man, and conveys mystery upon his final resting place without foisting blessings upon it.

A similar sympathy emerges from Thomas's more complex and more famous poem, "The Owl" (55). The speaker, a traveler, reports, "Downhill I came, hungry, and yet not starved; / Cold, yet had heat within me." The opening inversion sounds like Frost's in "Mending Wall," where "Something there is that doesn't love a wall," by forcing stress on "is," underscores the assertion the way "There is something" would not.[5] Thomas's "Downhill I came" begins the poem with a downhill rhythm, whereas the more idiomatic "I came downhill" would keep the stresses in a misleadingly rising iambic pattern. Arriving at an inn, the traveler feels his discomforts melt away, until an owl's "melancholy cry // Shaken out long and clear upon the hill" (recalling the wind, "Shaken out dead from tree and hill," and the melancholy psychological state of Rossetti's "The Woodspurge")[6] lifts his imagination beyond his own immediate mental and physical condition,

> telling me plain what I escaped
> And others could not, that night, as in I went.
>
> And salted was my food, and my repose,
> Salted and sobered, too, by the bird's voice
> Speaking for all who lay under the stars,
> Soldiers and poor, unable to rejoice.

The traveler's sympathy here travels outward not only to the literal soldiers in French and Flemish trenches, but also to all the poor and homeless, soldiers in a quite different but cognate war. The poem's power comes not from any perceived special protection for the traveler, any sense of "there but for the grace of God," despite the owl "telling me plain what I escaped / And others could not," because its cry contains "No merry note, nor cause of merriment." In the world of the poem, comfort is momentary and the speaker, whose moral imagination has transcended the self, also finds himself identifying with all the world's soldiers, "unable to rejoice."

Frost encouraged Thomas, already a well-known critic and editor, in his mid-life poetic ambitions, and from the first he wrote with astonishing facility. His supple blank verse poems about rural folk, such as his early "Up in the Wind" (3–6), at times seem a Welsh version of Frost in their easy colloquial phrasing and skillful dialogue, and the little lyric "A Tale" (here in its revised version) sounds like a modest sketch for Frost's great late poem "Directive":

> Here once flint walls,
> Pump, orchard and wood pile stood.
> Blue periwinkle crawls
> From the last garden down into the wood.
>
> The flowerless hours
> Of Winter cannot prevail
> To blight these other flowers,
> Blue china fragments scattered, that tell the tale. (69)

He can also sound like Wordsworth in his handling of pentameter, as well as in his occasional claims for an expansive imagination that participates in the creation of what it perceives, as in these lines from "Ambition":

> I could sit
> And think I had made the loveliness of prime,
> Breathed its life into it and were its lord,
> And no mind lived save this 'twixt clouds and rime.
> Omnipotent I was, nor even deplored
> That I did nothing. (47)

I wish Handsel's new edition of Thomas wore its learning a little less lightly: it needs an index of titles and first lines, as well as a few notes and some confirmation of the poems' chronology. But it is a gift once again to have in print a poet who cares so much about the meaning of what the world is trying to tell us, whether roosters "Cleaving the darkness with a silver blow" ("Cock-Crow" [115]), bugles who themselves alone "know / What the bugles say in the morning, / And they do not care" ("No One Cares Less Than I" [153]), or the thrush who in one poem sings "Over and over again, a pure thrush word" ("The Word" [103]), and in another "sings well / His proverbs untranslatable" ("Myrfen" [139]). Thomas, in his brief months as a poet, chronicled an entire lost world from beginning to end,

As when I was young—
And when the lost one was here—
And when the war began
To turn young men to dung. ("Gone, Gone Again" [169])

Handsel's new edition of thirty poems by Hafiz of Shiraz, the medieval Persian Sufi poet, amounts to a double recovery: a welcome paperback reissue of Peter Avery and John Heath-Stubbs's 1952 translations of these fourteenth-century poems. Most of Hafiz's more than six hundred poems take the form of the ghazal, five or more self-contained couplets loosely linked thematically but formally united by the device of rhyme leading into a refrain, and clinched by the inclusion of the poet's name or *nom de plume* in the concluding couplet. The rhyme and refrain appear in both lines of the opening couplet, then in the second line of every subsequent couplet: *aa ba ca,* and so on. A number of American poets have written what they have called ghazals, but almost no one adheres to any of the form's stringencies except for the couplet arrangement and, less often, the refrain. (John Hollander's "For Couplets, the Ghazal Is Prime" is a notable exception.)

Both the translators' original introduction and Avery's new foreword lament what they perceived as the necessary forgoing of any attempt to approximate Hafiz's meter, rhyme, and refrain; I, for one, join in the lamentation. Nevertheless, we get a bit of the formal flavor of Hafiz's originals in Heath-Stubbs and Avery's version of poem 82, which employs a refrain (as does their translation of poem 29), plus, in its final two couplets, an internal slant-rhyme preceding it:

> "Enjoy God's craftsmanship in your own face
> Revealed, as this reveals—the mirror I am sending you."

> Hafiz, we sing your praise in our assemblies:
> Hurry—a horse and a robe of honor I'm sending you. (47)

Hafiz writes a highly conventionalized poetry that celebrates the sensuous world of love, wine, nature, and fellowship, seen through the lens of strict literary conventions derived from Sufi devotion. For example, the translators teach us, "wine should stand as the symbol of esoteric knowledge," and "the nightingale, hopelessly enamored of the rose [the emblem of the Beloved, associated with God], represents the lover, as does the violet, with its humble growth and mournful hue" (9–10). Therefore, Hafiz's love poems work on a literal level, but also as an allegorical expression of the longing to be united with God; in addition, Hafiz is also writing court poetry, for this poetry of desire, celebration, and praise also elaborately exalts his patron. Poem 151 makes clear some of these relationships among wine, nature, divinity, and patron:

> When the one I love takes a cup of wine in his hand
> His beauty creates a slump in the market of idols.

> Everyone who has seen the look in his eye is saying,
> "Where's the police to put this drunkard in custody?"

> I have tumbled like a fish into the ocean of love,
> That he might come with a hook to haul me out.

> I have fallen down at his feet in my deep affliction:
> Will he be the one that will raise me up by the hand?

> His heart is unburdened, who, like Hafiz, takes
> A cup of wine as his covenanted destiny. (54)

The conventions intertwine, and the opening, with the beloved taking up the wine cup, prepares for the satisfying symmetry of the conclusion, where Hafiz himself raises his cup in commitment. Yet despite the translation's attractive informality, with its "slump in the market of idols" and the tumbling fish—appropriate for a poet whose work, we are told, "is remarkably colloquial in its tone" (3)—it still smacks of something put into English, not fully comfortable in its move from Persian.

At their best, Heath-Stubbs and Avery transfer the poems into the English idiom, and in such cases those of us untutored in Hafiz's tongue can taste his freshness in our own. By far, the strongest sample is 199, which begins,

> What good in being a solitary, secret drinker?
> We're all drunkards together—let's leave it at that.
>
> Unravel the heart's tangles, and leave the spheres alone:
> You won't solve Fate's paradox by parallax.
>
> Don't be surprised at Fortune's turns and twists:
> The wheel has spun a thousand yarns before.
>
> Respect the cup you hold—the clay it's made from
> Was the skulls of buried kings—Bahman or Kobad.
>
> For who can tell where Kai or Kaus are now,
> Or Jamshid's throne, gone on a puff of wind? (55)

Hafiz's instances of what we recognize as the *ubi sunt* theme, familiar to medieval Europe as well as medieval Persia, acquire remarkable vividness here from the metaphorical imagining of Fortune's wheel literally spinning yarn with "turns and twists," just like the yarns—the threads and stories—of our lives. The playfully macabre recycling of the dust of the ancient Persian kings Bahman and Kobad into wine cups gives Hafiz affinities with our Hamlet, both confident that such sporting with our mortality is not too curious to consider, even as we know that all the great ones are gone with the wind. But especially inspired is Hafiz's admonition to "leave the spheres alone: / You won't solve Fate's paradox by parallax." A translators' note (and this edition's notes are most helpful) gives the line's literal rendering as "That is a puzzle that no mathematician can solve" (81), and proceeds to cite "apparent discrepancies in the Ptolemaic system," but in a magical shorthand, Heath-Stubbs and Avery have created a beautiful line of English poetry, chock-full of gorgeous sound and intellectual tension. The poem ends just as impressively:

> Come, let's get drunk, even if it is our ruin:
> For sometimes under ruins one finds treasure.
>
> The breeze of Musalla, the waters of Ruknabad,
> They keep me still from wandering far from home.
>
> Like Hafiz, drink your wine to the sound of harp-strings:
> For the heart's joy is strung on a strand of silk. (56)

To know that Musalla would become Hafiz's burial site does not necessarily deepen the feeling; here the crucial impulse directs us to hedonistic pleasure, focused in the concluding images of the harp strings transformed into the multiple resonances of the strand of silk. We hear the silk strand echoing the harp music, but we also accommodate both its sensuous touch and its delicacy. The lush image binds together music, tactile richness, and human mortality in the book's most fully realized ghazal.

"Hafiz, expect no relief from the turning heavens," ends the book's last poem, number 528; "That wheel has a thousand flaws, and grants no favors" (74). But despite the poetic flaws of these English versions, Hafiz of Shiraz has received the small tribute of this able sample restored to circulation. May the west's newly urgent interest in Islamic culture bring him more translations and even more inspired translators.

Handsel's third rediscovery is not really a rediscovery at all but a remarkable archeological find. The scholar and critic Christopher Ricks, one of Handsel's guiding lights, excavated the poetry of James Henry when his eyebeams swerved upon it in the stacks of the Cambridge University library. Since Ricks is one of the wittiest literary men around, the scenario seemed rife with the makings of a literary hoax. I mean, James Henry? An anti-Christian Victorian poet? An Irishman to boot? Who died in 1876, at age seventy-seven, at Dalkey Lodge, a place name redolent of Flann O'Brien?

But Henry is real, a Dublin doctor who retired from medicine at forty-five upon inheriting his mother's fortune, and who dedicated the rest of his life to classical scholarship, chiefly Virgil, and, fitfully, to poetry. Happily, he's a real poet, too. Ricks has selected from several of Henry's self-published volumes what we might assume to be the cream of his work. At his dullest, he is intellectually engaging but poetically deficient, as in this untitled piece that sounds like an imageless version (save for the commonplaces of cart, horse, and hand) of Hardy's "Hap":

> Well! I'll be patient, to myself I said,
> And, though it's hard, do what I can to bear it,
> Not doubting but it's all to end in good.
> And yet, methinks, and with respect be it said,
> Heaven did not take exactly the right way
> To have me patient, giving me in hand
> The ill, and only promising the good.
> Ah, if instead of setting the cart so
> Before the horse, it had into my hand
> Given the good, and promised me the ill,
> What perfect model I had been of patience!
> With what sure hope looked forward to the future! (148)

Fortunately, Henry at his best is not only far, far better, but also far more mischievous. His underground version of Genesis in "Old-World Stories" raises in *faux naif* fashion some key theological and metaphysical issues, in unrhymed trochaic tetrameter quatrains with enough metrical variation to free them from the stultifying tomtom of Longfellow's "The Song of Hiawatha":

On the day before the first day,
God was tired with doing nothing,
And determined to rise early
On the next day and do something.

So, upon the next day, God rose
Very early, and the light made—
You must know that until that day
God had always lived in darkness. . . . (116)

It's hard to discern the degree of intention in Henry's metrical practice; in an introductory note Ricks reveals a maddening system of
accents, rather like a drunken Hopkins, which this edition thankfully
eliminates. But the playful blasphemies ("the day before the first day,"
God "tired" on that day "with doing nothing," "God had always lived
in darkness") are ingenious and continually entertaining, while raising
the kind of dilemma good Christians should not even imagine, much
less make the stuff of inquiry. From "Cain and Abel":

Bad boys both were; God had taken
Good care they should not be good ones,
For he had cursed both their parents,
Cursed the very ground they stood on. . . .

Of the ground's fruit Cain brought offerings;
Firstlings of the flock, brought Abel;
God a lover was of lamb's flesh,
Didn't care much for ears of green corn. (133)

In any event, despite his marking and exile, things turn out rather
well for Cain: "Who his wife was, I don't well know, / But suspect
she was an angel—/ Of an angel Cain had need, if / Ever man had
need of angel" (135). Henry refuses to suspend his skepticism, which,
together with his human sympathy, turns Genesis into a continually
fascinating dark comedy.

Henry is somewhat obsessive, which can make him tiresome at
times as he explores all the permutations of a phrase or relationship.

But his exhaustive mock-investigations can also entertain, as when he takes Milton grammatically to task by willfully misreading his lines, "Adam the goodliest man of men since born / His sons, the fairest of her daughters Eve," and spinning out a riff—

> So father Adam was his own born son,
> And her own fairest daughter, mother Eve:
> And father Adam was his own sons' brother,
> And sister of her daughters, mother Eve.

—for thirty-five lines until it jangles like a music hall song (162–63). But since his obsessiveness extends to his observations and enthusiasms, he appears capable of writing about anything. "Blessed be the man who first invented chairs!" he exults, not least because

> My Muse's visits I receive on thee,
> Semi-recumbent, make her sit beside me,
> And chat and banter with her to no end. (160)

And in Dresden he watches a woman pluck up her husband's cigar, dropped as he dons his coat,

> And puts into her own mouth, the cigar,
> And whiffs, and keeps it lighting, till the man's
> Ready and buttoned up, then gives it back,
> And takes her basket, and, all right once more,
> Away they go, the man with his cigar,
> The woman with the man, well pleased and happy. (161)

Henry finds this anecdote of the cigar curious, but more importantly, he sees in it a peculiar emblem of a marriage, a complete human relationship.

In a couple of Henry's poems we come movingly close to his own powerful feelings for his loved ones and his own thoughts on mortality, for example, "Anniversary of my mother's death," which ends with the candid and direct lines,

Full fifteen years ago this very day,
The longest lived of two loved parents died—
Their first born child's place should be nearly ready. (170)

And Henry's brief elegy for his wife comes close to taking the breath away:

She never in her whole life wrote one stanza,
She knew no Greek, no Latin, scarcely French,
She played not, danced not, sang not, yet when Death
His arms about her threw, to tear her from me,
I would have ransomed her, not Orpheus-like
With mine own song alone, but with *all* song,
Music and dance, philosophy and learning
Were ever, or to be were, in the world. (95)

The willingness to sacrifice not only one's own work but a worldful of poetry, music, art, and scholarship shows the other side of Henry's ironic restraint and intellectual play: a wild conviction that although poetry can't save us, it can express the heart's most radical understandings.

Though not a major poet, James Henry is a true original, adventurous, tart, and occasionally genuinely bittersweet. We owe Ricks and Handsel thanks for resurrecting him and his highly original poetic mind, thanks to a trick of fate and the assertiveness that pushed him to publish in the face of popular indifference. Thomas, through his concern with memorializing the anonymous soldiers of the Great War, as well as the workers and women of rural Britain, individualized his subjects and created in his poems an enduring, sympathetic self. And in his ghazals, a form that conventionally concludes with the signature-like flourish of the poet's name, Hafiz paradoxically turned the world's transitoriness into a lasting assertion of identity. All three of these poets, all long gone, left memorable work for us to know them by.

# Two Poet's Poets (2001)

*On Philip Booth and Jane Cooper*

Bill James, the shrewd baseball analyst, once wrote about Stan Musial, the Hall of Fame Cardinal outfielder, "Maybe I'm wrong, but it doesn't seem to me that you hear much about him anymore, . . . and to the extent that you do hear of him it doesn't seem that the image is very sharp, that anybody really knows what it was that made him different. . . . What he was was a *ballplayer.* He didn't spit at fans, he didn't get into fights in nightclubs, he didn't marry anybody famous."[1]

Since the Second World War, the cult of celebrity has threatened to supplant our cultural life, infiltrating even the relatively remote and peaceful republic of poetry. The best-known and most widely read poets of our time have often achieved their popularity through their standing as personalities in the public imagination. The confessional mode of the past four decades promoted this trend by creating the illusion that poetry consisted of the poet's most intimate agonies and embarrassments. Lowell and Berryman's personal and psychological illnesses, and Plath and Sexton's suicides, for example, encouraged the creation of Romantic myths in which each poet became demonized as a self-destructive genius or cherished as a victim, myths many readers have misused as a rigidly narrow lens on the poetry. Poets have also achieved cult status through their public behavior, and Allen Ginsberg's combination of hero and buffoon—the political activist and the exhibitionist—is only the best-known example. For poets also gain fame via their power as public readers—a tradition descended to us from Tennyson through Dylan Thomas to many of today's poets justly renowned for their spellbinding expressive abilities before an audience—as well as for their ability to network in "po-biz," making themselves predictably ubiquitous on reading tours and at workshops and conferences.

In such a cultural atmosphere, the careers of Philip Booth and Jane Cooper bear some resemblance to that of Stan Musial. Though both have been writing and publishing for more than fifty years, each building an impressive, durable body of work, neither is as much a household word among poetry readers as many less-accomplished poets. They haven't led scandalous lives, they haven't written scurrilous confessions, they haven't led political marches, they haven't paraded around the readings-and-workshops circuit. For half a century they have been *poets,* and fine ones. Each spent decades building a creative writing program at a single school, Booth at Syracuse and Cooper at Sarah Lawrence, and during that time neither devoted much effort to the direct pursuit of fame, focusing instead on the less flashy but more lasting marks made through teaching and the poet's craft. A further complication for Booth is that by consciously placing himself "in the long shadow of Robert Frost," as the dustjacket of his new selection, *Lifelines,* has it, he may have unnecessarily encouraged readers to imagine his mentor looming over his work, obscuring its clear, unique light. Cooper's complication is the eccentricity of her publishing career: she stopped writing for several years in her youth, did not put out a book until her mid-forties, and even as recently as ten years ago had difficulty finding an American publisher.

Booth and Cooper are exact contemporaries, now in their mid-seventies. Both began writing tight, elegant, formal poems before relaxing their prosody in mid-career, and both have continued to experiment with the relationship between form and expressiveness. Their poetry differs markedly in the stance it takes towards the world, for where the energy driving Booth's poems is largely centripetal, taking landscapes, objects, and language out in the world and pulling them into a complex consciousness, the impulse behind Cooper's work feels centrifugal, identifying feeling and desire in the mind and projecting the self out upon the landscape.

The names of their two books illuminate these contrasting Romantic tendencies. Booth's choice of *Lifelines,* a characteristically punning title, conjures up imagery from sailing, one of his great loves, as well as the palmist's speculations on our human future, both individual and collective, and attendant meditations on aging and death, themes which permeate his work. More metaphorically, it suggests an obsession with our inextricable ties to each other, lifelines providing the multitudinous practical and emotional ways we seek aid and provide rescue. Cooper's own nautical coinage, *The Flashboat,* on the other hand—perhaps, as she has suggested, an amalgam of "flashlight" and "lifeboat"—takes a word invented in a dream and set sailing in the currents of her poem of that title. In the speaker's nightmare, "the Queen Mary is sinking. / All is bustle. . . . / The crew makes ready the boats," and then, mysteriously,

> A smaller dory rocks
> in and out of our lights; black fists grip the oars.
> Room only for six—we will
> all need to row.
> For a moment I hesitate, worrying about my defective blood.
> A rope ladder drops over. My voice with its crunch of bone
> wakes me: *I choose*
> *the flashboat!*
> > work,
> > > the starry waters (144)

Connotations of illumination and rescue in the word "flashboat" mingle with hints of explosions and disaster, compounded by those black fists rowing, the "defective blood," the "voice with its crunch of bone." These ambiguous feelings burst into the world of the poem and recreate perceptions and objects: we finish reading and *know* there is such a thing as a flashboat. While Booth's "lifelines" offer a solid world in which we are mutable beings, in Cooper's vision the mind tries to change a world in which nothing seems steady in its nature or identity, in which everything may be a changeable product of the imagination.

The contrast between these two poets' tendencies emerges clearly in their elegies. Writing about his friends, Booth looks outside and lets the objective correlatives accumulate. "This Day after Yesterday," for Robert Lowell, starts by reiterating its title before turning outward to the mood of the weather, "Morning rain small on the harbor, / nothing that's not gray" (137). That latter line transcends the grammar of its double negative through its context in a 1980 book, *Before Sleep,* that employs a running motif of little gnomic poems with knowing Donne-like or Stevensian puns on "nothing" and "nothingness":

> *We used to say* Nothing's
> too good for our kids.
>
> *Now we don't know what to say.*
>
> *Nothing seems to be good enough*
> *for them. If everything isn't*
> *just right, nothing will do.* (120)

Among these *petits riens,* the "nothing" of the morning after Lowell's death is assuredly "not gray" but vivid with pain, and while the poem's attempt to balance anguish, gravitas, and linguistic restraint is not consistently successful, it stands as something of a model of Booth's moral and mortal process. The world enters the mind and the mind attempts to accommodate it through the complex defense of language.

Cooper, instead, approaches "Hotel de Dream," her elegy for Muriel Rukeyser and James Wright from an entirely personal pose—actually a personal *sup*pose:

> Suppose we could telephone the dead.
> Muriel, I'd say, can you hear me?
> Jim, can you talk again?
>
> And I'd begin to tell them the stories they loved to hear. . . .

Muriel, I'd say, shall we swing along Hudson Street
underneath the highway and walk out together on the docks? (189)

The poem begins in the mind and tenderly desires to alter the harsh
world: through the retelling of stories about Cora Crane, Stephen
Crane's widow and also the madam of the Jacksonville whorehouse
commemorated in the poem's title, the speaker attempts not only to
resuscitate her beloved dead but to learn from them, that wish culminating in a sonically luscious progression of adjectives:

tell me how to redress the past,
how to relish yet redress
my sensuous, precious, upper-class,
unjust white child's past. (190)

Booth found early success at thirty when Viking, publisher of all
his books, issued *Letter from a Distant Land*. The few poems from
that volume selected for *Lifelines* show an early mastery of varied
and colloquial moods in formal poetry, as implied in one poem's title,
"Storm in a Formal Garden." Here is its opening stanza:

Where my struck mother stays,
she wakes to thunderstorms
of doubt. Squalls blacken
her bright-surfaced dreams,
and she stands coldly shaken,
lost in the dripping trees. (8)

While we might want to blue-pencil "of doubt" and "bright-surfaced"
(and edit even more that first book's title poem, a homage to Tho-
reau in which "Machines as murderous / as mad bulls gore the land,"
and a roadkill skunk's "flowering intestines lie halfway / in sun" [12,
14]), this is a confident style, waiting for its poet to grow into it. The
delight in metrical variation and repeated sound for abrupt shocks
("struck mother," "Squalls blacken") continued to mature and deepen
throughout Booth's career, especially after he abandoned end-rhyme.

Though Booth took Frost as his master, his wordplay soon departed from Frost's in its higher density and greater consciousness of angst. His much-anthologized early poem "Was a Man," from *The Islanders* (1961), demonstrates how his diction was rarely Frost-folksy but always colloquial, and how his metaphysics strove less for the cosmic and more for the psychological than Frost's:

> Was a man, was a two-
> faced man, pretended
> he wasn't who he was,
> who, in a men's room,
> faced his hung-over
> face in a mirror hung
> over the towel rack.
> The mirror was cracked.
> Shaving close in that
> looking glass, he nicked
> his throat, bled blue
> blood, grabbed a new
> towel to patch the wrong
> scratch, knocked off
> the mirror and, facing
> himself, almost intact,
> in final terror hung
> the wrong face back. (18)

John Thompson once talked of Lowell's early poems as being carved in granite, and Booth's carving here, while less daunting, is similar: it would be hard to dislodge a single word of this brilliantly constructed poem. The enjambments create a taut linguistic and dramatic suspense between the lines, a lesson from William Carlos Williams that Booth has kept practicing throughout his career together with his aim to place each word and sound perfectly.

Most impressive about Booth is the career-long authority of his voice, and how skillfully that voice transmutes the world into striking and moving language. Listen to the ending of "After the *Thresher*," from *Weathers and Edges* (1966), spoken by a dead sailor on a lost submarine, imagining life continuing above:

> the lawnspray squeaks,
> and traffic begins to thunder
>
> as if it were Sunday somewhere.
> But we have been sunk for months,
> under tons of possible air. (40)

Or the multiple personalities of the snow in "Entry," from *Available Light* (1976), with its "flakes in / large sizes / lazing against / a small sun," a poem wherein Booth's Frostian New England–speak is again steeled by a Williams-like tension in his lineation:

> Around here
> they call
> these days "open
> and shut," by
> sunset the wind
> will veer and
> stiffen; tomorrow
> will build on
> a windblown
> crust. (61)

Or how what begins as description in "Stonington," from *Relations* (1986),

> Fog come over us.
> Come under sea wind
> over cold tide, fog
>
> blown home against
> the sharp ebb.. ,

gets delicately transformed into prayer by the poem's end:

in small bedrooms,
the harbor bell close.

Spruce full of fog,
fog all this night,
come over all of us. (176)

Or the similar mixture of resignation and blessedness in "Presence,"
from *Selves* (1990), where the world seems to the speaker by lightning-
quick turns magically immanent and maddeningly random:

Still, as the physicist said, *the mystery is*
that we are here, here at all, still bearing with,

and borne by, all we try to make sense of:
this evening two does and a fawn who browse

the head lettuce we once thought was ours.
But no. As we chase them off mildly, and make

an odd salad of what they left us, the old stars
come casually out, and we see near and far we own nothing. (216)

This appearance of casualness held in place by a structure of bed-
rock persists in Booth's most recent work. One new poem, in fact,
"Writing It Down," hearkens all the way back nearly forty years to
"Was a Man," but with its wordplay focused more poignantly to evoke
the emotional complexities of aging:

Was an old man, no
jazz left. No doubt
about it, tired as

Hell. Fell asleep
early, woke somewhere
near two. Mostly woke

screamless, half-awake
quick. Felt for his
pretty ones, found his

wife took them. Flown
on his ticket, flown
long since. (267)

The powerless speaker, bereft as Macduff, rages like Lear to rediscover
himself, then sinks "back toward sleep, flat / as a flounder," remembers
the life of language, "the spider-webbed world, // which snatched out
of print / the old language of trees," and decides that although he is
"No wonder now," he must keep up the difficult enterprise:

Odds were against him.

A mere five words.
A pre-posthumous poet's
raw self-sentence. (268)

Philip Booth's late poems continue to ravel out that "raw self-sentence,"
with its paradoxical tension between condemnation and self-assertion
in the face of the world's hostile storms. Readers of *Lifelines* will wish
for many more years of his terse, strong, pre-posthumous work.

While Philip Booth's poetry has steadily evolved and deepened in its
technical and emotional mastery, Jane Cooper's underwent a signal
revolution in mid-career. She talks eloquently about the biography of
her poetry and the changes it underwent in her now-classic 1974 essay
about writing and female identity, "Nothing Has Been Used in the
Manufacture of This Poetry That Could Have Been Used in the Manufacture of Bread," reprinted in *The Flashboat*. Steeped in Hopkins,
Yeats, and Hardy, Cooper deliberately wrote from the stance of "a non-
combatant, a witness" (101), producing poems whose feelings, she later
concluded, "were often distanced by their forms," even those "that
promised most in the way of love and growth" (107). In the 1960s, however, she strove to stop writing "as an observer, almost too patiently,"
in favor of making a poetry that created the illusion of more direct
emotional engagement: "I had to get through the perfectionism of

those early poems, to learn that no choice is absolute and no structure can save us" (122).

The funny thing about Cooper's escape from formalism is that, far from stiff and distant, her early formal poems are often deeply moving in spite of—or maybe because of—their technical polish and emotional restraint. Here are the opening stanzas of "The Faithful," a 1955 poem from her first book, *The Weather of Six Mornings* (1969):

> Once you said joking slyly, *If I'm killed*
> *I'll come to haunt your solemn bed,*
> *I'll stand and glower at the head*
> *And see if my place is empty still, or filled.*
>
> What was it woke me in the early darkness
> Before the first bird's twittering?
> —A shape dissolving and flittering
> Unsteady as a flame in a drafty house.
>
> It seemed a concentration of the dark burning
> By the bedpost at my right hand
> While to my left that no man's land
> Of sheet stretched palely as a false morning. . . .

The drama inheres in the speaker's continuing to be haunted "after ten years of grieving" her lover dead in the war, and the substitution of grief as a way of life for grief as catharsis is so skillfully rendered that the pun on "no man's land" works brilliantly: she keeps the war and her self-martyrdom alive through the deliberate emptiness of her bed. These tensions culminate in her recognition in the stunning final stanza:

> What if last night I was the one who lay dead
> While the dead burned beside me
> Trembling with passionate pity
> At my blameless life and shaking its flamelike head? (28)

The *abba* envelope rhyme scheme works beautifully here as an emblem of the speaker's containment, her determination to persist nobly as an empty vessel until her intimation that emptiness permeates *her* more terribly than it does her bed. Cooper used many envelope schemes in her early poems—*abccba, abbcaca,* and *abccbba* are just three other permutations—and they clearly symbolized for her a containment, a penting-up, a being-told-by-the-masculine-world-to-shut-up feeling that she felt the need to break free of.

From the beginning Cooper's language sang—listen to the lyricism in lines like "Snow is a process of thinking. Down the street / I see the flakes ballooning from the west" ("Snow in the City" [31]); or "she is still not beautiful but more / Moving than before, for time has come / When she shall be delivered" ("Eve" [78]); or "I take your hand. I want to touch your eyes. / They are water-soft. I know. I could push them in" ("Blind Girl" [29]). When she burst out of her meters and rhymes, her language became more direct and colloquial but also, curiously, less rhapsodic, the freeing from form allowing the illusion of greater candor. Here is "Rent," from her collection *Scaffolding* (1984):

> If you want my apartment, sleep in it
> but let's have a clear understanding:
> the books are still free agents.
>
> If the rocking chair's arms surround you
> they can also let you go,
> they can shape the air like a body.
>
> I don't want your rent, I want
> a radiance of attention
> like the candle's flame when we eat,
>
> I mean a kind of awe
> attending the spaces between us—
> Not a roof but a field of stars. (154)

The poem starts as a witty, informal contract in the first five lines but then begins to take off into Romantic reverie ("shape the air like a body"), before moving into a desire for ecstasy ("a radiance of attention") and the final dream of revelation, all the while skillfully tempered by matter-of-fact negotiations ("I don't want your rent," "when we eat") in an intercourse growing increasingly less mundane. Throughout *The Flashboat* Cooper has interwoven her poetry with lyrical prose, and the sneakily seductive ordinariness of her diction makes her memoirs as compelling as her later poems, especially "From the Journal Concerning My Father" and "In the Children's Ward," an account of Cooper's hospital stays as a sickly child.

Cooper's longer sequences, involving the lives and words of Rosa Luxemburg and Willa Cather, are impressive interactions of the personal with the historical. But among my favorite poems in *The Flashboat* are those she has "reclaimed" and published in this volume for the first time, both early ones and more recent examples like "Olympic Rain Forest":

> I left the shutter open, the camera
> flooded with light, the negatives
> were abstract and damp as the undersides of leaves.
>
> So much greenish light, I had never
> imagined a transfusion of so much tenderness.
>
> Why can't it all be printed? How can I stand here
> holding in one hand a fossil fern, in the other
> a colored guide from the Sierra Club?
>
> Travel isn't originality. I
> left the shutter open.

That enjambment, with its emphatic "I," perfectly captures the process in Cooper by which the imagination conceives feeling, which in turn acts upon the world, changing it utterly, a world that continues changing even more quickly than our feelings can accommodate. The poem ends:

> What I need is a new medium, one that will register

the weight of air on our shoulders, then
how slowly a few hours passed,

one that will show
the print of your heels that morning on the spongy forest floor,
there, not there. (149)

These poems create the impression that Cooper's shutter is always left open to discover that new medium. They make us believe we can feel the air upon our bodies and fix our evanescent footprints in the moss. These are the lasting marks of *The Flashboat,* and it is a great pleasure to have its two Jane Coopers: the "collected" Cooper of five decades and the "reclaimed" Cooper affording us enriched discoveries.

# Shocking,
# Surprising Snodgrass (2006)

In 1987, when W. D. Snodgrass's first *Selected Poems* appeared, another poet told me how different she felt revisiting his *Heart's Needle* sequence after many years. Back in the 1960s, she said, those poems had shocked her—had shocked everyone—with their subject matter, the guilt and anger of the speaker's divorce and the anxious difficulty of maintaining a loving relationship with his estranged young daughter. But the poetry now seemed tame, decorous in its formal restraint, and she had difficulty perceiving what had created such a fuss. And truly, it was quite a fuss: the 1959 *Heart's Needle*, Snodgrass's first collection, took the Pulitzer Prize over, among others, *Life Studies*, the now-iconic book by Snodgrass's teacher Robert Lowell that, together with *Heart's Needle*, brought family trauma and psychological disturbance out of the closet and made them fair game for verse, inspiring M. L. Rosenthal to create the label "confessional poetry." These books shocked readers in 1959 precisely because Snodgrass and Lowell presented themselves not as wild-man outsiders like Allen Ginsberg, who, guided by Blakean vision and elegiac Whitmania, ran naked through America, but strong traditionalists who clothed disturbing personal dramas in technical beauty, so the rawness of the wounds they examined seeped through the gold tissue of their poems' finery.

Our difficulty today in seeing Snodgrass's special quality actually derives from his success and his influence, as well as the influence of Lowell, John Berryman, Sylvia Plath, and others: what looked forbidden in his poetry, what made it new and startling at the time, has become the norm. The wrong turns that in the nineteen-fifties counted as dirty secrets of private life—divorce, adultery, and the emotional snarls they make of parent-child relationships—have become common American experience, and therefore common poetic subjects. The culture has caught up with Snodgrass and Lowell, and poetry, as always, has pushed beyond the culture, outing all of its skeletons from the closet into cold print.

If *Heart's Needle*'s subject no longer piques our lust for gossip or scandal, its compelling technical mastery still argues for the sequence's enduring power. Snodgrass has included all ten of its sections in his new book of selected poems, *Not for Specialists,* and it demonstrates how, early on, he had achieved an impeccable craft. Here is its opening poem:

Child of my winter, born
When the new fallen soldiers froze
In Asia's steep ravines and fouled the snows,
When I was torn

By love I could not still,
By fear that silenced my cramped mind
To that cold war where, lost, I could not find
My peace in my will,

All those days we could keep
Your mind a landscape of new snow
Where the chilled tenant-farmer finds, below,
His fields asleep

In their smooth covering, white
As quilts to warm the resting bed
Of birth or pain, spotless as paper spread
For me to write,

And thinks: Here lies my land
Unmarked by agony, the lean foot

> Of the weasel tracking, the thick trapper's boot;
> And I have planned
>
> My chances to restrain
> The torments of demented summer or
> Increase the deepening harvest here before
> It snows again. (19–20)

The poem's complex grammar unrolls in a single sentence whose long parenthetical phrases interrupt his address to the child, suggesting the constant interruptions in their love. It embodies the difficult balancing act the speaker has assigned himself: to salvage some harvest in his emotional winter, to control his sometimes violent feelings (the sequence's third poem describes how he "tugged your hand, once" so hard he "dislocated / The radius of your wrist"), and to establish a lasting bond with his daughter (the same poem boasts that "Solomon himself might say / I am your real mother," since he has surrendered her to his rival parent, rather than tearing her in half like "Love's wishbone" [21–22]). If the movement from the Korean War to the divorced couple's "cold war" seems presumptuous, the development of the snow metaphor for the child's mind resonates richly. The "new snow," her *tabula rasa,* presents a comforting purity but also induces anxiety, implicit in the preceding image of Asian snows "fouled" by death, in the guise of "fallen soldiers," "new" in both their youth and their sacrifice. By turns, her "new snow" recalls the trauma "Of birth or pain," offers itself "spotless as paper" for the poet-father to make his mark upon, and demands protection from "the weasel tracking, the thick trapper's boot," and other predatory dangers.

Yet the speaker also feels temporary and helpless, like "the chilled tenant-farmer" who neither owns the land nor can, in the dead of winter, cultivate "His fields asleep." His lack of rights eliminates any certainty in his life with her: he has "planned" only to leave much between them to chance, realizing that any paternal protection he can provide must be hit or miss. The poem's stanza, swelling from three beats to four in the second line, then to five in the third, before dwindling to two at the end, plays out his swelling love and shrinking hope, while the language details his restrained and terrible acceptance. Later, in poem seven, set in summer, the rhythm of a playground swing enacts precisely his combined adoration and despair in their periodic relationship, ending, as she returns through the air to him, with an emblem of their tentative love: "Once more now, this second, / I hold you in my hands" (27). That the subject matter of *Heart's Needle* has grown commonplace reflects on us, not on the poetry, which still succeeds in its skillful designs.

In his letters from the late 1950s, Lowell repeatedly judges Snodgrass "better than anyone [of the new poets] except [Philip] Larkin,"[1] and his best early poems warrant the comparison. Snodgrass is more flamboyant than his English contemporary, as in this stanza I often quote to my students from "Mementos, 1," from his second book, *After Experience* (1968), a poem unfortunately omitted from *Not for Specialists:*

> Sorting out letters and piles of my old
>    Canceled checks, old clippings, and yellow note cards
> That meant something once, I happened to find
>    Your picture. *That* picture. I stopped there cold,
> Like a man raking piles of dead leaves in his yard
>    Who has turned up a severed hand.[2]

Here is the sense of shock my poet friend missed in *Heart's Needle,* a rancid memory instantly transforming domestic life into gothic horror, landing on a dissonant slant-rhyme. Snodgrass comes closer to Larkin, however, in presenting the accumulated disappointments of modern daily emotional life, cast into formal structures that keep them art, as in "Leaving the Motel," whose mildly despondent, postcoital mood highlights the tawdry side of adultery:

> An aspirin to preserve
> Our lilacs, the wayside flowers
> We've gathered and must leave to serve
> A few more hours;

That's all. We can't tell when
We'll come back, can't press claims;
We would no doubt have other rooms then,
Or other names. (48)

Yet Snodgrass's particularly American confessionalism—his lack of reticence in appropriating his own life and family for poetry—also distinguishes his early work from Larkin's. *Not for Specialists* includes six poems from his 1970 chapbook *Remains,* a bitter exposé of unhappy family life centering on the early death of a hopelessly mousy wallflower sister, a sequence apparently so personal that he first issued it under the anagrammatic pseudonym S. S. Gardons:

The unworn long gown, meant for dances
She would have scarcely dared attend,
Is fobbed off on a friend—
Who can't help wondering if it's spoiled
But thinks, well, she can take her chances. (65)

This poem, "Disposal," also describes how "One lace / Nightthing lies in the chest, unsoiled / By wear, untouched by human hands," and notes "those cancelled patterns / And markdowns that she actually wore, / Yet who do we know so poor / They'd take them?" That "actually" serves a vital role, not just filling out the meter, but expressing quiet amazement at her impoverished taste and acceptance of her shriveled emotional circumstances. As in Donne's elegy, "Going to Bed," clothing becomes a synecdoche for the woman who wears it, but here creating a scenario of isolation and misery rather than erotic play.

As a student I loved Snodgrass's poetry, especially how its formal elegance domesticated the worst shocks of our emotional lives, intensifying them by ironically pretending they participated in an orderly universe we could endure. I chose Syracuse University's writing program expressly to study with him, and found a man as boisterously outspoken as his poems were movingly restrained. He attended intensively to detail, the minutiae of rhythm, rhyme, and sound, as you would expect from a poet with such an impeccable ear, but he also encouraged a tendency to sarcasm I wished, at the time, to exorcise from my work. He would declaim poetry to us each week, and if his exuberant performances of "Frankie and Johnnie," Wyatt, Wordsworth, and Whitman, designed for a thousand-seat hall with no amplification, felt overbearing at the seminar table, they offered an antidote to 1970s poetry-reading syndrome—a monotonous delivery distanced from expressiveness, punctuated by a rising inflection at the ends of lines or sentences. Snodgrass helped me learn to read aloud by demonstrating that, yes, poetry could stand dramatic emotion in oral delivery, and I borrowed from his approach while softening it by several decibels. When I tested my new style one Sunday, reading at the local art museum, Snodgrass joined our quiet chatter afterwards to congratulate me in his booming voice: "That was woNderful! That was deLISHious! And you used to read so BADly!"

With the first installment of his poetic cycle *The Führer Bunker* (1977), the first book ever published by BOA Editions, Snodgrass's subject shocked us all—interior monologues in the voices of Hitler and his circle during the war's final days—as did its explosive, often obscene language: "if any foe rejects us, / We'll broil their liver for our breakfast / And fry their balls like bacon!" ("Chorus: Old Lady Barkeep" [93]). It showed an encyclopedic understanding of form—ballads, tetrameter couplets for Goebbels, envelope sextets for Goering, a pantoum for Magda Goebbels—in addition to experiments in free verse, especially for Hitler. (Snodgrass had used free verse in *After Experience* for some of his poems based on paintings. "Van Gogh: 'The Starry Night,'" the lone example included in *Not for Specialists*, is unfortunately rather slack; I prefer the psychological drama of his Vuillard poem, on *The Mother and Sister of the Artist*, which harmonizes chillingly with the tensions of Snodgrass's other family poems.)

As a sequence, a gesture towards a long poem, *The Führer Bunker*, which Snodgrass kept expanding and revising until the complete cycle appeared in 1995, fails for all the reasons that his other work succeeds: the monstrous nature of many of the characters resists his attempts to humanize them, and we don't feel the force of poetic revelation; a more sympathetic Hitler and company might have created a literary sensation. In Snodgrass's bunker, the most successful poems belong to the women. The pantoum's repetitions circle around Magda Goebbels' mind as she meditates on how to save her children ("Now Joseph's sister's offered us the chance / To send the children somewhere farther West / Into the path of the Americans / To let them live. It might be for the best"), several days before she and her husband will hit on the final family solution of poisoning them all (109). In contrast, Eva Braun flounces about the bunker, ecstatic at the new life she has defined for herself and Hitler: "Today He ordered me to leave, / To go back to the mountain. I refused. / I have refused to save my own life and He, / In public, He kissed me on the mouth" (119).

In the 1980s Snodgrass began a series of collaborations with the painter DeLoss McGraw, resulting in humorously sinister books with titles like *The Death of Cock Robin* and *W. D.'s Midnight Carnival*. If Nazi history moved Snodgrass towards the prosaic, McGraw's paintings helped him discover a new musicality, mixed with grotesquely comic intimations of mortality, in a set of nursery rhymes for adults:

> Who'll start out—shebang and applecart
> Go along; so what's wrong? Who'll buy a heart?
>
> I, said the fly, I go for the eye.
> Me, said the beetle, I'll buy me a bone.
> Mine, said the earthworm, I take the heart.
>
> ("Auction" [146])

> By lurch and stumble, change and growth,
>     Struggling from all fours, we rise
> Cranking the backbone up, though loath,
>     To lift our skull into the skies. . . .
>
> ("A Strolling Minstrel's Ballad of the Skulls and Flowers" [148])

Snodgrass jumbles into this vaudeville an open embrace of all his traditions, alluding more obviously than before to writers ranging from the troubadours (he has ably translated Provençal poetry), to the seventeenth-century cavalier poets, to modern masters like Wallace Stevens ("They say, 'Your songs do not compute. / Your music's mixed; your moral's moot'" [154]) and Auden ("In the perspective of the heart / Those dearly loved, when they depart, / Take so much of us when they go / That, like no thing on earth, they grow / Larger..." [155]). Working with McGraw relieved Snodgrass of the overbearing obligation to seriousness with which *The Führer Bunker* saddled him, and by letting himself have more fun, he created more interesting and important poetry. In their try-anything, on-with-the-show, shuck-and-jive spirit, Snodgrass's McGraw poems owe something to Berryman, and while they do not possess *The Dream Songs'* wild, manic power, they constitute a significant accomplishment.

*Not for Specialists* concludes with forty new poems written over the past decade or so, which provide many satisfying symmetries with the early work. Snodgrass has always acknowledged the comical nature of his name ("poor ill-named one," sympathized Randall Jarrell)[3]: his early "These Trees Stand ...," which opens the book, notes, "Your name's absurd," and turns on a delightfully ludicrous refrain, "Snodgrass is walking through the universe" (13). The recent poem "Who Steals My Good Name" returns to the name blame game: it casts spells upon a Snodgrass masquerader "who obtained my debit card number and spent $11,000 in five days," after beginning with a complaint from "My pale stepdaughter": "Well, that's the last time I say my name's / Snodgrass!" (210). Even better, his homage to Andrew Marvell, "Chasing Fireflies," exploits his name's literal sense, since "to snod" means "to make smooth, trim, or neat":

I am the mower, Snodgrass, known
Through fields and meadows run to seed,
Undertended and overgrown
With ragweed, sneezewort and neglect,
Where moths lay eggs and fireflies breed—
You are the harvest I collect. (220)

The *Heart's Needle* sequence also earns a reprise, in "For the Third Marriage of My First Ex-Wife," which speaks once more of the woes of wedlock past—

> not once in twelve years had we laid
> each other right. What we *had* made
> were two nerve-wracked, unreconciled,
> spoiled children parenting a child

—in order to look benignly ahead and wish everyone well. This moving gesture acknowledges all the hearts badly in need of repair, including that of the daughter, as well as providing some comic and benevolent surprises:

> Our daughter, still recovering from
> her own divorce, but who's become
> a father, in her call at least
> as an Episcopalian priest,
> will fly down there to officiate
> in linking you to your third mate;
> only some twenty years ago
> that daughter married me also
> to the last of my four wives. (238–39)

"Also, save the best for last," the poem ends. Not all the new poems that end *Not for Specialists* rank with Snodgrass's best, but several decidedly do. All told, they provide a delightful and absorbing range of subjects and moods: splenetic political poems denouncing the Bush administration's war in Iraq, satiric Ben Jonson-like epigrams on a contemporary literary culture designed (his book's title implies) increasingly *for* specialists, wry observations on the foibles of advancing age, and generous accounts of love for wife, children, and friends. Through it all, Snodgrass remains undiminished in his technical skill and unapologetic about his formalism, the secret subject of "Warning," a poem ostensibly about "rumors that Richard Wilbur has had a hip replacement so he could go on playing tennis":

Wilbur's ball and ceramic socket
Propel him like a racing sprocket
To where his artful serve and volley
Dole out love games and melancholy.
Tremble, opponents: learn by this
What power's secured through artifice. (231)

The poem is not just a charming tribute to his important fellow poet, but a witty manifesto, recalling Robert Frost's quip that writing free verse is like playing tennis with the net down. After more than fifty years refining his "love game," Snodgrass remains mindful of the rules, and the rules have enabled him continually to surprise and delight us. If his poems dare to commit the occasional fault, they can still move and enchant us with the power artifice can secure.

# A Formal Garden
# with a Real Poet in It (2003)

*On Daniel Hoffman*

Reading Daniel Hoffman's *Beyond Silence,* his selected poems of the past fifty-five years, we stroll through a garden expansive as an entire landscape. Now eighty, perhaps less heralded but certainly no less accomplished than other poets of his generation, Hoffman has accumulated a stunning oeuvre. In his book, he has also taken the daring approach of organizing his work thematically, so poems written in his twenties stand cheek by jowl with others written in his sixties and seventies, early crocuses with summer lilies. Such an arrangement has its limitations—I find, for example, the thematic arrangement of Randall Jarrell's own *Selected Poems* frustrating, because it denies the reader an understanding of the biography of the poetry. But in Hoffman's case it works because over the decades he has maintained a remarkable consistency and maturity of voice. Listen to this excerpt from "That the Pear Delights Me Now":

> Some squash remains, though,
> some meat around the seed.
> When Indian Summer strains
>
> the last warmth through the orchard
> pearpits feast and feed
> and stir, & burst, & breed:

Earthward plunge the tendrils.
    That the pear delighted me
is wholly incidental,

for the flower was for the fruit,
the fruit is for the seed. (80)

And this one from "A Comfort":

    Won't you have a dipper
of this birch beer? I've just put a chunk of ice in—

taste of homebrew still remembered,
skinny freckled hands and yellow flowers
fading on an apron, her gaunt smile

a comfort remembered still
years and years
after she squanched the burning of the day. (208)

At least fifty years separate these poems, the first from Hoffman's debut
Yale Younger Poets book, *An Armada of Thirty Whales* (1954), the second from one of *Beyond Silence*'s handful of new poems. They are not
the same—the new poem is more flexible and colloquial, the early poem
more self-conscious in its rewriting of Keats and the lovely, mimetic
trochaic inversion of "Earthward plunge the tendrils"—but they iden-
tifiably come from the same hand, sharing a sharpness of eye, a precision of ear, a pleasure in satisfied memory, and a delight in language
that extends to onomatopoetic coinages ("squush" and "squanched").
Neither embarrasses the other; rather, Hoffman's poems gain illumination from their new thematic contexts.

Those contexts, sorted into eight untitled sections, include the
world and public events, love, nature and myth, the eternal or spiritual
realm, the personal past, homages to other artists, elegies and meditations on mortality, and so on. Only the homages section seems less

vital than the others, and only in those poems dedicated to other poets, where Hoffman is prone to settle for writing in the manner of his subjects rather than using that manner to achieve new revelations. But that section concludes with "High Society," a wonderfully anecdotal account of hearing Cozy Cole, Art Hodes, Max Kaminsky, and Ed Hall play a Connecticut bar in September 1939, jamming with "insouciant, plangent joy" as the world is about to blow itself up (197–200).

Hoffman's encounters with the violence of twentieth-century history can be profoundly moving. In a dream-poem called "A Special Train," the speaker, disoriented, asks "What am I / Doing in the Orient?" before recognizing his kinship with the innocent victims of war:

> And look, in this paddy
> A little boy is putting in the shoots.
> He's naked in the sunlight. It's my son!
>
>        . . . See, his hands are smeared
>
> With mud, and now his white
> Back is flecked with ash, is seared
> By embers dropping from the sky—
>
> The train chuffs past. I cry
> *Stop! Stop!* We cross another paddy.
> He's there, he's fallen in the mud, he moans my name. (13)

The poem remarkably conflates imagery from Hiroshima, the Nazi camps (including a "chuffing" train that recalls Sylvia Plath's "Daddy"), and Vietnam, immersing the reader in suffering with an unusual immediacy. Ironically, in a recent poem, "Violence," an audience member at a poetry reading turns the tables on the poet by confronting him with just this kind of responsibility:

> After I'd read my poem about a brawl
> between two sidewalk hustlers—one,
> insulted, throws the other down and nearly
> kills him—over coffee and cookies a grave

senior citizen reproved me: *How*
*could you see such violence and you*
*didn't try to stop them?*—Oh, I explained,
it wasn't like that, really—I saw

two guys in a shoving match and thought
I'd write about aggression, what
anger really feels like. . . . *Yes,*

*and if the one got killed*
*it would be on your head.*
*You should've stopped them,* he said. (26)

Though Hoffman writes in his preface that his sonnets will be collected in a future volume, this is, of course, a sort of sonnet, like some others in the book, but one that plays with the formal borders, shrinking its lines after the opening pentameter, and rhyming when it needs to, evolving from slant-rhymes ("How" / "you" / "saw"; "thought" / "what") to the only full rhyme, to end the poem with an appropriate knock on the head. Many subtleties make the poem vivid: the ordering of speech patterns, the idiosyncratic phrasing of the old man's question, the possible momentary misreading that "coffee and cookies" might have incited the fight, and the poem's shift from past tense into present for its brief description of the violent act, a cameo of epic heightening. But it wittily deals with one of a poet's demons, the ornamenting of an actual event for poetic purposes, only to have the work of art taken for truth. And further, it raises the fascinating question of whether we are morally responsible for the universes we create—whether we must lie in the beds we have lied to make.

One of the great pleasures of reading Hoffman is his delight in mixed diction that always feels exquisitely controlled, a deliberate strewing of pansies among the roses, as in the ending of "Who Was It Came," a modern personification of Death:

Just when we thought to repossess
The taut frenzies of Chicago jazz
And bridal ardor

Here he comes,
Inexorable gaffer in an old hat
Croaking our names. (57)

Or in "O Personages," a hip invocation to the muse:

O Personages who move
Among me, why don't you
Guys come on call? . . .

Musebaby, what good are you to me
In the dark spirit of the night?
Who needs you more than when the will,
Exhausted, finds dry clay
Where imagination's fountains were—dry clay. . . . (110)

Hoffman's versions of origin myths gesture at ways of animating our dry clay through the transformative power of language. An early poem, "In the Beginning," ends with the desire to domesticate the world by possessing it through speech, the speaker envying his infant daughter's triumph at giving things their proper name:

Kate's word names the vision
that's hers; I try to share.

That verbal imagination
I've envied, and long wished for:

the world without description
is vast and wild as death;

the word the tongue has spoken
creates the world and truth. (61–62)

The trimeter couplets pair into quatrains barely rhyming *ab//ab,* the stanza break perhaps suggesting the unbridgeable distance between signifier and signified, and although "and truth" feels written to complete the rhyme, it does convey our confidence in language's ability to order our lives, even while the speaker understands the impossibility of the task. In a recent poem, "Summer," from his fine 2002 volume *Darkening Water,* Hoffman continues to be obsessed with the simultaneous power and impotence of poetry to shape our experience.

> A breeze tentatively comes from somewhere
> Far at sea, searching for a lover,
> For bestowal, bringing its caresses,
>
> Bringing words etched on this page,
> A white prow I launch now
> To cleave the darkening water. (203)

The breeze, recalling Wordsworth's literal inspiration in *The Prelude,* is here tentative yet loving, profligate yet cautious. This late version of Hoffman's muse gives and takes away. The new poem becomes a ship, its prow cleaving the water the way a plow—and Hoffman's career-long sensitivity to sound calls up the rhyming association unmistakably— cleaves the earth in order to bear fruit. Yet the poem plows only water, and ominously "darkening water" at that, upon which it is launched with a hint of despair like that plaguing Keats, who feared his poems were "writ on water." The poet finally must be bold in launching the proud, full sail of his verse, but also despairing, ultimately working without hope.

This generous harvest of poems from Hoffman's lifetime of work, however, offers ample proof of his lasting power; one more ingredient in the mix is his accomplished love poetry, particularly the poetry of love enduring into middle age and beyond. These lines come from "It Cannot Come Because Desired":

> It's with these
> Banal bodies
> That we must
> Make do,
> Their strangely bulged and cherished
> Curvatures, their folds, their flanks,

> Their impermanent
> Ageing surfaces
> Concealing
>
> Messages that we
> Discover, each
> The other's own
> Rosetta Stone— (49)

The loving acceptance, touching but unextraordinary, of each other's changing bodies works towards the glory still concealed within, set off brilliantly by the sudden formality of the little quatrain and its clinching rhyme. Literally and figuratively, the two lovers become translated, transformed into pure analogs of each other, defined by their ability to read and understand each other thoroughly. They inhabit a pre-Babel world in which everyone speaks the same language, a world before any tower has yet collapsed. Hoffman has poetically imagined us back to the formal garden, his Eden, and it is a garden of love.

# Mary Oliver's Divided Mind (2005)

Mary Oliver's new book, *Blue Iris,* gathers poems of the past twenty-five years together with ten new ones into a thematic bouquet redolent with plants and the creatures that live among them, including Oliver herself. Punctuated by illustrations derived from electronically scanned flower specimens, it is a handsome book filled with excellent work. As a result of this tight focus on theme, many of the traditions in which Oliver operates lie sheer and clear. She evokes the spirit of Whitman, for example in "Some Questions You Might Ask," which catalogs several natural creatures, asking whether they, as well as we, might possess souls. It concludes,

> What about roses, and lemons, and their shining leaves?
> What about the grass? (9)

Similarly, a new poem, "Just Lying on the Grass at Blackwater," in pondering death as glamorous, hypothesizes

> that it might be wonderful to be
> lost and happy inside the green grass—
> or to be the green grass!— (46)

Hopkins also turns up, as in "Morning Glories," which celebrates the "fling of their bodies their / gear and tackle" (1), as well as in the dense appositives for swampy water—"that mud-hive, that gas-sponge, / that

reeking / leaf-yard"—that pile up in "The Lilies Break Open over the
Dark Water" (22).

Nevertheless, the poet to whom Oliver appears most indebted
for her technique is William Carlos Williams. One of her new poems,
"Old Goldenrod at Field's Edge," demonstrates how her short lines
and shrewd enjambments slow the reader down, making us study
everything. In doing so, the poem enacts how the speaker wants us
to slow down and establish communion with the natural world:

> Ice upon old
>   goldenrod
>     stops me at the edge
>       of the field, how
>
> gleaming,
>   this morning,
>     the stiff stalks
>       stand,
>
> slender, exhausted,
>   the gray boss—
>     all that is left of their
>       golden hair—
>
> holding
>   a crown of snow. . . . (64)

It is difficult to stop quoting, since the poem's deliberate motion keeps
us moving inexorably down the page. Each line is an event, each enjambment holds us in suspense, the poem itself becoming Williams's
"machine made of words" with an organic bias, though clearly also a
humanly manufactured thing, as Oliver's rhymes ("old / goldenrod,"
"gleaming / morning," "their / hair") alert us. No one alive uses the
short poetic line as effectively or as excitingly, and few other poets
working in free verse have as precise and seductive a sense of rhythm.

These machines express the complexity of her speakers' relationship with nature, and they continually strive for revelation in their

quest of the force uniting all living things. In "Touch-me-nots," whose speaker has freed a raccoon from a trap and imagines the trapper returning, the poem's interactions of self and not-self, as well as the speaker's attempts to merge with the organisms surrounding her, are immensely touching, ironically so, given the title. Yet Oliver's vital attempt to maintain herself as a citizen-activist of the earth, pursuing relationships with all living things, lands her speaker in the midst of a dilemma pushing her poetic psyche into the opposed roles of scientifically clear-eyed naturalist, at one extreme, and natural senti-mentalist, at the other. The sentimental emerges in the personifica-tion of the flowers, who nod, affirm, and possess bodies in a way that strains credulity. The speaker not only personifies the "little raccoon" in the trap, but has it "praying, / as it felt, over and over, / the mesh of its capture" (34). The touch-me-nots and the raccoon become cute pawns in Oliver's poesis. Such sentimental caricatures of the natural world, by which she forces plants and animals to operate on the basis of emotion rather than genes and instinct, crop up again and again: "the chickadee, singing his heart out" in "October," for example (61), or violets greeting us, "looking up as you pass by" in "Spring" (13), or the sweet swamp flowers that release "such happiness it enters the air as fragrance" in "Morning at Blackwater" (40), adding up to an ecstatic vision of nature that contradicts her scientific scrutiny.

This, then, is Oliver's psychomachia, though what keeps her work from turning into a Disney cartoon is her sweeping command of tone, so that the poetry's conflicted mind rarely diminishes her po-etic power. At her best, she can strike a prophetic pose and get away with it, uttering such attractive saws as "Eternity is not later, or in any unfindable place," from "Count the Roses" (59), or "Attention is the beginning of devotion," from her essay "Upstream" (56). Her powers coalesce vigorously in the new poem "Just Lying on the Grass at Black-water," where the speaker's anti-Wordsworthian insistence that the world was *not* created expressly for her meshes with the entirely Words-worthian credo that we nevertheless can, "In a wise passiveness," enjoy Nature's "privilege . . . to lead / From joy to joy." This paradoxical resolution overcomes the sentimental notion that the singing sparrow is "enjoying his life" and legitimizes the prophetic ending:

> The little sparrow
> with the pink beak
> calls out, over and over, so simply—not to me
> but to the whole world. All afternoon
> I grow wiser, listening to him,
> soft, small, nameless fellow at the top of some weed,
> enjoying his life. If you can sing, do it. If not,
>
> even silence can feel, to the world, like happiness,
> like praise,
> from the pool of shade you have found beneath the everlasting. (46–47)

Salvation, in Mary Oliver's poems, consists of the living of a natural life, the dying of a natural death, and the ability to look clearly in both directions while keeping the two processes in balance.

# New Bottles (2011)

*On Kay Ryan, Robert Dana, Michael Jennings, and Edward Hirsch*

Just as a good poem collapses immensities of feeling or experience into a single page, a devotion to reading and writing poetry condenses time. Poets you consider your contemporaries, whose first books you recall reading with varying combinations of admiration and envy, suddenly stare out from their dustjackets with weathered faces or, for laurels, a wreath of white hair, and you realize with a shock that all of you have sixty or more winters on your heads. Suddenly you hold in your hands the poet's "new and selected," where work from that first book, some of it still vivid in memory, no longer marks the adventurous uncertainty of setting forth but a first firm step toward a destination the poet continues to pursue and continually redefines.

In recent decades the "new and selected" volume has evolved into a standard shape as rigid as a bottle's, into which the poet has decanted the best or most representative of a career's worth of work. The shoulders may slope or ride high, the punt may vary in its depth, but our method of tasting remains constant: we uncork it and first sample the "new poems," whose familiarity might bring comfort, or whose novelty might strike our palates strangely. Then, as the poetry breathes, we leap back in time to early pressings, proceeding chronologically, book by book, through the poems the poet has selected as those likeliest to age most gracefully and enduringly, from youthful fruitiness to mature complexity. The analogy ends, of course, when we finish the selection, since we can lay the volume back down in the rack for cellaring until we wish to sample it anew, curious how renewed acquaintance will color our enjoyment of the *cru* while we anticipate vintages still awaiting the press.

Recent months have brought a new selection of several "new and selecteds," with volumes by Kay Ryan, Robert Dana, and Edward Hirsch following the typical model, opening with their newest work. Only Michael Jennings—less well known than the other poets—has followed the sometimes frustrating lead of Randall Jarrell by grouping his poems thematically, heedless of autobiography. Nevertheless, either approach can result in a satisfying volume, and each of these volumes contains work that should continue to bring immediate pleasure to the nose and a long finish to the palate.

In both her poetic development and her poetry itself, Kay Ryan offers the headiest intensity of these four poets. Because her first full book, *Flamingo Watching,* only appeared in 1994, when her voice had already matured, even the early work in *The Best of It* shows a poet fully formed, with a consistent, identifiable style that for two decades has indulged one of today's most musical ears. Her idiosyncratic method accumulates both end- and internal rhymes and slant-rhymes to propel her poems over a series of heavily enjambed short lines, creating, at her best, the impression that every word has found its perfect habitation and function. Her delightful sound, and her confident voice that bestows upon almost every poem the impression of wise insight about how to live our lives, chime simultaneously on the ear and in the mind, making her work appeal both to connoisseurs of the minutiae of technique and to folks who rarely read poetry. One of her new poems, "Bitter Pill," typifies these qualities:

> A bitter pill
> doesn't need
> to be swallowed
> to work. Just

reading your name
on the bottle
does the trick.
As though there
were some anti-
placebo effect.
As though the
self were eager
to be wrecked. (18)

As we flip from new poems to early ones, we find these sonic, syntactic, and tonal strategies inexorably in place—for example, in "Is It
Modest?" which complains about God's penchant for hiding in his creation and punningly criticizes divine reticence as "un-becoming / on
and on, leaving us like this":

Is it modest or arrogant
not to enter the scene;
instead to push a parrot
forward or make the air
apparent in the spring. . . . (41)

Ryan's own reticence, combined with her stylistic eccentricities,
has made it a critical commonplace to compare her with Emily Dickinson and Elizabeth Bishop. Yet while Dickinson hid in her house, Ryan
hides in her poems. Though she alludes to Dickinson occasionally—
when she discusses "the valves / of the attention" ("Attention" [198])
or "the pharaohs, / shutting their / cunning doors" ("The Pharaohs"
[15])—her stances feel far more armored and impersonal, less willing
to admit any psychological upheaval in her speakers' minds. Without
actually tallying them, I would guess that all the poems in *The Best of
It* spoken by an "I"—the standard pronoun of contemporary poetry,
and one Dickinson used without hesitation—could be counted on
the fingers of one hand. (One of those poems ferries us all the way
back to "After Xeno," Ryan's 1965 elegy for her father, which begins,

"When he was / I was. / But I still am / and he is still" [29], poignantly bandaging personal grief in layers of wordplay and rhyme.) She has also learned much from Bishop, whose dimeter "Sonnet" anticipates Ryan's syntax and compression, and whose last line in "The Bight," "awful but cheerful," stands both sonically and semantically as a model for Ryan's philosophy of slant-rhyme. But even Bishop—famous, ironically, for her privacy—gives "One Art," her villanelle-elegy for Lota Soares, a jolt of personal intensity by having her speaker enumerate her own losses—a house, cities, a continent, and, finally, "you"—in first person.[1] Decades after "After Xeno," by contrast, we can only guess that Ryan might have intended one of her new poems, "Polish and Balm," as an elegy for a lover: "No unguent / can soothe / the chap of / abandonment. / Who knew / the polish / and balm in / a person's / simple passage / among her things. / We knew she / loved them / but not what / love means" (19).

The impression of personal feeling in Ryan's poetry results, paradoxically, not from her accounts of psychological experience, but from the eccentricities of her technique. Following the mind of someone who writes with her precision of diction, her ambushes of rhyme, and her apparently throwaway remarks gives us the illusion of understanding how she thinks and feels. Her rhyming creates surprising, imaginary relationships among words and their referents that recall Hopkins, and her sonic patterns can produce aural anagrams that rival those of "God's Grandeur," "and wears man's smudge and shares man's smell":[2] in "The Silence Islands," its title another aural anagram, Ryan speaks of "a refinement / so exquisite that, / for example, to rhyme / anything with *hibiscus* / is interdicted anytime / children or anyone weakened / by sickness is expected" (182). Ryan's "Blandeur," in fact, takes on "God's Grandeur" directly by coining the title word, as well as concluding, in prayer, with a Hopkinsian imperative: "Unlean against our hearts. / Withdraw your grandeur / from these parts" (158).

While the high-flown Jesuit also provides a possible antecedent for her virtuosic compression, Ryan often ends her poems not with Hopkins's explosions into immanence, but with what seem throwaway lines, as if the poem were simply giving up. Not throwaways at all, their carefully casual diction resembles that of Stevie Smith, another poet whose wit and eccentricity, like Ryan's, mask depths of feeling, and whose willful misunderstandings spark sudden recognitions in the reader of intellectual and emotional crisis. In "Doubt," Ryan warns against welcoming Coleridge's "Person from Porlock," the hero of one of Smith's best-known poems, but she recalls Smith more particularly in the grumbling, world-weary, offhand style that sometimes dares to sound childish and often leaves her poems feeling a bit loopy—to cite just a few instances, in "Apology" ("how we have to leap in the morning / as early as high as possible, / we are so fastened, we are so dutiful" [45]), "Bestiary" ("*Best* is not to be confused with *good*— / a different creature altogether, / and treated of in the goodiary—" [99]), and "Great Thoughts" ("Standing in a / grove of them / is hideous" [185]). In this vein, she also brings to mind her exact contemporary, English poet Wendy Cope, who likewise can disguise her deadly seriousness as light verse.

An intensively aural, rhyme-thick style like Ryan's can spring traps for the poet when flamboyant technique drives the poem instead of providing the vehicle for imaginative event and feeling. In "Osprey," Ryan describes the bird capturing its prey: "He fishes, riding four-pound salmon / home like rockets. They get / all the way there before they die, / so muscular and brilliant / swimming through the sky" (80). This marvelous, ironic transformation of the helpless salmon into a creature whose capture has bestowed majesty upon it encounters a problem, though: an osprey carries its catch transversely to the path of its flight, so depicting the salmon "like rockets . . . swimming through the sky" falsifies perceptual appearance—and such perceptions must register accurately for Ryan's playful visual puns to ring true—for the sake of the poem's conceit. All poets bend the world to fit into their poems—casting phenomena and feeling into language marks the first step—but a willful misrepresentation like this one pulls the reader up short and turns Ryan's style into gimmickry.[3] This puffing up of Ryan's fancy overinflates her recent book *The Niagara River,* where poems like "Felix Crow," "Hailstorm," "Rubbing Lamps," and "Tar Baby" feel forced, rather than the result of emotional or intellectual revelation that appears coincidentally, and miraculously, to chime with the revelations of language.

The good news, however, is that Ryan's new poems show a return to form and truly merit inclusion among the best in *The Best of It,* a cleverly punning title that suggests dogged stoicism, making the best of it, while also summing up the excellence of this poet whose ear, syntax, and wit place her among the best of our current best.

Moving from Ryan's new work to her earliest published poems resembles swimming in the same river twice: though time has passed, the currents feel familiar and we welcome the splashy surprises. Robert Dana presents a strikingly different case, and after beginning *New and Selected Poems 1955 to 2010* by encountering his casual-sounding recent poems, with their syntax-defying accumulations of present participles and noun phrases scattered in free verse about the page, readers new to his work may bark their shins on the elegant formalism of his 1950s poems. Dana, a generation older than the other poets discussed here, died in February 2010, at eighty, and his late poems snatch at the world's mutable scintillations, piling up details, musings, and impressions in "a poetry," as he writes in the prose-poem/essay "In Panama," "less compositional and more improvisational. Less predictable" (239). Here are two brief sections, about half of a typical new poem, "3:10. July. 2009.":

Is the sacred ever silent?
                    Or does it babble and hum and whistle.
Continually. Invisibly.

The tongues of the leaves wagging.
                    Wash of wind through the grass.

A young woman wearing it on a hot day as a long flowing dress made of something just this side of air.

∾

What do I wish?
                   Or wish for?
At eighty and holding a short string
                   strummed to a thread by cancer.
Short fuse.

An entirely different story? Or the same story?
                   How would I know?
         It's all so obvious in its secrecy. (10–11)

Dana domesticates and personalizes high modernism, stripping it of Pound's daunting scholarship and foreign tongues. The passage feels random, a succession of items passing through consciousness, yet it also contains sensuous moments of transport, like that imagining of the young woman wearing the wind.

Like the poetry of many of his contemporaries, Dana's work grows pointedly autobiographical throughout his career, but without scandal, complaint, or self-pity. Cancer thins the old poet's "short string," but it does so by strumming upon the poet, making him an instrument for extending his music while also providing a "short fuse"—like Shakespeare's dying fire in Sonnet 73, "Consumed with that which it was nourished by."[4] Unlike Kay Ryan's, Dana's tunes come stuffed with details about personal situations, landscapes, rooms, even cats—he identifies at least ten by name in his various poems. The late poems feel open, capacious, a place where anything can happen, and while they can grow obvious and sentimental ("And the glossy lip of the long wave shall have the last kiss," from "Beach Attitudes," a title punning on "beatitudes"), they also exhibit their wit ("And blessed be the pacemakers and the peacemakers," from earlier in the same poem [278–79]), as well as finding epiphanies in images of daily life, as in "Looking for Sharks' Teeth": "a five-year-old blond stick of a boy shouts insults at the waves, / slapping at them, / holding out his arms, // the water barely past his knees" (277).

The early poetry plunges us into quite another world. In the 1950s, Dana studied at Iowa under Lowell and Berryman, alongside Donald Justice, Jane Cooper, and Henri Coulette, and his early poetry shares with that of his contemporaries a rage for formal order that would strive ironically against the emotional traumas of the personal past to accommodate them and make them bearable. "For Sister Mary Apolline," a poem in ten-line stanzas from his 1957 book *My Glass Brother and Other Poems*, addresses the speaker's half-sister, who has become a nun (the speaker charmingly observes, "When I called 'Sister' half the convent turned / And smiled" [21]):

> Sister, we share no common heritage.
> A son who does not wear his father's name,
> My birth engendered all; the public shame
> That rattled mother screwloose in her bed;
> Your father, shattering in his rage
> The sideboard glass, the radio, and the clock;
> Your trembling prayers, and your bowed head.
> Above my crib dry birds of paper twirled,
> And I, startled by the sounds, the shock,
> Woke weeping in the dark and adult world. (22)

This poem, a fascinating model of a 1950s artist's exploitation of repression, performs a marvelous balancing act, imposing an order with its rhymes that threatens to break down at the enjambments on the key words "shame" and "rage." The emotions run wild: the mother, "rattled" and "screwloose in her bed," her violently jealous husband, the innocent speaker feeling stained, "weeping in the dark and adult world." But the poem's formality pretends that everything is normal, just as the family continues in spite of the scandal of the mother's adultery and the speaker's bastardy.

Dana's poetry got quieter after these early poems as it began to use the present more than the past. After some experiments in syllabics, including syllabic sestinas, he eventually embraced free verse as his poetic mode, though returning occasionally to the sonnet, the villanelle, and other forms. His experiments in using haiku as stanzas, in books like *The Power of the Visible* (1971) and *In a Fugitive Season* (1979), eventually led to his abandoning haiku form for haiku feeling. In the manner of A. R. Ammons, he began pulling anything he wished into his poems—though with his short phrases, he does not share Ammons's syntactical and intellectual sinuousness—and his poems look casual but often reveal careful construction and, again, an endearing weakness for puns. "Thyme," which winningly begins, "I'm drying herbs. A bumper crop / of oregano, and all the thyme / in the world," proceeds to discuss a friend's heart trouble; meditate on the botanical and architectural cognates of the friend's diagnosis, "fibrillation in the atrium"; study the squirrels out the window; and finally return to the task at hand, "crumbling sweet thyme between / my fingers," weighing the sweetness of his time, crushing it as a means of preserving it (189–91).

Dana's work kept metamorphosing beyond the point where aesthetic or emotional closure provided a suitable or desirable aim. Finally, sick with cancer, he seemed to have found endings less significant even than Whitman, who inspires his invitation to "look for me, Reader, in the dapple of these lines, in the late-summer morning or evening of these poems" (242). If the zigs and zags of his last poems seem to resist settling on a theme, an image, or a feeling, that mutability seems part of Dana's point: as he says in "In Panama," he wants his work to emulate "the butterfly, dipping and slanting and jagging little flashes of color into the air on its jazzy stagger toward whatever far edge of creation may still be breathing out there" (242).

For over thirty years, Michael Jennings's strong work has appeared in small press books and chapbooks, and with several of these editions long out of print, his new selection of sixty-six poems, *Bone-Songs and Sanctuaries,* introduces his poetry to a world that should know it better. But if the scarcity of his early work denies us its acquaintance, the thematic organization of *Bone-Songs* still prevents us from enjoying his poetry's chronological development without doing a little detection. For example, an acknowledgment thanks the New York Creative Artists Public Service program for a grant to write "Dust and a Good Wind," the book's closing section of nine poems inspired by Dorothea Lange photographs—but since the CAPS program ended in 1981, these likely stand as the collection's earliest work. In contrast, a section called "Lamentations" begins with Jennings's most remarkable poem, "Alexandra," a fourteen-sonnet sequence about the poet's mother; since she died in 2001, it shows his mature poetic gifts at their height.

"Alexandra" portrays a "damaged princess," a woman of personal magnetism, sexual power and license, and social pretension, whom the speaker, her son, both loves and hates. "You're done, Mom," he says cruelly in the opening sonnet and crows, in both parody and grammatical protest, "you shan't / correct my English, nor nothing rail nor rant / against forever more" (95). A later sonnet paints her as "Powdered, perfumed, your beauty cool as ice," in "red coat, stiletto heels," nightly "whisked away into a world of eyes / and mouths and random men" (97). Yet the sequence also develops a powerful sympathy that lets us understand the mother without mitigating the emotional damage she inflicts upon herself and her son. We see her at age ten in divorce court, forced to choose between her own "mother drug addicted, / [and] your rich daddy a secret queer and crazy" (96), circumstances that grimly repeat in her own marriage to the speaker's stepfather, who "stood only five foot six and favored boys" (98). Yet the triumphs of "Alexandra" belong more to Jennings's poetry than to psychoanalysis. He daringly and playfully rhymes "You sang your own mantra" with "You changed your name to Alexandra" (101), and gives his speaker point-blank observations like "You desired to be impossible" (102). Most powerfully, after surveying "several boxes" of portraits after her death, the final sonnet crystallizes Alexandra's unique combination of charm and repulsion, mixing her outrageous fascination together with an incestuous queasiness—a combination demanding a slew of hyphenations:

None of [her portraits] hold the look I cherish—
that devil-may-care, slightly-over-the-top,
what-the-hell grin. That wink. It all said come
dance, little broody boy, it's all there is. (108)

Jennings's early poems, especially the Lange sequence, show
youthful virtuosity—one, for example, is a double sonnet consisting of
two octaves followed by two sestets—and in the strongest of them, like
"Damaged Child, Shacktown, Elm Grove, Oklahoma, 1936," we would
feel the power of Lange's images even if we had never seen them:

> She reminds me
> of the future. I give her names.
> The names change. Today she stands
> in front of four pieces of dark sheet-metal
> and almost smiles. It is her birthday.
> She has just turned eight.
> Her one rag
>
> is held together at her right shoulder
> by a small knot that is almost a bow. (138)

This is exquisitely skillful in its documentary pretense. Although the
title and the straightforward description gesture toward objectivity,
Jennings has contrived everything as shrewdly as in a monologue by
Browning—in fact, the abrupt syntactical rhythm and diction here recall the climax of "My Last Duchess": "This grew. I gave commands. /
Then all smiles stopped together. There she stands / As if alive."[5] Yet
even as the poem focuses our attention on the girl, even as the speaker
becomes an interpreter of the photograph and an ironic prettifier of
her wretched circumstances—the "almost" smile, the birthday, the
"almost" bow—even because of these efforts, the poem deliberately
remains outside her, holding the picture at an aesthetic distance and
keeping her an object.

In other early work, Jennings channels other poets, especially Ted
Hughes and Robert Lowell, to whom he dedicates individual poems.

Some of the animal poems that open the book, while powerful, smack of Hughes's poetic paganism—"Before Speech" depicts "the wolf pack, the moon's children, / her insignia borne in the whites of her faces" (3), and in "Squandered by the Hundred Millions" the spirits of slaughtered bison "rose into stars, numberless as stars. / And the night came / lifting him up with his black rage" (4). Jennings discovers his voice, however, in "Crocodile," an apostrophe to the reptile he addresses humorously as "Old bubble brain":

> Mountain ranges grow from his back.
> His each scale anticipates
> the iron age by eons.
> He is the Hindu calendar
> written in Braille. (5)

While the poem still owes to Hughes its feeling of the primal, the diction here has become entirely Jennings's own: the internal rhyming and sonic anagrams ("each scale," "iron age," "eons," "Braille") sound almost like Kay Ryan in a prehistoric mood.

But Jennings's unique gifts display most thoroughly in two more poetic sequences that fully imagine the emotional sweep and subtleties of personal experience—in addition to "Alexandra," these include "A Dance of Stone," a striking set of poems about growing up in Iran, where the speaker's stepfather works in the oil industry, and "This, of Course, Is What Money Won't Buy," eight short love lyrics. In both these sequences, the poetry grows rich with both sympathy and invention. The Iran poems overflow with riveting stories, some perhaps apocryphal, like that of "The Egg Woman," now toothless but once "far the richest whore / in all Khuzistan, with silks and tapestries to boot" (67), and others all too chillingly plausible, like "Hanoon," a portrait of the family's cook whom "we'll lure . . . with money to another town / far from his family and tribe, / to live, displaced, . . . / And he will service us, less smiling than before, / and steal our silver, and we will fire him, / and I will know what it is like / to steal a man's joy and pride / and break his heart" (69).

Reading the love lyrics, "This, of Course, Is What Money Won't Buy," feels like falling in love. We follow the development of a romance that—to our delighted surprise—turns the tawdry dross of adultery into the gold of clean-washed emotion. Everything sparkles freshly in these poems—Jennings even gets away with rhyming "exotic" with "quixotic," preparing for the speaker's awakening not only to foolhardy new quests but to life's deeper shadows: "I'm new—grinning ear to ear, hearing windmills. / Death is new here, too, and moves like water underfoot" (28). As in Donne, the speaker sees love as resolving all paradoxes: "Clothed in purple and black, / you're naked. Naked, raspberries and cream, / you're clothed. It's magic" (29); "seeing / is much like blindness, blindness like pure sight" (33). But for these "new ghosts / wakened to Elysian Fields," the world never loses its nature, never floats away into fantasy. The lovers "smile at all that is sensuous / and literal" (35), confident of a love dependent on the body and the organic renewal not only of the heart but of the entire world that houses it:

> But here, your walk is so much like the sun
> or prayer, I must stoop
> and touch the place you've stepped, knowing
> come spring, something will grow there. (32)

Opening Edward Hirsch's *The Living Fire* and revisiting "Song against Natural Selection," the first poem in his first collection, *For the Sleepwalkers* (1981), brings back all the excitement of his initial appearance on the poetry scene:

> The weak survive!
> A man with a damaged arm,
> a house missing a single brick, one step
> torn away from the other steps
> the way I was once torn away
> from you. . . . (25)

For all its startling freshness, however, the poem also reveals a tendency that pervades Hirsch's early work: the doomed romance in this stanza never becomes convincing as a real love affair, despite nostalgic allusions to "when we were young" and how "losing itself becomes a kind / of song, our song" (26). The anonymous lovers here serve as a stage prop for the poem's true performers, the words making love under Hirsch's direction. These early poems are amazing for how thoroughly they create the illusion of completeness out of little but Poetry itself—how the title poem notes "the worn path / that leads to the stairs instead of the window" and how sleepwalkers "raise their arms and welcome the darkness" (32), how in "Still Life: An Argument," "The milk on the table is always / about to spill" (35). Everything seems about to happen, the world feels full of linguistic and affective potential, and Hirsch's language is so strong and memorable that we scarcely notice that the poems barely touch the real world of human interaction and feeling.

"Omen," from Hirsch's second book, *Wild Gratitude* (1986), awakens us to this fact when, as the moon poetically "comes out to stare," and the clouds poetically "gather like an omen above the house," the speaker suddenly puts away Poetry and instead creates the sense of a real person undergoing real suffering: "I can't stop thinking about my closest friend // Suffering from cancer in a small, airless ward / In a hospital downtown" (49). Suddenly the great agon of Hirsch's poetry crystallizes into a conflict between wanting to create art about art—and he has written many fine ekphrastic poems—and producing poems expressive of human life and feeling. In Hirsch's art poems, apparently real people, like the "you" of "Song against Natural Selection," become extras intended to give gravity to the artistic exploration that really interests him. The bag lady the speaker follows in "Three Journeys," "on her terrible journey past Food Lane's Super-Market" and beyond, finally exists not as a sympathetic woman suffering the terror and solitude of poverty and homelessness, but as a figure who functions solely to let us "know what it meant for John Clare / to walk eighty miles across pocked and jutted / roads" (67).

But Hirsch's third book, *The Night Parade* (1989), marks a poetic maturation. It introduces a series of family poems that in every detail feel more intensely imagined, more fully alive and sympathetic than either his bag lady or his John Clare: the bubbe in "My Grandmother's Bed," who "pulled it [her Murphy bed] out of the wall / To my amazement" (79), and the zayde in "My Grandfather's Poems," who "wrote them backwards, / In Yiddish, in tiny, slanting, bird-like lines / That seemed to rise and climb off the page" (81). This exciting, entirely believable world sets up the emotional nakedness of the powerfully imagined "Infertility," an exploration of the speaker's childless marriage that will re-emerge in several poems, here as a threat to terminate the genetic and poetic lineage *The Night Parade* has lovingly presented:

> We don't know how to name
> > the long string of zeros
> Stretching across winter,
> > the barren places,
> The missing birthdates of the unborn. (94)

The argument for Hirsch's enduring power as a poet depends on these poems that, intelligent as they are, still favor the heart over the head. The 1998 volume *On Love* introduces *The Lectures on Love,* a series of monologues in which the likes of Diderot, Heine, Baudelaire, Margaret Fuller, Gertrude Stein, Colette, and others hold forth. It feels like a symposium where, except for Fuller's lively pantoum and Stein's lyrical free verse chop-logic, you can't imagine how such a sexy topic could sound so dull. Hirsch's formal experiments here are intriguing and innovative, but the several poems using his inventive *rime riche* envelope stanzas—octaves, for example, in which pairs of identical words end lines 1 and 8, 2 and 7, and so on—tend to feel labored and, strangely, make the repetitions of the sequence's sestinas and pantoums sound almost natural. The point seems almost to be that *talking* about love instead of practicing it becomes a dull, redundant round.

But in *Lay Back the Darkness* (2003), Hirsch's poems truly conceive and enact powerful romantic and sexual feelings, making it his most fully achieved book, the one that truly merits the title *On Love*. *Lay Back the Darkness* is just as literary as *On Love*, but Hirsch reimagines moments from Homer, Virgil, Dante, and the personal life of his speaker and gives them shape and intensity through his masterful use of form, especially the difficult terza rima sonnet. The speaker and his partner, reading Dante's episode of Paolo and Francesca in "The Sentence," become the doomed medieval lovers: "When you read Canto Five aloud last night / in your naked singsong, fractured Italian, / . . . // I suspected we shall never be forgiven / for devouring each other body and soul" (176). The idea of being sentenced extends to the marriage's fruitlessness, which becomes entwined in "The Asphodel Meadows"—a kind of Limbo—with all the deaths the speaker witnesses and imagines:

> the loved ones, the deaths we had tended,
> the work we had made, the desperate charms
> we had uttered on behalf of our child,
>
> but the god was indifferent to our terms,
> and then I woke with you in my arms. (201)

This theme of lost children, of blasted potential, emerges most fully in Hirsch's great poem of heaped fragments, "Two Suitcases of Children's Drawings from Terezin, 1942–1944." The poem's ten sections pretend simply to present a series of lists—"Artist Unknown," "Parables," "The Art Teacher"—but the brief sections accumulate great emotional power. Here are a handful from "What Some of the Class Drew":

> Zuzga drew the saddest elephant in Block 4

---

> Karel scribbled his name upside down
> under a scrawny camel in the desert

———————

Liana painted her face on a tin plate

———————

Franta sketched a sleepy ballerina
lifting her leg over a wooden practice bar

She called it *Memory of a Dancing Girl*

———————

Petr signed his name in the water
that swirled around the deportation train (188)

Hirsch's list operates in a *faux naïf* fashion, and we intuit that despite
his pretense of objectivity, the speaker has an intensive emotional in-
vestment in his material: he interprets the drawings for us and nudges
our response, even to the point of alluding to Keats's deathbed wish
to have his name "writ in water." But the wise spareness of Hirsch's
language here, apparently so simple a child could understand it, has
brought him light years beyond the self-consciously poetic diction of
his early work. "Two Suitcases of Children's Drawings" is one of the
most subtle and powerful Holocaust poems I know.

The new poems that open *The Living Fire,* which I have left for last,
though they begin the book, prove a mixed bag. A couple are wonderful:
"Early Sunday Morning," with its memory, like a Richard Thompson
song, of "that red-haired girl / who left you stranded in a parking lot /
forty years ago," whom the speaker imagines "disappearing / around the
corner of your dream / on someone else's motorcycle" (17), and "Last
Saturday," a brief poem in which "The new exterminator" comes calling "without warning," an unidentified death-figure whom the speaker
"never expected . . . to be so young" (20). But some of the new poems
feel either careless or cavalier, qualities that have rarely marred Hirsch's
past work. *The Living Fire* opens with a four-line lyric, "The Beginning
of Poetry":

> Railroad tracks split the campus in half
> and at night you'd lie on your narrow cot
> and listen to the lonely whistle
> of a train crossing the prairie in the dark. (3)

The poet's humble undergraduate beginnings slyly suggest economic class—that in his "narrow cot," he comes from the wrong side of the tracks. But short as it is, the poem gets lazy: "lonely whistle" seems a sentimental instance of pathetic fallacy, while "a train" and "in the dark" repeat what Hirsch already has clearly presented. Further, while that whistle seems to embody the poetic impulse, the poem ignores the metrical rhythm of the distant train, the persistent undercurrent of poetry from which the whistle arises to punctuate loneliness in an expressive climax. In the conclusion of that other nocturne of inspiration and vocation, "My Grandfather's Poems," Hirsch captured the interplay of rhythm and melody, of drive and lament that make poems urgent:

> For years I fell asleep to the rhythm
> Of my grandfather's voice rising and falling,
> Filling my head with his lost, unhappy poems:
> Those faint wingbeats, that hushed singing. (82)

More troubling, Hirsch has included a number of poems that, in their resort to silly puns, feel like throwaways. A line like "Hell was sinking in" destroys any chance of our taking seriously "Once, in Helsinki" (15), and "Dark Tour" relates the near-breakup and reconciliation of a love affair in thirty trivial haiku, each set in a different world city: "Budapest," for example, goes, "No sign of Buddha, / but a history of pest— / ilence and beauty" (10), while "Madrid" shows the lovers "Mad at each other / in a romantic city. / Love got rid of us" (11). There's nothing wrong with punning that enriches a poem's themes or expressiveness, as in Kay Ryan and Robert Dana's work; though Hirsch's trifles don't aspire to the profound wit of Donne, say, they do little harm—with one exception, "Belfast":

Let the bells quicken.
We've lived through enough troubles
for a few lifetimes. (12)

The opening line's pun on "Belfast" conjures up church bells pealing
in celebration of the Good Friday accords, an analogy for the truce
between the lovers, but using the "lifetimes" of Irish "troubles" to represent the problems of two little people feels woefully inappropriate.
What next? "No, never again / love concentrated like ours, / which
went up in smoke"?

I hope Hirsch has gotten these frivolities out of his system. When
he writes with fidelity to the world and the feelings it evokes in us, he
has few peers, and as the excellent majority of *The Living Fire* demonstrates, his best poetry's continually shifting forms, whether sonnets
or free verse, blaze with energy, surprises, heat, and the intensity of
a first-rate poetic imagination. Robert Dana will be missed, but as
Hirsch, Ryan, and Jennings continue to mature, their poems should
continue to feel good in the mouth and bring a buzz to the intellect
and the bloodstream.

In so doing, they give the lie to the proverbial complaint about
repackaged goods as "old wine in new bottles," itself a corruption of
the Gospels' warning against putting new wine into old wineskins.
On the contrary, these "new and selecteds" allow us to taste a variety
of vintages from the same stock, revisiting old and rare poems that
have aged remarkably well, while sampling the latest harvest of these
fine poets, fresh and oozing from the press.

# Better Poetry
# through Chemistry (2007)

*On David Wojahn*

Reading David Wojahn's impressive new book of selected poems, *Interrogation Palace*, kept reminding me of T. S. Eliot's metaphor for the poetic imagination in his essay "Tradition and the Individual Talent": the catalyst, the filament of platinum that, in Eliot's example, induces oxygen and sulfur dioxide to react:

> This combination takes place only if the platinum is present; nevertheless the newly formed acid contains no trace of platinum, and the platinum itself is apparently unaffected; has remained inert, neutral, and unchanged. The mind of the poet is the shred of platinum. It may partly or exclusively operate upon the experience of the man himself; but, the more perfect the artist, the more completely separate in him will be the man who suffers and the mind which creates; the more perfectly will the mind digest and transmute the passions which are its material.[1]

Eliot's chemistry-class metaphor for his "impersonal theory of poetry" pretends that the poet's life and art live peculiarly divorced from each other, that the imagination creating the most "perfectly" realized works does not itself react—chemically or emotionally—to betrayals, celebrations, sudden deaths, and other upheavals in the poet's daily world. For support, he even pulls in Keats and his nightingale, an imaginative encounter most readers find overflowing with personal reaction: "The ode of Keats contains a number of feelings which have nothing particular to do with the nightingale, but which the nightingale, partly, perhaps, because of its attractive name, and partly because of its reputation, served to bring together" (9). The feelings in the ode, Eliot insists, derive neither from anything Keats personally felt at the jug-jug of a particular live bird in his plum tree nor from the heartaches of his own pale, specter-thin existence, but rather from the wish to have such heartaches universally understood by translating them into the symbolic realm of art. The bird therefore represents no real bird, but everything ever associated with nightingales, a tradition to which Keats adds his own considerably individual talents. The nightingale behaves as the catalyst *in* the poem to produce feeling in the speaker, just as Keats's mind catalyzes the poem's imaginary materials to get them—and consequently us—to react.

In our current, ever-later-Romantic poetic world, even after nearly fifty post-Eliot years of highly personal-sounding, confessional poetry, the catalyst idea still makes psychological sense, however much we despise the "impersonal" label. Keats himself subscribed to the theory in his letter explaining that the imagination "is every thing and nothing," for "it has as much delight in conceiving an Iago as an Imogen": the "camelion [that is, chameleon] Poet . . . is the most unpoetical of any thing in existence; because he has no Identity—he is continually in for—and filling some other Body."[2] He does not mean that poets don't write about the personal, but that poetry "is not symptomatic," as Susanne K. Langer explained about art in general: "An artist working on a tragedy need not be in personal despair or violent upheaval; nobody, indeed, could work in such a state of mind. . . . Art is congruent with the dynamic forms of our direct sensuous, mental, and emotional life."[3] That emotional life, of course, can produce works that convince us they have deep personal roots in personal joy or anguish. But the poem succeeds only when the poet has devised ways of turning individual joy and suffering into congruent forms—what Eliot calls, notoriously, "the objective correlative" and Langer "expressive form." The poet combines materials into new compounds, leading us to respond with an emotional reaction. Both these operations are symbolic and imaginary: the poet's mind creates the illusion of reaction and, reading, we experience a vicarious response that, however profoundly we feel it, remains imaginary and need not draw on our personal emotional circumstances at all. In even the most personal-sounding poem, the poet engineers emotional catharsis so we can first perceive the poet's imaginary surrogate—the "I" of the poem—undergoing it, and then respond imaginatively.

Such complex chemistry underlies the biography of David Wojahn's poetry, for as much as any contemporary poet, he uses such combinations in an Eliot-like, almost metaphysical way. He is a maximalist, constantly experimenting by interweaving in a single poem accounts of two or more apparently disparate events or persons. Developing each at length, he then trusts both his platinum imagination to produce a flash of insight, and the reader's imagination to understand suddenly the new thing he has created by bringing these materials together in the lab. *Interrogation Palace* provides the great pleasure of watching Wojahn develop this technique over the past two decades.

But success with such a technique has come only with great difficulty. In poems from Wojahn's second book, *Glassworks* (1987), he began to experiment with this scientific method, and while we see how he expects his ingredients to produce that sudden flash, his results remain more hypothetical than emotionally fulfilled. The speaker of "Pentecost," for example, imagines his father as a World War II corporal in Pisa, guarding Ezra Pound, "the old man / who claims that he's American himself, / who speaks in whispers from within / the bars, in the corny mannered slang / of a movie cowboy." After drinking "sick- / sweet grappa at a café with the men," the corporal obeys a sudden, mysterious urge to write, "to take down / the details of this light, its shimmer," having no idea why. The poem concludes by detailing

how he felt, for a moment,
he'd had the power to speak in Greek,
Italian, and Chinese, his thoughts

churning forth in swirling cadences,
like oars striking brightly
against a sea so vivid
he's blinded and must turn away. (51–52)

Wojahn aims for a miraculous, pentecostal moment, in which Pound's
unholy/holy spirit fills the father and then vanishes, leaving both revelation and fear in its passing. But the miracle feels more like a poet's
imaginary concoction forced onto our attention, and less like a natural
reaction bursting from the potential of the elements Wojahn introduces.
In other poems, like "Dates, for Example," the elements ingeniously
brought together—John Dos Passos and Eugene O'Neill's former gardener on Cape Cod; the speaker next door imagining the Turkish poet
Nazim Hikmet, whom he is reading, admiring from his prison cell a
poem the speaker's wife is busy writing decades later—run admirably
parallel but still leave us waiting for the flash. When, at the end, the
gardener appears with gifts (*"I brought you some rhubarb! / I brought
you some peppers!"*), we understand only intellectually how the two
harvests, vegetables and poems, should ignite sparks (53–55).

*Mystery Train* (1990) marks an important departure for Wojahn.
By exploring forms, especially the sonnet, but also the villanelle and
others, he devises appropriate containers for his inventions, flasks to
contain his experiments. Though many of his sonnets take the Shakespearean or Italian form, he slant-rhymes heavily and adopts variant
rhyme schemes, a flexibility that extends to his poetic line, which over
the years has ranged from four to nine beats, even in a single sonnet.
These prosodic liberties might drive purists crazy—some of them even
drive me crazy—but taking them has helped Wojahn make just about
any subject fit for verse. The "Mystery Train" sequence itself, twenty
of whose poems appear here, examines the darker side of rock and
roll through the lens of political and literary culture. Some of Wojahn's
pairings would surprise no one—Buddy Holly watches *Rebel Without
a Cause,* Bob Dylan visits Woody Guthrie, Delmore Schwartz hears
his student Lou Reed's Velvet Underground play at Andy Warhol's

Factory—but some of them prove startling and lovely: William Carlos Williams watching Elvis Presley on *Ed Sullivan,* John Berryman meditating on Robert Johnson in a neo-Dream Song, a Robert Goulet *Carol Burnett Show* skit juxtaposed with the famous Vietnam image of a point-blank street execution.

But in addition to his discovery of the sonnet, *Mystery Train* also marks Wojahn's greater mastery in getting his historical and personal materials to react. In "Posthumous Life (London: Hampstead Heath)," the speaker combines a visit to Keats's house in Highgate, a blind couple playing chess on a nearby bench, and memories of his last hospital visit with his blind grandfather:

> I scarcely know him, and it was my groping
> smooth-faced self I mourned as I left.
> Cheap cliché of turning at the doorway
>
> a final look at his face, *gloom-pleased eyes*
> *embowered from the light,* the nurse's heels
> clicking toward me on the floor,
>
> antiseptic hallway smell. How does
> forgiveness come? I have your pocket watch,
> have lost the only photograph. It's late.
>
> The lamps click on, the rain, how fresh it must feel
> against their faces. *Teddy,* she says,
> and touches, gently, his shoulder,
>
> *I think there's someone watching us.* (83)

The ending turns us away from the grandfather, then back to the blind couple, commuting smoothly among the poem's multiple scenarios, showing their imaginary fusion without confusion. Though the self-conscious young speaker calls that "final look" at his grandfather's face a "cheap cliché," the real cliché here is the sudden burst of invented self-consciousness that overemphasizes the personal emotion, "How does / forgiveness come?" Here Wojahn doesn't trust us to react in the way he has so well prepared for us, having brought together lines from Keats's sonnet "To Sleep" to react with the speaker's sense of inadequacy and his voyeuristic fascination with the blind couple, whose loving warmth spurs his guilty memory of his solitary grandfather. As catalysts in the poem, both poet and speaker have convened all the essential elements, rendering unnecessary such an awkward fingerposting of personal sensitivity and shame.

Also from *Mystery Train*, "The Resurrection of the Dead: Port Glasgow, 1950" sets Stanley Spencer's painting of Judgment Day dawning in a Scotch churchyard against an account of a grotesquely burned boy "whose father, drunk, had hurled a pan of scalding / cooking oil on his face and shoulders." Wojahn's description of the dead arising is as beautiful as that of Carlos's wounds is awful:

> They don't all wake at once. This couple: the wife's
> 	kiss startling her husband to life, her shroud
> 		a kind of negligee she fidgets with,
>
> suddenly shy, while her man dusts off his bowler hat,
> 	and taps his pocket watch alive again.

The details give the scene's full emotional value: the husband's tapping his watch in disbelief—has time gotten going again, or has it ended?—and the sexuality of the kiss and the shroud / negligee, underscoring not only the resurrection's physicality but the power of love that underlies it. Sometimes Wojahn too obviously juxtaposes this miracle against the boy's suffering, as when observers can't "help but cringe / in secret at the doctor's botched salvation / of his face." But the speaker ends by confronting the risen dead, so newly reanimated by love, conjuring them to acknowledge the ruined Carlos: "Moon-faced, grinning immortals, / what can you say to him, a man by now ... ?":

> I want you to move closer. Feel
>
> his breath on the napes of your living necks.
> 	Stroke, if you can, his face. You—the risen,
> 		The born again—how can you turn away? (86–88)

The fact that the speaker addresses the reader as well as the painting's blithe spirits does not diminish the poem's power. Unlike the speaker's self-accusation in "Posthumous Life," this conclusion grows brilliantly out of a charge to accept the responsibilities of love, even eternal love, as well as its joys.

The role of the dead has swelled in Wojahn's work since 1994's *Late Empire*, both the numberless dead of history he attempts to re-cover and humanize and the more personal deaths he investigates and reacts to, particularly the losses of mother, father, and wife. "White Lanterns," the crown of sonnets about his mother's death, though powerful in individual poems, takes a studied, impersonal pose, an uncomfortable attempt to seduce us ironically by pronouncing family photographs "Colorless now, outside of history" (104). The stance remains cool and restrained, in spite of our wish to see the shaping imagination suddenly startled into feeling, like Coleridge in "Frost at Midnight" exclaiming, "My babe so beautiful!"[4] The personal-sounding moments in the sequence sound the most convincing, for example, the way her ordinary goodbye on a snowy morning anticipates her final departure, "The bus laboring off into snow, her good-bye kiss / Still startling my cheek with lipstick trace" (102). The full sequence feels skillful but pinched. More expansive elegies follow, however, like "The Ravenswood," from *Spirit Cabinet* (2002), which, in triadic feet like William Carlos Williams's, intertwines images of the dying mother with the speaker's childhood memory of accompanying her by train to a family funeral and feeling sexually excited by "the fur & her smell so close / they are breathing me." This complex of memories ignites against a background of Milton's rebel angels falling for nine days to burn in hell, for his mother's sexy cigarettes ("the Salem she lit / pulsing down") and the heat of emotion swallow everything like the train tunnels, combusting it all together: "The tunnel yawning / receives us whole. . . . // Then vortex, spasm, / sudden dark /within the car. / *The glow, the flicker.* / Ash" (161–63).

Elegies come to dominate the spirit of the book, but deftly intertwined with other materials that deepen the sorrow and broaden the significance of personal grief. "The Shades," a seven-sonnet sequence, presents the speaker's father's suicide attempt, hospitalization, and death against a literary/anthropological landscape populated by feral children, theories of language, and Aeneas trying and failing to embrace his father in the underworld. The themes proliferate, but Wojahn mixes them skillfully so his elements react, we react, and his speaker reacts as well: he achieves that Coleridge-like illusion of the catalyst suddenly catalyzed, as when he tries and fails to accommodate the image of his "father in the locked room lying still":

> a scowling nurse
> > brings his white paper cup of pills.
> He's scarcely breathing, face turned toward the wall.
>
> Not a jump cut: the film itself unspools,
> celluloid melting, or ribboning the floor, subtitles
>
> blurred. *Describe this empty screen.*
> > Opal? Pearl?
> Cancel. Cancel, fading like a vapor trail. (126)

We can see the maturation of Wojahn's chemistry in the less complex but equally moving sonnet "God of Journeys and Secret Tidings," one of several elegies for his wife, the poet Lynda Hull:

> Eurydice is better off in hell.
> Isn't that what Rilke says? Hermes
> guides her back, unspools black gauze
> to shroud her anew, and Death again is merciful,
> is grave goods, unguents, clove-scented fluids,
> his lips pressed deftly on nipple and thigh,
> the god's long fingers, his laving hands, their slide
> as they stroke and roil and spool her shroud.
>
> And how, indeed, could such beauty be borne,
> except by the shoulders of a god? Here on the dome

of hell it rains, and you are six months dead.
The answering machine tonight spins down—
February's messages, a half-year un-erased,
another mistake to tally. And on them is your voice. (130)

Caught between the opposed compounds of conventional mourning
and personal anguish, between the comfort of the classical tradition
and the void of lost love, the sonnet starts with the speaker trying to
convince himself the dead are happier dead, enlisting Rilke—but in
an uncertain question—as his authority and anchor. But the images of
Hermes's or Death's—the "his" is ambiguous—sexual intimacy with
Eurydice provoke discomfort, which the speaker tries to allay with
that over-rhetorical "indeed," instead of immediately exploding, "How
could such beauty be borne?" But the reaction—a small explosion, but
an explosion nonetheless—comes in the final four lines. The world
is no longer the land of the living but "the dome / of hell," where the
emotional climate grows increasingly bleak, for that half-year sepa-
rating the lovers can never be erased as long as her messages remain.
The kicker, "And on them is your voice," is in a way superfluous—we
already know what he hears. Yet that incantatory ending provides
a gesture essential for the poem's closure, a ritual that provides no
comfort but further torture.

More recently Wojahn's work has experimented further with
mixing his chemicals, and the results are likewise mixed. The seven
sections included from his sequence "Crayola" stuff as much as they
can into their baggy sixteen lines, slant-rhymed *abba*. They feel
overstuffed, their sentence fragments proliferating in an attempt at a
pop *Waste Land,* complete with notes in the form of postmodernish
marginalia, ranging from allusions to Plato's Parable of the Cave and
the Gospels' account of the Crucifixion to facts from a childhood
epileptic episode and speech bubbles from Green Lantern comics.
Each line constitutes a single stanza, a mannerism Wojahn has used
several times in his recent work, yet few of the lines merit such em-

phatic isolation—"DC & Marvel, to my mother = *trash*" and "The Blind Man has a braille watch. It clamshells open" are fairly typical (175, 177)—and the marginal material might have fleshed out those gaps more profitably. Ambitious as it is, "Crayola" reduces history, literature, popular culture, and personal life to a big, sloppy coloring book with the poetry working too hard to color outside the lines.

I will end where *Interrogation Palace*'s readers will begin, with "For the Poltergeists," a set of nine new poems that opens Wojahn's book. As always, they demonstrate intellectual adventure, seeking new elements to catalyze into new works of art. The life and work of Theremin, the Russian electronic music pioneer, spark the larger problem of "a century where all inventions / will in time be used to rip the world asunder" (13), lines that may disclose a new interest in prosaic rhythms after the overfragmentation of "Crayola." "Scrabble With Matthews," William Matthews, that is, provides a fitting tribute to the mind of the late poet, its wittiest moment finding the speaker "minding my *p*'s & *q*'s, the latter of which // I could not play, failing three times to draw a *u*," playfully suggesting the impossibility of adequately sketching his subject, "*u*," then startlingly bursting into "The dead care nothing for our eulogies" (20). "Eulogies," of course, cannot be written without "*u*," and it would not surprise me if Wojahn here implied a punning definition of the term as "*you*-words."

The most intriguing of the new pieces, though, the six-poem sequence "Dithyramb and Lamentation," sees the war in Iraq against a background of twentieth-century historical horrors and literary history. It has brilliant sections, such as "E-mail," a variant villanelle about our abusive interrogation tactics, which makes poetry from the vicious, colloquial refrains "Make sure he has a bad night" and "He'll break down real fast," surely a feat more of alchemy than mere chemistry (24). But one of its most ambitious efforts, "George W. Bush in Hell," a serious parody of the *Inferno*'s twenty-sixth Canto, fails because it ennobles the politician by assigning him an implausible self-awareness—he confesses, "Truth was my toy. No counsel

could dissuade // My certainty, nor satisfy my cronies' greed"—and
an undeserved tragic dignity:

> "But see where this has taken me,
>    Who brought two countries to shame & ruin.
>    My every cell is napalm. Take pity
>
> On me, you who may leave this fiery tomb
>    & walk again among the living." (27)

The real triumph of "Dithyramb and Lamentation" lies in its final
section, "Child's Drawing, Spanish Civil War," in which Wojahn's materials once more come both from without—CNN Iraq War images of
violence and detainees, viewed during an airplane trip; the eponymous
child's drawing of a battlefield being cleared of the dead—and, quite literally, from within—not only the speaker's twin sons, but "my come /
streaking the beaker's sides," required for the *in vitro* fertilization that
will produce "Baby A & Baby B." As he quickly recounts the closely
observed growth of the two fetuses, we somehow feel as though we
were witnessing the scientific development of our species:

> What case,
>    what tactic, what rite? Exfoliation
>          & its psalms: twenty fingers opening
>
> in amniotic brine & opening still
>       even as the night comes on, & beside me now
>             my voyagers thrash, belted to their seats,
>
> selah selah selah. The cabin lights
>       flicker & the plane bucks,
>             but their sleep is unperturbed. (28–30)

The poem expresses wonder at how we got here and how we can endure,
introducing, via a sly allusion to Berryman, a bit of turbulence that
doesn't trouble the children but participates in the larger turbulences
operating on the speaker, and on our entire planet. All these elements

in Wojahn conspire in their operations upon us: we find ourselves opening still, horrified and awed by our world, but lucky to have poems with such complex combinations of feeling as this, to spark our reactions and increase our awareness, even as the night comes on.

# III.

## *The Ear*

# Why Poetry
# Doesn't Count as Song (2012)

One traditional commonplace about poetry holds that it enjoys an intimate relationship with music, not only in the practical sense of providing lyrics for composers to set, but in its very nature as an art form. The generally accepted origin of poetry as an element of song has allowed the identification of these two arts to persist as a romantic fiction. Ezra Pound insisted "that music begins to atrophy when it departs too far from the dance; that poetry begins to atrophy when it gets too far from music."[1] He had, early on, exhorted aspiring poets "to compose in the sequence of the musical phrase, not in sequence of a metronome."[2] Similarly, in a letter to Cleanth Brooks, T. S. Eliot once called "the conscious problems" of writing poetry "more those of a quasi musical nature, the arrangement of metric and pattern, than of a conscious exposition of ideas."[3] Coming from the two poets who most famously made poetry modern, these authoritative-sounding pronouncements on poetic composition reflect a long history of considering poetry as a species of music. Their notion of music as the purest, most abstract of the arts, particularly alluded to in Pound's dictum about music, dance, and poetry, likely derived from the aesthetics of Walter Pater, whose well-known aphorism *"All art constantly aspires towards the condition of music"*—emphatically italicized—provided a kind of blueprint for Modernism's push towards greater and purer abstraction in each of the arts.[4]

In earlier centuries, poetry and music shared a closer identification than in our time, as suggested by the countless sixteenth- and seventeenth-century lyrics simply identified as "Song," like John Donne's "Go and catch a falling star" or Edmund Waller's "Go, lovely Rose—" But already by the Elizabethan period, poets distinguished between poems composed for singing and poems that called themselves songs by way of metaphorical convention. Although no one believes Shakespeare wrote his Sonnets to be sung, the speaker/poet informs his young man in 102 that "I sometime hold my tongue, / Because I would not dull you with my song," and in 105 turns this charge of monotony into the virtue of constancy: "all alike my songs and praises be."[5] Similarly, Edmund Spenser's "Prothalamion" declares itself a song at each refrain, while George Herbert's speaker in "Virtue," a few decades later, refers to the poem as "my music." The convention of poets calling their poems "songs," although not designed for singing, survives to this day, even—perhaps especially—in free-verse works that have deliberately eliminated the patterns of meter and rhyme that most closely linked the two arts in earlier times. Whitman insisted on calling his revolutionary free-verse sequence *Song of Myself,* Pound's speakers continually refer to poems as "my songs," John Berryman devised 385 *Dream Songs,* and Michael S. Harper called a 1985 collection *Healing Song for the Inner Ear.*

Jon Stallworthy's "Versification" essay for *The Norton Anthology of Poetry* perpetuates the ideas that poetry equals song and that it achieves its full form only when read aloud, or heard aloud in the imagination: "A poem is a composition written for performance by the human voice. What your eye sees on the page is the composer's verbal score, waiting for your voice to bring it alive as you read it aloud or hear it in your mind's ear." Building on this analogy, he argues that a knowledge of prosody makes us appreciate poetry in the same way that understanding "musical notation and the principles of musical composition" will enhance our understanding and enjoyment of "a composer's score."[6] While knowing prosody *does* make us better readers of poetry, his musical score/poetic text analogy ultimately rings false. It breaks down because we live in a literate culture, where our primary experience of poems comes through reading them privately on the page, but we also live in a functionally illiterate musical culture, where most of us, by far, experience music through direct listening to live or recorded performance, rather than by reading printed scores. The fact that both art forms commonly originate in written compositions directed to the eye, which provide the basis for performance directed to the ear, does not make them interchangeable. On the contrary, the two arts essentially differ, and not simply because of the historical accident that linguistic literacy has grown nearly universal while musical literacy remains a specialty.

Poetry is not song because we do not experience the two arts in the same way. While music appeals directly to the "sensual ear," as Keats understood, poetry's "ditties of no tone" invoke both the interpretive and the emotional imagination—or, as Pater wrote, "Poetry, again, works with words addressed in the first instance to the mere intelligence."[7] Further, the nature and purpose of rhythmic and sonic effects in poetry differ qualitatively from effects believed to resemble them in song. The irony that Keats's phrase "no tone" stands as one of the most beautifully toneful moments in the "Ode on a Grecian Urn"—a moment some might call a highlight of poetic "musicality"—would likely disappear in a setting of the poem as a song, because composers have intrinsically musical rather than poetic priorities and aesthetics. Only in reading the poem, where we can dwell on "no tone," not having to chase after it as it swims past on the currents of a melodic and instrumental setting, can we appreciate that the speaker has created a frozen moment in time where the language leads directly from sensuous impact into the poem's imaginative world—a frozen moment that, because of the overwhelming illusion of musical motion, a composer's setting would likely negate. In that moment, with Keats's language unfettered by melody and instrumentation, we realize that the appeal to our imagination of "no tone"—music that does not exist—imitates precisely the experience the speaker is about to undergo, imagining himself first into the scenes on the urn and then, ultimately, off the urn and back into life, mourning for the "little town" he imagines—a town that also does not exist—"by river or sea shore" grown "desolate."[8] To take a more recent example of poetic "music," the sonic relationships William Carlos Williams creates in *Spring and All* 22 ("The Red Wheelbarrow"), both consonance ("de-pends / upon") and assonance ("glazed with rain," "beside the white"), provide an aurally satisfying analog for the visual relationships in the poem created by the three prepositions "upon," "with," and "beside."[9] But no matter how often we repeat these lines aloud, and no matter how much sensuous pleasure they provide, these sonic devices do not make the poem a song. Setting it to music would transform it into a song, but it would no longer be a poem.

Susanne K. Langer long ago investigated this illusory relationship between poetry and song, both forms dependent on sound to achieve their effects, but each an art we experience in a qualitatively different way. All arts, she proposed, operate upon our senses or imagination through a "primary illusion" (a term she later renamed "primary ap-parition"), the means by which we apprehend the work through either our senses or our imagination. Music's primary illusion, according to Langer, is the creation of virtual time, "the sonorous image of passage, abstracted from actuality to become free and plastic and entirely per-ceptible."[10] Music's strict manipulation of time—its use, for example, of duration, rhythm, rests, and the sustaining of sung syllables over two or more different pitches—sets our experience of songs apart from that of poems. Poetry's primary apparition, on the other hand, unlike music's, depends only peripherally on the direct sensory per-ception of its art's elements; its major mode enlists the reader's imagi-native entry into an apparition of lived experience, what Henry James called "felt life": "the appearance of thought and feeling or outward events that [the poet] creates." "The poet's business," Langer main-tains, "is to create the appearance of 'experiences,' the semblance of events lived and felt, and to organize them so they constitute a purely and completely experienced reality, a piece of *virtual life*" (*Feeling* 212). What we think of as poetry's music—the direct sensory appeal of such devices as meter, rhythm, and sound—is in truth a means to serve that imaginative end, not an end in itself.

That poetry can be considered song only in a metaphorical sense—Langer calls such comparisons "deceptive analogies"[11]—becomes clear when we examine the relationship between words and music in songs, for whether we consider song lyrics good poetry or not, they are undeniably poetic texts. Some art forms, she maintains, tend to assimilate, or "swallow," others (*Problems* 85–89). When two forms combine, we tend to experience them as one art or the other, not an equal combination of both. This does not mean that some arts are "better" than others, only that one or the other tends to take precedence in our perception or our imagination (*Feeling* 149ff.). We experience musical comedy, for example, as theater rather than as music or dance, while a film of that same musical tends to feel predominantly like a movie instead of a play. The relationship between poetry and song serves as one of her chief examples:

> Consider, for instance, a good poem successfully set to music. The result is a good song. One would naturally expect the excellence of the song to depend as much on the quality of the poem as on the musical handling. But this is not the case. Schubert has made beautiful songs out of great lyrics by Heine, Shakespeare, and Goethe, and equally beautiful songs out of the commonplace, sometimes maudlin lyrics of Müller. The poetic creation counts only indirectly in a song, in exciting the composer to compose it. After that, the poem as a work of art is broken up. Its words, sound and sense alike, its phrases, its images, all become musical material. In a well-wrought song the text is swallowed, hide and hair. That does not mean that the words do not count, that other words would have done as well; but the words have been musically exploited, they have entered into a new composition, and the poem as a poem has disappeared in the song. (*Problems* 84)

Schubert's setting of Müller's poems in his song cycle *Winterreise*, to which Langer alludes above, inspired comments by the music critic Alex Ross that implicitly demonstrate her point. Ross calls the work "twenty-four numbingly beautiful songs [not poems] on texts by Wilhelm Müller," and quotes musicologist Karol Berger's claim that "Schubert's cycle [not Müller's poetry] is 'our civilization's greatest poem [not musical work] of existential estrangement and isolation.'"[12] Ross's comment that the work consists of "beautiful songs," combined with Berger's metaphorical use of "poem" to describe a musical work, not a literary one, reinforce the impression that with the help of Schubert's genius, Müller's poetry has undergone a significant transformation through its participation in a transcendent work of music. We can also appreciate that great songs do not require great poetry when we realize we love many songs without knowing all their words, or the foreign language in which they are sung.

The assimilation of poetry by music, whether the adaptation of an extant poem into a song or the fitting to a melody of words written expressly for that purpose, provides endless opportunities to examine how poetry becomes something quite different when music swallows it. The special demands of musical settings turn the poem into a song—that is, into music—and the resulting changes remove the text from the sphere of literary experience and turn it into an object of musical interest. This transformation can occur in several ways. In some cases, music can submerge a text, transforming its expressive content through use of a setting that, on its own, expressively contradicts the feelings enacted by the lyrics. Such a strategy can create fruitful ironic tensions between text and music, resulting in a complex expressive form absent from either the music or the lyric on its own. More frequently, music distorts poetry in a variety of ways that remove its rhythms—one of the major bases for literary discussions of poetry's "music"—from the conventional accents of speech. A setting often shifts the metrical emphasis of a text in ways that make it musically expressive but also underscore the artifice of song by exposing the unnaturalness of its manipulation of spoken language. Such common vocal music devices as slurring and melisma compound these expressive distortions, leading to the perception that the music is somehow wringing the words. These very devices that songs use for musical expressiveness intensify our feeling that the poem set to music has lost its literary identity. Musical rhythm and melody, in other words, turn poetry into music—and poems just do not count as music.

Countless examples exist of texts—both poems written as independent literary works and poems written as lyrics, to serve the needs of a musical setting—that have strikingly different effects when read on the page from the way they sound to the ear when transformed by their music. Even a poem so close to song as Yeats's early "Down by the Salley Gardens," when heard in the well-known setting by Benjamin Britten, exhibits several of these distortions that make it expressive as music while depriving it of much of its poetic identity. Yeats maintained, in fact, that he derived the poem indirectly from a musical work, in "an attempt to reconstruct an old song from three lines imperfectly remembered by an old peasant woman in the village of Ballysodare, Sligo."[13] We perceive Yeats's debt to folk song, even the faded memory of a folk song, in the way the poem combines conventionalized love imagery and diction in its hexameter couplets. Its kinship to folk ballads emerges strongly when we consider how Yeats substitutes a strong central caesura for an expected stress, immediately following the unstressed seventh syllable of each line. Those emphatic pauses make us experience the couplets as if they were the fourteeners of traditional ballads, as the first of the poem's two stanzas demonstrates:

Dówn bў | thĕ sál | lĕy gár | dĕns ‖ mў lóve | ănd Í | dĭd méet;
Shĕ pássed | thĕ sál | lĕy gár | dĕns ‖ wĭth lít | tlĕ snów- | whíte féet.
Shĕ bíd | mĕ táke | lóve éas | ў, ‖ ăs thĕ léaves | grów ŏn | thĕ trée;
Bŭt Í, | bĕĭng yóung | ănd fóol | ĭsh, ‖ wĭth hér | wŏuld nót | ăgrée.[14]

Although Yeats introduces a number of minor metrical substitutions, "Down by the Salley Gardens" looks perfectly ripe for a musical setting that would preserve its speech rhythms.

Britten's setting, however, transforms the text from a literary work into a musical element by altering its rhythms from spoken to musical accents, and by employing considerable slurring:[15]

Dów-ŏwn bý thé-ĕ Sál-lé-ĕy Gárdĕns mý-ў lóve á-ănd Í dĭd méet;
Shé-ĕe pássed thé-ĕ Sál-lé-ĕy Gárdĕns wí-ĭth líttlé-lĕ snów-whĭte féet.

Dividing these lines, as sung, into poetic feet would challenge even the most ardent student of prosody; feet have become irrelevant, yielding to musical measure. Britten's shifts of accent in general, as well as the division of syllables created by slurring, have introduced such rhythmic complexity that we can no longer perceive Yeats's caesuras as rhythmic events; the pauses have disappeared, swept along in the music's steady tempo, for as Langer reminds us, "All music creates an order of virtual time, in which its sonorous forms move in relation to each other—always and only to each other, for nothing else exists there" (*Feeling* 109). Nevertheless, the caesuras survive in the melody: we hear them when the pitch rises a fourth from "dens" to "my," creating a psychological break in the line, if not a temporal one. Britten has violently abducted Yeats's poem into his song—yet not only is it a beautiful song, but its method of assimilating its literary text typifies how music swallows poetry.

The major key of Britten's music presents a peculiarly unmelancholy setting for this poem of loss and regret. Yeats's opening line locates the lovers' meeting "Down by the Salley Gardens," and he therefore begins the poem with a falling rhythm by substituting a trochee for the expected iamb. Britten's melody turns this melancholy hint into a rising melody line, which seems to belie the text's initial downward rhythm and meaning but expresses a youthful optimism appropriate for the lovers' engagement. The song's final line, however, repeats this jaunty melody identically, hardly an appropriate mood for a man regretting that "I was young and foolish, and now am full of tears." Nevertheless, Britten's melody, even in its major key, conveys a wistful nostalgia that parallels the poem's long-ago feeling, and perhaps even the rose-colored partial amnesia of Yeats's attempt to recreate the old woman's folk song.

A sizable minority of melodies contradict their texts, and as mentioned above, the disjunction can give composers opportunities for ironic enrichment. In *Orfeo ed Euridice,* Gluck follows the canons of neoclassical musical decorum in giving Orfeo one of his most sweetly optimistic melodies in which to mourn Euridice, "Che farò senza Euridice?" and the tradition of tension between music and text persists in popular music, as evidenced by three examples from the early 1970s. My students invariably listen more intently to Pete Townshend's mount-the-barricades guitar chords in the Who's "Won't Get Fooled Again" than to what the lyrics say, and they therefore miss the song's cynicism about the very kinds of revolutionary change the music sounds as though it endorses. Harry Nilsson's 1972 "You're Breakin' My Heart" never received the airplay it merited because its barrelhouse piano and frolicsome melody support a lyric that proclaims, loudly and cheerily, "You're breakin' my heart, / You're tearin' it apart, / So fuck you." We experience it not as an angry song about an ended affair, but as a rollicking, good-time number. We can attribute to it as a musical work the feelings expressed by the lyrics only by thinking of it as a comic parody of songs about heartbreak, which Nilsson likely intended. And Lou Reed's 1973 album *Berlin* ends with a stirring anthem in a major key, "Sad Song," that builds majestically and inexorably to its chorus, which features the nasty lines, "I'm gonna stop wastin' my time; / Somebody else would have broken both her arms," though Reed's vocal performance on both the original recording and the 2008 concert revival carries, beneath its crowing, hints of both violence and tears.

Poetry, dependent entirely on its text, cannot easily present itself in an ironic "setting," although some poems expressively overturn the expectation of their form. Philip Larkin's "This Be The Verse," in part through its cheery profanity, but chiefly by casting its lines in tetrameter quatrains, gives an air of jauntiness to the despondency of

They fuck you up, your mum and dad.
   They may not mean to, but they do.
They fill you with the faults they had
   And add some extra, just for you.[16]

More subtly, the tetrameters and trimeters of several of Blake's *Songs of Innocence*—another metaphorical application of "song" to literary texts that have, in fact, been set by several modern composers—permit the forms' apparent simplicity to disguise the poems' complex ambiguity. At times, however, even a major poet's inappropriate casting of a poem into a form and meter unsuited for its concerns can severely undercut expressiveness, as in Tennyson's "The Higher Pantheism":

> Speak to Him, thou, for He hears, and Spirit with Spirit can meet—
> Closer is He than breathing, and nearer than hands and feet. . . .
>
> And the ear of man cannot hear, and the eye of man cannot see;
> But if we could see and hear, this Vision—were it not He?[17]

Tennyson's faintly absurd use of triple meters for a purportedly serious philosophical poem results in a work far less memorable than Swinburne's lampoon of it:

> Body and spirit are twins: God only knows which is which:
> The soul squats down in the flesh, like a tinker drunk in a ditch. . . .
>
> God, whom we see not, is: and God, who is not, we see:
> Fiddle, we know, is diddle: and diddle, we take it, is dee.[18]

The shifting of accent in Britten's setting of Yeats, with ordinarily unaccented words like "the" and "my" receiving emphasis, is one way in which music swallows poetry and makes it song, a work of art we experience not through the poetic imagination, but through the sensuous ear. "Extraordinary Machine," a terrific 2005 song by Fiona Apple, illuminates this transformation. Its opening lines read this way as a literary text:

> Ĭ cér | tăinlў háv | ĕn't bĕen shóp | pĭng fŏr án | ў nĕw shóes, | ănd
> Ĭ cér | tăinlў háv | ĕn't bĕen spréad | ĭng mўsélf | ăróund.

The meter resolves itself more or less into regular anapests, which feel even more regular if 1.) we consider that Apple's opening line begins not on the downbeat but after it, and 2.) we consider the terminal "and" in line one as the opening syllable of line two. Apple's melody underscores this conversational rhythm as well, since she sings the first line as triplets, all on a single pitch. But after "shoes," something strange happens. She pauses, and then, as her voice rises to a sixth, she heavily accents "and" as we seldom do in speech:

Ĭ cér | tăinlў háv | ĕn't bĕen shóp | pĭng fŏr án | ў nĕw shóes, ‖ ánd
Ĭ cér | tăinlў háv | ĕn't bĕen spréad | ĭng mўsélf | ăróund.

The shifted accent expressively breaks the line out of its rut, the rise to a new pitch conveying the hope that, beyond the grind of daily life, someone will discover the secret the singer confides to us, that she is an "extraordinary machine." To reproduce that stressed "and" silently on the page, however, demands special notation, which Apple's lyric sheet provides:

I certainly haven't been shopping for any new shoes
-And-
I certainly haven't been spreading myself around

Her musical decision to accent "and" requires extraordinary machinery on the page, like Gerard Manley Hopkins's eccentric use of accent marks and, in the extreme case of "The Windhover," capital letters:

Brute beauty and valour and act, oh, air, pride, plume here
    Buckle! AND the fire that breaks from thee then. . . . [19]

The accentual distortions we accommodate as idiomatic practice in song, with barely a moment's thought, become major expressive events in poems because of the intensity of their disruption of our expectations for speech, as opposed to those for sung language.

These distortions happen constantly in music—they are the ordinary mode of song, although they constitute exceptional events in poetry. In the Young Rascals' 1967 number-one hit "Groovin'," the lyrics' floating feeling of lazing with a lover, expressed in the dactyls

Lífe wŏuld bĕ | écstăsȳ,
Yóu ănd mé | éndlĕsslȳ
Gróovĭn'. . . .

shifts violently from its natural rhythm when the band syncopates
the second line—

Lífe wŏuld bĕ | écstăsý,
Yóu ănd mé | ĕndlésslý
Gróovĭn'. . . .

—leaving listeners, in the days before rock musicians thought to provide printed lyrics, titillated by the apparent ménage à trois of "You
and me and Leslie." But such distortions can create considerable
power as well. Lou Reed has probably committed more violence upon
the natural accents of English than any other popular songwriter, but
the results usually prove expressive. In "Caroline Says," another song
from his angst-ridden 1973 album *Berlin,* the simple anapestic meter
of "Shĕ tréats | mĕ lĭke Í | ăm ă fóol," with the shifting of one stress
and the addition of two others, becomes the angry

Shé tréats | mé || líke | Ĭ ám | á fóol.

And lest we assume that these distortions of accent occur solely in
rock and roll, in *West Side Story,* Stephen Sondheim's simple line
"Thĕre's ă pláce fŏr ús" becomes transformed by Leonard Bernstein's
stately, emphatic melody into

Thére's á pláce fŏr ús

with almost every syllable making its case.

Sometimes the way accents shift when words become song produces the odd phenomenon of greater metrical regularity, rather than
greater expressive freedom, a seeming contradiction of the idea that
melody can liberate formal poetry from its rhythmic chains.

In "Paint It, Black," the Rolling Stones' torturing of "Ĭ cŏuld | nót fŏre | sée thĭs | thíng háp | pĕnĭng | tŏ yóu" into

Ĭ cóuld | nŏt fóre | sĕe thís | thĭng háp | pĕníng | tŏ yóu-ŏu

might result from the unaccustomed insistence of the song's driving sitar-and-tabla rhythm—it was the band's first recording with Indian instruments. Curiously, though, the song forces the line into the iambic meter in which they all would have been drilled as English schoolboys. Such wrenching of lyrics from their pronunciation as natural speech back *into* stilted iambics in order to accommodate melody and musical rhythm creates a truly eccentric surprise in the 1967 musical *Hair,* a show usually associated with breaking rules and violating taboos concerning what the stage could present. For "What a Piece of Work Is Man," Galt MacDermot sets Hamlet's act 2 speech to Rosencrantz and Guildenstern in such a way that it resolves largely into iambics:

Whát | ă píece | ŏf wórk | ĭs mán,
Hów | nŏblé | ĭn réasón,
Hŏw ín | fíníte | ĭn fác |ŭltíes,
Ĭn fórm | ănd mó | vĭng hów | ĕxpréss | ănd ád | mĭráblé,
Ĭn ác | tĭon hów | lĭ-íke | ăn án | gĕl-él,
Ĭn áp | prĕhén | sĭŏn hów | lĭ-íke | ă gó- | ŏ-ód,
Thĕ beaú | tў óf | thĕ wórld,
Thĕ pár | ăgón | ŏf án | ĭmáls.

The regular, pulsing rhythm seems especially peculiar here because Shakespeare has Hamlet meditate on Renaissance humanism not in blank verse, but in emotionally soaring, rhythmically varied prose. In order to cast it into iambics—possibly because of Americans' own school associations of Shakespeare with iambic pentameter—Mac-Dermot has taken liberties with both the text (Hamlet actually says, "What a piece of work is a man," and "How infinite in faculty") and English pronunciation, bizarrely making "noble" iambic, for example, and using slurring more extensively than the Stones, so the singers transform "like" into an iamb and "a god" into a pair of iambs. We experience the language not as gorgeous prose, not as a heightened expression of Hamlet's paradoxical vision of humanity as angelic one minute, depraved the next, but as a metronomic swallowing of his meditation by MacDermot's charming but mechanical setting.

Slurring, which we have just noticed in the Stones and in *Hair*, is another musical device that, especially in its frequent combination with shifted accents, emphasizes how poems do not count as songs. We can see both strategies operating in one of the Beatles' greatest recordings, "Tomorrow Never Knows," whose first and third lines on the page scan as nearly orthodox iambic pentameters:

> Tŭrn óff | yŏur mínd, | rĕláx, | ănd flóat | dŏwnstréam.
> Ĭt ĭs nót | dýĭng; || ĭt ĭs nót | dýĭng.
> Lăy dówn | áll thóught, | sŭrrén | dĕr tŏ | thĕ vóid.
> Ĭt ĭs | shínĭng; || ĭt ĭs | shínĭng.

The lines follow a generally rising iambic or anapestic pattern, abruptly reversed by a falling trochee at the end of each *b* line. But in John Lennon's singing, accents accumulate, contributing to the trancelike quality created by the dense electronic musical setting and driven by one of Ringo Starr's most hypnotic drum figures:

> Túrn óff | yóur mínd, | rĕláx, | ănd flóat | dównstréam.
> Ít ís | nót dý- | ĕe-íng; || ít ís | nót dý- | ĕe-íng.
> Láy dówn | áll thóught, |sŭrrén | dér tó | thĕ vóid.
> Ít ís | shí-ĕe-níng; | ít ís | shí-ĕe-níng.

Almost all the iambs become spondees, as Lennon's words, assimilated into the song and absorbed into its layered texture through an electronic experiment that, later in the piece, fed his vocal through a revolving organ speaker, become an unearthly chant. He magisterially slurs the most crucial two-syllable words, the rhymes "dying" and "shining," into three syllables, two of them stressed, their high-pitched vowels extending the spiritual quest the song enacts.

When such slurring in music extends over several notes, it becomes a device called melisma. Since melisma assigns several pitches to a single syllable of text, it stretches words out musically to such an extent that the poetry becomes nearly unrecognizable and a linguistic utterance becomes a sheer musical event. A quick example, again from the Beatles, comes this time from their early recording of Arthur Alexander's rhythm-and-blues song "Anna." The bridge, the recording's remarkable expressive highlight, has a lyric that alternates a basic iambic pattern in the middle lines with expressive anapestic and dactylic variations before and after:

> Áll ŏf mў | lífe Ĭ bĕen | séarchĭn' fŏr | ă gírl
> Tŏ lóve | mĕ lĭke Í | lŏve yóu.
> Ŏh nów, | bŭt év | 'rў gírl | Ĭ've év | ĕr hád
> Bréaks | mў héart | ănd léave | mĕ sád.
> Whăt ăm Í, | whăt ăm Í | sŭppósed | tŏ dó?
> Óh. . . .

But John Lennon's extraordinary vocal performance, which owes much to rhythm-and-blues style but doesn't steal significantly from Alexander's original, stretches the lyrics through his use of melisma, which, in his reedy baritone, expresses the shredding ache of unrequited sexual desire:

> Áll ŏf mў lífe || Í bĕen séarchĭn' || fór ă gír-ír-ír-ír-írl
> Tŏ lóve mĕ-ée || líke Í-Í || lóve yóu-óu-ŏu-óu.
> Óh nów-ów-ŏw-ów-ów, || bŭt év'rў gírl Í've évĕr hád
> Bréaks mў héart ănd léave mé-ĕe sád.
> Whát ăm Í, || whát ăm Í || sŭppó-ŏ-ósed tŏ dó?
> Óh-óh-óh-óh-óh-óh. . . .

Once again, I have abandoned the attempt to divide the text as Lennon sings it into feet, but I have introduced caesuras to give some sense of the rhythmic effects of his phrasing. His stylistic choices, coupled with the plaintive melody, result in distortions of the lyric that look absurd on the page. There is no logical reason for the slurring of the word "me" into two syllables stressed first as "mĕ-ée" and then as "mé-ĕe," but there is every expressive reason for it. The melismas on "girl," "you," "now," "supposed," and "oh" intensify the song's yearning while simultaneously removing these words from the realm of poetry and assimilating them into the song. They cease being denotative instances of imaginative language, transformed instead into immediately sensuous musical events.

Through this role in helping transform poetry into song, melisma makes possible equally voluptuous expressive effects in so-called serious music. In Handel's *Messiah*, for example, in the glorious chorus "For unto us a child is born," each of the sections in turn—soprano, bass, tenor, and alto (together with the sopranos)—sings a melisma on "born" that lasts fifty-seven notes, fifty-six sixteenths and a final quarter note. The word becomes unrecognizable because the language, even the marvelous English of the King James Version, loses its imaginative appeal as poetry, seducing us instead as pure sound. Yet listening, we experience the continuous motion and invention of this pure sound as embodying the joy expressed in the words. As with Lennon's yearning in "Anna," the singing provides an immediate sensory presentation of what the words mean, even though anyone not knowing the text, from Isaiah, must guess at what the chorus is actually singing. The music and the poetry clearly are not identical—the poetry has turned into song—but it becomes a matter of subjective opinion as to which of the two stands as a metaphor for the other.

Melisma, slurring, shifting of accent to accommodate melody and musical rhythm—these devices partly describe what happens when poems become songs. The texts' language ceases to behave as poetry, letting go of denotative meaning, which recedes in importance or, in some cases, evaporates entirely. As their sounds become music, the music swallows them and we hear them as song, not literature. In that light, the pronouncements on poetry and music quoted at the start of this essay bear closer examination. We continually use poetry and music as metaphors for each other, but any identity between them remains imaginary or hopefully willed. Poetry may, as all arts, "[aspire] *towards the condition of music,*" as Pater maintained, but this consummation, however devoutly wished, can never bear fruit: the two arts will never be identical because identity is not in their nature; we do not experience the two in the same way. Pound may be correct that "poetry begins to atrophy when it gets too far from music," but the distance he points out between the two arts—far but not "too far"—is just as necessary to our understanding of each as their nearness. And perhaps we have misread Eliot's labeling of the problems of writing poetry as "those of a quasi musical nature"; we have long assumed his statement essentially equates poetry with song, but we should pay more attention to that telling qualifier, "quasi." It warns us that we have wandered into misleading metaphorical comparisons that, like all metaphors, assert identities more imaginative than genuine.

# Heard and
# Unheard Melodies (1990)

Where do poems exist? "A poem," says Jon Stallworthy in his *Norton Anthology of Poetry* "Versification" essay, "is a composition written for performance by the human voice. What your eye sees on the page is the composer's verbal score, waiting for your voice to bring it alive as you read it aloud or hear it in your mind's ear."[1] Stallworthy pushes this analogy between musical notation and the printed text of a poem, quoting T. S. Eliot's famous remark that a poet's concerns "are more those of a quasi musical nature . . . than of a conscious exposition of ideas,"[2] but much as the parallel might alert Poetry 101 students to the importance of poems' sound and rhythm for their felt life, it oversimplifies the issue. The primary experience of music is always aural: that we can learn to read a score and thereby imagine hearing a work does not alter the fact that for the great majority of us, musical experience demands live or recorded performance directed to the ear. Music does not exist for our sensuous understanding until we hear it; only then does it acquire what Susanne K. Langer called its primary illusion of virtual time, the mode by which it creates feeling.[3] Stallworthy is right that we *do* hear poems in our head as we read them, but in a literate culture we apprehend them primarily *by* reading, all the while listening imaginatively—far more alertly than we listen to prose—in order to fine tune the experience. Literacy gets us the news from poems right off the page, and while the printed text cues us to the role of sound, rhythm, and suspense in the voice, it also transmits those qualities directly to the reader, with no need of a performance medium. Tell me, where are poems said? Both in the mouth *and* in the head.

That reading essentially defines our experience of poetry also separates it from drama, another art form where a "score" requires performance to fulfill the artist's intentions. The play on the page, even Shakespeare's page, appears a nonwalking shadow of the humanly embodied work, whether the ideal *Lear* in our minds or the imperfect one before us onstage. Hearing a poem read aloud, especially by its author, can teach us something essential about it, but it doesn't have to. Having grown up in New York City, I recall my amazement on first hearing Eliot's recording of *The Waste Land* and realizing that "cruellest" is not a two- but a *three*-syllable word, thereby learning, of course, that the poem does *not* open with three trochees. But much as I love the sound of Pound's bardic brogue or Wallace Stevens's ponderous sonorities, I would go mad if those voices played in my head whenever I read their work; to a considerable extent, their unheard melodies are sweeter.

Rhino/Word Beat's new boxed set, *In Their Own Voices: A Century of Recorded Poetry,* a handsomely produced, four-hour audio collection of 121 poems by eighty poets, implicitly raises this issue of reading versus listening, and it's gratifying to have the poets' voices in our heads as they read their work, whether their renditions produce fresh revelations or not.[4] When the revelations come, they bring news of how an individual poem operates on us, or about the obsessions and idiosyncrasies of particular poets. For example, the anthology includes Sections I–V of *Hugh Selwyn Mauberley* (alas, only I–V—not the album's only problematic excerpting decision), where Pound's quirky brogue-and-twang prolongs the stresses so strangely alongside the other poets' reading styles as to suggest that his scheme for great literature in English required its transformation into a quantitative language, a perverse attempt to rival the classical tongues as a kind of Nouveau Greek. On the level of the individual poem, it delights me to hear such feats as James Wright's audible communication of an enjambment at the end of "A Blessing." By pausing for nearly a full second at the final line break—"if I stepped out of my body I would break / Into blossom"—Wright's reading both sums up the fragility and awe at the heart of that wonderful poem and teaches us how it moves on the page.

Other pleasures come from hearing well-known, powerful poems powerfully read: William Carlos Williams's "To Elsie," his Jersey accent calmly keening the lines, "as if the earth under our feet / were / an excrement of some sky"; Stanley Kunitz's beautifully elegiac tones in "King of the River"; Robert Lowell's sudden discovery of vigor and stoic fortitude towards the close of "Skunk Hour," when his skunks "march on their soles up Main Street: / white stripes, moonstruck eyes' red fire"; or Sylvia Plath's lightly English-accented "Daddy" and "Ariel," the former a chilling incantation, the latter directly conveying what defies paraphrase in that poem: the desire to have mind stripped away and burst into sheer energy, angelic and self-destructive. These recordings all startle us into discoveries about the text, even on repeated listening.

On the other hand, some performances, even strong performances, reveal disappointing limitations in the poetry itself: for example, the attractive, longshoremanly gruffness of Roethke's "I Knew a Woman" unfortunately underscores how much that poem reads like secondhand Yeats. Other fine poems get done in by monotonous or chilly reading, so that from Stevens's oceanic basso you would never suspect his "So & So Reclining on Her Couch" is a very funny poem (a smarter choice would have been the better-known "Idea of Order at Key West"). Similarly, Auden's "In Memory of W. B. Yeats" comes across far less expressively than his much later recording of "The Shield of Achilles," a poem not included here; what's worse, the producers give us only part 1 of the Yeats elegy, eliminating the essential "You were silly like us," as well as the beautiful homage of the finale. And Ogden Nash, an odd inclusion in light of how many fine poets the collection has snubbed, reads "Portrait of the Artist as a Prematurely Old Man" so as to convince you he knows next to nothing about poetry, reading aloud, *or* humor—he has no clue how to time his comic rhythms and rhymes. But overheated performance can also corrupt our enjoyment of a good poem, such as Anne Sexton's "The Truth the Dead Know," which possesses far greater delicacy and restraint on the page than her vampiric reading would lead you to believe.

The producers' decisions to include or ignore particular poets and poems raise key canonical and political issues, not least because of the album's ambitious subtitle. *In Their Own Voices* at times seems peculiarly undecided about its own significance. While a promotional sticker on the box hypes it as "The Definitive Collection of Modern Verse! The Greatest Poets of the 20th Century Reading Their Own Work," co-producer Rebekah Presson's enthusiastic but inadequate introductory essay—packaged in an attractive hardcover booklet that contains the program notes, a brief essay by Erica Jong, and a fine one by Al Young—emphasizes that "the twentieth-century American poetry community in all its diversity of style and participation is represented," including many poets of whom she remarks, "whether their work will be celebrated 100 years from now remains to be seen."[5] It is impossible to be at once definitive and exploratory, and as good as most of this collection is, some strange things happen in the attempt, and some great poets get lost in the shuffle—though Eliot's absence, as Presson points out, results from the producers' inability to obtain permission for his work, a pity, since I would love to hear his fine reading of "Prufrock" among this company. (In addition, Gwendolyn Brooks refused to allow her work to appear.)

As Presson's remarks suggest, the anthology has a very American sound to it, right from track 1: Whitman reading four lines of his late, bland six-line poem "America." Presson confesses the Whitman is the only uncertainly documented recording: no original wax cylinder has been found, though evidence exists that Thomas Edison planned to record Walt around 1890. Still, she is probably right that the poem's obscurity makes the recording unlikely to be a later forgery; its recency would support its genuineness as well, since it had just come out in *Sands at Seventy*.[6] Through the whirling scratchiness of the recording, Whitman sounds oddly like a faint cross between his two later Jersey progeny, Williams and Allen Ginsberg, and *In Their Own Voices* cleverly picks up on Walt's "America" by including more cynical modern visions from the later poets, Williams's aforementioned brilliant reading of "To Elsie" ("The pure products of America / go crazy") and Ginsberg's own sardonic "America," delivered in a slightly revised and occasionally improvised version to an enthusiastic audience. The anthology furthers this implicit commentary upon the nature of American identity through its inclusiveness, as evidenced by the fourth disc's smorgasbord of readings by African American, Latino, and Native American poets, which range from extremely fine to extremely dull.

But how differently things might have turned out had the project embraced not only Whitman but Tennyson, whom Edison *did* record in May 1890. In those recordings, according to Tennyson biographer Robert Bernard Martin, "a ghost of his powerful voice emerges from the mechanical scratching, but it is still possible to fall under the hypnotic quality of his reading."[7] The Whitman excerpt is not really an icon but a nifty curiosity, a few abstract lines from a bad poem, but clearly the producers consider it an important symbol. Alternatively, *In Their Own Voices* could profitably have begun with the eighty-year-old Tennyson—ten years Whitman's senior—inviting us into a poetic arboretum with "Come into the garden, Maud," one of the poems he read for Edison. The fruitful garden might have provided a more humanly welcoming metaphor for the whole project than Whitman's patriotic monument, for under the spell of Whitman and democratic inclusiveness, the producers have excluded all British and Irish poets born after Dylan Thomas. This decision absurdly neglects some of the best poets—and readers—of our times, such as Philip Larkin, Ted Hughes, and even Seamus Heaney, whose omission is especially amazing, since the collection proudly displays such other Nobel laureates as Yeats, Joseph Brodsky, and Derek Walcott. Many other overseas transplants might have enriched such a garden in addition to the few who bloom all too briefly here—Yeats, Graves, Auden, Spender, and Thomas.[8]

Yet every poetry lover will also construct a long list of American melodists unheard on *In Their Own Voices*. Just for starters, it's upsetting not to have Berryman, Jarrell, May Swenson, or James Merrill, four superb poets who also read wonderfully. The first of the set's four discs runs just under forty-nine minutes (the other three run well over an hour each), so surely there must have been room to include a couple of the Dream Songs, or Jarrell's "Next Day," or Merrill's "The Broken Home." And it's a mistake to have omitted Elizabeth Bishop: though she read her own work indifferently, the anthology, as noted, includes several subpar performances. Surely her recording of "The Fish" might have landed here, in lieu of some of the more recent poets' bland or superficial pieces that go on endlessly.

The anthology's Americanness also extends to several poets' absorption of American music, and here it triumphs with a series of poems playing with jazz subjects or rhythms. Al Cohn and Zoot Sims's sax solos wonderfully transform Jack Kerouac's "American Haikus," and Amiri Baraka's "Bang Bang Outishly" spotlights his great a capella rendition of Thelonious Monk's "Misterioso" in a poem as "interplanetary" as the Hit Parade it shoots for. Paul Zimmer's "Zimmer Imagines Heaven," Michael Harper's "Dear John, Dear Coltrane," and Al Young's "Lester Leaps In" offer up another three powerful, swinging examples of how jazz has given American poetry a fresh transfusion. Unfortunately, rock-and-roll fares less well, and the electric music performed behind Anne Waldman's "Uh Oh Plutonium," Juan Felipe Herrera's "Logan Heights & the World," and Joy Harjo's "For Anna Mae Pictou Aquash" fails to throw the poems into higher relief; as for rock music that aspires to performance poetry, I'd much rather listen to Laurie Anderson, Lou Reed, or Patti Smith. Canadian folkie poet Leonard Cohen sings "The Story of Isaac," though unlike some of Cohen's other songs, like "Suzanne," its lyric has never been published as a poem.

This issue of poetic musicality—to let us end where we begun—recalls Yeats's famous introduction to one of his BBC broadcasts: "It gave me the devil of a lot of trouble to get into verse the poems I am going to read, and that is why I *will not* read them as if they were prose."[9] A trip through *In Their Own Voices* maps what Yeats would have mourned as the changing performance styles of lyric poets. The self-consciously bardic readings of Yeats, Pound, Dylan Thomas, Edna St. Vincent Millay (whose haughty recitation of "Recuerdo" is delightful until the poem's sappy ending), and others, let us imagine how ancient poets might have woven their enchantment upon an audience. Poets like Tennyson needed to project, without amplification, to audiences numbering in the hundreds, but because of the poetry of our time's increasing illusion of privacy, as well as the psychological difference between reading into a studio tape recorder and reading to a live audience, the vast majority of the poets in the anthology read quietly, with conversational tones instead of declamatory power, striving for a feeling of intimacy rather than prophecy. While most still do not read poems as if they were prose, their voices clearly have become less public and more personal; even performances as differently lovely as Muriel Rukeyser's "The Ballad of Orange and Grape," David Ray's "The Greatest Poem in the World," and Edward Hirsch's "Wild Gratitude" share a feeling of privacy, of confession, of something observed or felt or believed that needs sharing not with the tribe as a whole, but with each of us as a feeling individual, as a friend.

For this reason, in spite of Rebekah Presson's hope that the anthology marks a recovery of oral poetic tradition, it instead reinforces key distinctions between spoken poetry in an oral culture and in a literate one, and especially between live and recorded spoken poetry in our time. "Poetry existed in all parts of the world probably as soon as there was language; certainly long, long before there were books, before there was writing. And, like the works in this collection, the first poems were spoken," Presson writes.[10] But *In Their Own Voices* offers us not oral poems, but literary compositions read aloud, poems quite unlike any from the oral tradition. The collective, shared experience of the spellbound hearers in the meadhalls may resemble the way poetry enraptures those of us who still love it in our technological age, but printed texts and, less often, live reading, not CD technology, remain the media through which we become possessed. Poetry-lover that I am, I can't imagine slapping a CD into the stereo at a party and announcing, "Hey, let's all listen to some Galway Kinnell, Richard Howard, and Adrienne Rich!" a scenario doomed to mortification, rather than the elevation collective listening to poetry can produce.

The technology that enables us to play confessor to today's poets, whose work has evolved steadily towards the personal-sounding, and who have built the illusion of confidentiality into their reading styles, can let us imagine that the poet has become the poetry. With our experience limited to nothing but voice and audible text, the flesh-and-blood human being comes alive as words in the air, making the poet one with the work. Yet oddly, perhaps paradoxically, the confessional intimacy of these contemporary ghosts in the machine makes listening to *In Their Own Voices* an often splendid but essentially private experience—like reading.

# Notes

### Becoming Poetry: An Introduction

1. William Shakespeare, Sonnet 144, in *The Norton Shakespeare,* gen. ed. Stephen Greenblatt (New York: W. W. Norton, 1997), 1972.

2. *The Poems of Emily Dickinson,* ed. R. W. Franklin, 3 vols. (Cambridge, MA: Harvard University Press, 1998), Fr425.

3. For a detailed elaboration of these ideas, see Susanne K. Langer, *Feeling and Form: A Theory of Art* (New York: Charles Scribner's Sons, 1953), 208–35.

4. *The Letters of Emily Dickinson,* ed. Thomas H. Johnson and Theodora Ward, 3 vols. (Cambridge, MA: Harvard University Press, 1986), L268. I thank Patrick Keane for drawing my attention to this letter.

5. Allen Ginsberg, *Howl: Original Draft Facsimile, Transcript, and Variant Versions,* ed. Barry Miles (New York: Harper and Row, 1986), 12, 44.

6. Shakespeare, Sonnet 130, in *The Norton Shakespeare,* 1967.

7. John Keats, *The Complete Poems,* 3rd ed., ed. John Barnard (London: Penguin Books, 1988), 344–46.

8. Stephen Booth, "On the Value of *Hamlet,*" in *Bloom's Shakespeare through the Ages:* Hamlet, ed. Brett Foster, with an introduction by Harold Bloom (New York: Infobase Publishing, 2008), 328.

### Certain Slants: Learning from Dickinson's Oblique Precision

This 2008 essay, written for a special issue of the *Emily Dickinson Journal* on Dickinson and contemporary poetry, considers her poetic practice alongside my own. Quotations from *The Poems of Emily Dickinson,* ed. R. W. Franklin, 3 vols. (Cambridge, MA: Harvard University Press, 1998) are cited internally by poem number as assigned by Franklin.

1. *The Letters of Emily Dickinson,* ed. Thomas H. Johnson and Theodora Ward, 3 vols. (Cambridge: Harvard University Press, 1986), L342a.

2. Jay Rogoff, *Venera* (Baton Rouge: Louisiana State University Press, 2014), 48.

3. Jay Rogoff, *The Long Fault* (Baton Rouge: Louisiana State University Press, 2008), 3. Subsequent quotations cited internally by page number.

4. Randall Jarrell, *The Complete Poems* (New York: Farrar Straus and Giroux, 1969), 313.

## Adding Feathers to the Learned's Wing

This 1999 essay examines Shakespeare's Sonnets through the lens of Helen Vendler's study *The Art of Shakespeare's Sonnets.*

1. Surrey also seems to have invented blank verse for his translations of sections of the *Aeneid,* suggesting that poetry's great innovators are not necessarily its greatest practitioners.

2. Helen Vendler, *The Art of Shakespeare's Sonnets* (Cambridge, MA, and London: Harvard University Press, 1997), 25. Subsequent quotations cited internally by page number.

3. John Keats, *Complete Poems,* 3rd ed., ed. John Banville (London and New York: Penguin, 1988), 221.

4. The Acting Company. *Love's Fire: Seven New Plays Inspired by Seven Shakespearean Sonnets* (New York: Morrow, 1998), 99–100.

5. *Shakespeare's Sonnets,* ed. Stephen Booth (New Haven and London: Yale University Press, 1977, rev. 1978).

6. William Shakespeare, *A Midsummer Night's Dream,* in *The Norton Shakespeare,* gen. ed. Stephen Greenblatt (New York: Norton, 1997), 4. 1. 189–90. Subsequent quotations from the plays cited internally by act, scene, and line number.

## The Aesthetics of Contemporary Sonnet Sequences: The Examples of Salter and Muldoon

This article, first presented at a conference session on the sonnet at the Association of Literary Scholars, Critics, and Writers, appeared in 2010 in a special issue of *Literary Imagination* dedicated to that poetic form.

1. M. L. Rosenthal and Sally M. Gall, *The Modern Poetic Sequence: The Genius of Modern Poetry* (New York and Oxford: Oxford University Press, 1983), 9. Subsequent quotations cited internally by page number.

2. In addition to criticizing sonnets' "undifferentiated form"—though Emily Dickinson's devotion to the ballad stanza does not hamper their insightful investigation

of her fascicles—Rosenthal and Gall lament the "pointless gaps in development" of Shakespeare's sequence, "its more boring poems, and its general unevenness," as well as how "Shakespeare often throws away the endings" (19), all problems that largely evaporate under the laser-like intensity scholars like Stephen Booth and Helen Vendler have trained on them.

3. Mary Jo Salter, *Open Shutters* (New York: Knopf, 2003); Paul Muldoon, *Horse Latitudes* (New York: Farrar, Straus and Giroux, 2006). In quotations from both poets, the letter-markings at the line endings indicate my understanding of a given sonnet's rhyme scheme. Salter, especially, frequently uses slant-rhyme, as do many twenty-first-century formalists, for reasons discussed above. Quotations from both poets cited internally by page number.

4. George Herbert, "Love (III)," in *The English Poems of George Herbert*, ed. C. A. Patrides (London: J. M. Dent and Sons, 1974), 192; Sir Philip Sidney, *Astrophil and Stella* 1, in *The Major Works, including* Astrophil and Stella, ed. Katherine Duncan-Jones (Oxford: Oxford University Press, 2008), 153.

5. Sidney, *Astrophil and Stella* 1, in *The Major Works*, 153.

6. William Shakespeare, Sonnet 18, in *The Norton Shakespeare,* gen. ed. Stephen Greenblatt (New York: Norton, 1997), 1929.

7. Quoted by James Fenton, "A Poke in the Eye with a Poem," *Guardian* 20 October 2006, http://www.guardian.co.uk/books/2006/oct/21/featuresreviews.guardian review6. Accessed 28 September 2009.

8. John Hauer, *The Natural Superiority of Mules* (Guilford, CT: Lyons Press, 2005), 26.

## Pound-Foolishness in Paterson

First presented at the Ezra Pound Centennial Conference at Hamilton College, this 1987 article explores how William Carlos Williams used his economic, political, and poetic agon with his friend Pound as a tonal and structural element in his long poem *Paterson.*

1. M. L. Rosenthal and Sally M. Gall, *The Modern Poetic Sequence: The Genius of Modern Poetry* (New York and Oxford: Oxford University Press, 1983), 236, 248.

2. Michael André Bernstein, *The Tale of the Tribe: Ezra Pound and the Modern Verse Epic* (Princeton, NJ: Princeton University Press, 1980), 194; Joel Conarroe, *William Carlos Williams'* Paterson*: Language and Landscape* (Philadelphia: University of Pennsylvania Press, 1970), 18; and Paul Mariani, *William Carlos Williams: A New World Naked* (New York: McGraw-Hill, 1981), 712–14.

3. William Carlos Williams, *Paterson,* rev. ed., ed. Christopher MacGowan (New York: New Directions, 1992), 138. Subsequent quotations cited internally by page number.

4. Walter Scott Peterson, *An Approach to* Paterson (New Haven, CT: Yale University Press, 1967), 171–72.

5. William Carlos Williams, *Autobiography* (New York: New Directions, 1951), 385.

6. Anne Janowitz, "*Paterson:* An American Contraption," in Carroll F. Terrell, ed., *William Carlos Williams: Man and Poet,* The Man and Poetry Series (Orono, ME: National Poetry Foundation, 1983), 305–6; see also Benjamin Sankey, *A Companion to William Carlos Williams'* Paterson (Berkeley: University of California Press, 1971), 158.

7. Roy Harvey Pearce, *The Continuity of American Poetry* (Princeton, NJ: Princeton University Press, 1961), 128. See also Conarroe, *William Carlos Williams'* Paterson, 127, and Sankey, *A Companion to William Carlos Williams'* Paterson, 192.

8. Randall Jarrell, "Three Books," in *Poetry and the Age* (1953, rpt. New York: Farrar Straus and Giroux, 1972), 262–63.

9. Paul Mariani, *William Carlos Williams: A New World Naked,* 620–21.

10. I mean "monetarism" in the now-archaic sense of a system that severely limits credit because its currency is based strictly on specie and therefore becomes a commodity in itself.

11. John Berryman, "From the Middle and Senior Generations," in *The Freedom of the Poet,* ed. Robert Giroux (New York: Farrar, Straus and Giroux, 1976), 314.

12. Perhaps composed in 1876, in Dublin, by William Percy French, and collected, for example, in James J. Fuld, *The Book of World-Famous Music: Classical, Popular, and Folk,* 3rd ed. (New York: Crown Publishers, 1967), 73.

13. Wendy Stallard Flory, "The Pound Problem," in *Ezra Pound and William Carlos Williams: The University of Pennsylvania Conference Papers,* ed. Daniel Hoffman (Philadelphia: University of Pennsylvania Press, 1983), 116–19.

14. John Addington Symonds, "Peer of gods he seemeth to me," 1883, in Henry Thornton Wharton, *Sappho: Memoir, Text, Selected Renderings, and a Literal Translation,* 5th ed. (London: John Lane, the Bodley Head, 1908), 69.

## *Andrew Hudgins's Blasphemous Imagination*

This 1998 article closely examines three of Hudgins's ekphrastic poems, each inspired by a Renaissance painting and each confronting the challenges of religious faith with the poet's characteristic wit.

1. Randall Jarrell, *The Complete Poems* (London and Boston: Faber and Faber, 1969), 332.

2. Poems from Andrew Hudgins, *The Never-Ending* (Boston: Houghton Mifflin, 1991), cited internally by page number.

3. Leo Steinberg, *The Sexuality of Christ in Renaissance Art and in Modern Oblivion,* 2nd ed. (Chicago: University of Chicago Press, 1996), 81–90.

4. Stephen Dobyns, *Cemetery Nights* (New York: Penguin, 1987), 47, 54.

5. Frank O'Hara, "Poem" ("Lana Turner has collapsed!"), in *Selected Poems,* ed. Mark Ford (New York: Knopf, 2009), 234.

6. Andrew Hudgins, *The Glass Hammer: A Southern Childhood* (Boston: Houghton Mifflin, 1994), 3. Subsequent quotations cited internally by page number.

7. Andrew Hudgins, "The Humor Institute," *Shenandoah* 46, no. 2 (1996): 62. A significantly revised version appears in *A Clown at Midnight* (Boston: Houghton Mifflin / Mariner, 2013), 49.

## On Writing the Sonnet Sequence Danses Macabres: An Interview with Stefanie Silva

This interview marked the occasion of my receiving the Robert Watson Poetry Prize, which included publication by Spring Garden Press of my 2010 chapbook *Twenty Danses Macabres.* The chapbook consisted of a selection from *Danses Macabres,* a sequence of thirty-four sonnets that subsequently appeared in *The Art of Gravity* (Baton Rouge: Louisiana State University Press, 2011).

1. *Ballet Review* ended publication in 2020. I continued as *Hopkins Review*'s dance critic through the end of 2021.

2. Baton Rouge: Louisiana State University Press, 2008.

## Credentials

This 2000 discussion of Rachel Hadas's *Halfway Down the Hall: New and Selected Poems* (Hanover, NH, and London: Wesleyan University Press/University Press of New England, 1998); Eamon Grennan's *Relations: New and Selected Poems* (Saint Paul: Graywolf Press, 1998); and Karl Shapiro's *The Wild Card: Selected Poems, Early and Late,* ed. Stanley Kunitz and David Ignatow, introduction by M. L. Rosenthal (Urbana and Chicago: University of Illinois Press, 1998) was one of my first considerations of the use and significance of books of New and Selected Poems. All quotations cited internally by page number.

1. William Carlos Williams, *Selected Essays* (New York: New Directions, 1969), 258–62.

## Archeological Gifts: Thomas, Hafiz, and Henry

First published in 2004, this essay, excerpted from a longer discussion of the new imprint Handsel Books, considers *The Poems of Edward Thomas,* introduction by Peter

Sacks (New York: Handsel Books, 2003); *Hafiz of Shiraz: Thirty Poems, An Introduction to the Sufi Master,* trans. Peter Avery and John Heath-Stubbs (1952; rpt. New York: Handsel Books, 2003); and *Selected Poems of James Henry,* ed. Christopher Ricks (New York: Handsel Books, 2002). Quotations cited internally by page number.

1. An imprint of Other Press, Handsel Books itself appears to have ceased publication by 2012. Some of its titles remain available from Other Press.

2. Rupert Brooke, "The Soldier," in *Collected Poems* (Cambridge, UK: Oleander Press, 2010), 139.

3. Christopher Ricks, *Reviewery* (New York: Handsel Books, 2003), 21.

4. Thomas Hardy, *Complete Poems,* ed. James Gibson (London: Macmillan, 1976), 90–91.

5. *The Poetry of Robert Frost,* ed. Edward Connery Lathem (New York: Holt, Rinehart, and Winston, 1969), 33–34.

6. Dante Gabriel Rossetti, "The Woodspurge," in *The Pre-Raphaelites: An Anthology of Poetry by Dante Gabriel Rossetti and Others,* ed. Jerome H. Buckley (Chicago: Academy Chicago Press, 1986), 67.

### Two Poet's Poets

This 2001 essay discusses Philip Booth's *Lifelines: Selected Poems, 1950–1999* (New York: Viking, 1999) and Jane Cooper's *The Flashboat: Poems Collected and Reclaimed* (New York: W. W. Norton, 2000). All quotations cited internally by page number.

1. *The Bill James Historical Baseball Abstract,* rev. ed. (New York: Villard Books, 1988), 391.

### Shocking, Surprising Snodgrass

This 2006 essay considers W. D. Snodgrass's *Not for Specialists: New and Selected Poems* (Rochester, NY: BOA Editions, 2006). All quotations cited internally by page number.

1. *The Letters of Robert Lowell,* ed. Saskia Hamilton (New York: Farrar, Straus and Giroux, 2005), 299, 301, 321.

2. W. D. Snodgrass, *After Experience* (New York: Harper and Row, 1968), 7.

3. *Randall Jarrell's Letters,* ed. Mary Jarrell (Boston: Houghton Mifflin, 1985), 286.

### A Formal Garden with a Real Poet in It

Excerpted from a longer discussion of several poets published in 2003, this essay examines Daniel Hoffman's *Beyond Silence: Selected Shorter Poems, 1948–2003* (Baton Rouge: Louisiana State University Press, 2003). All quotations cited internally by page number.

## Mary Oliver's Divided Mind

This excerpt from a longer 2005 essay discussing several poets focuses on *Blue Iris* (Boston: Beacon Press, 2004), a selection of Mary Oliver's nature poems written throughout her career. All quotations cited internally by page number.

## New Bottles

This 2011 essay considers Kay Ryan's *The Best of It: New and Selected Poems* (New York: Grove Press, 2010); Robert Dana's *New and Selected Poems 1955 to 2010*, ed. C. L. Knight (Tallahassee: Anhinga Press, 2010); Michael Jennings's *Bone-Songs and Sanctuaries: New and Selected Poems* (Riverdale-on-Hudson, NY: Sheep Meadow Press, 2009); and Edward Hirsch's *The Living Fire: New and Selected Poems* (New York: Knopf, 2010). All quotations cited internally by page number.

1. Elizabeth Bishop, *Poems* (New York: Farrar, Straus and Giroux, 2011), 59, 198.

2. Gerard Manley Hopkins, *A Hopkins Reader,* ed. John Pick (Garden City, NY: Doubleday/Image, 1966), 47.

3. I owe Ryan an apology. Since publishing this article, I have seen an osprey in the Adirondacks carrying a fish in exactly the way the poem describes.

4. *The Norton Shakespeare,* gen. ed. Stephen Greenblatt (New York: W. W. Norton, 1997), 1947.

5. *Poems of Robert Browning,* ed. Donald Smalley (Boston: Houghton Mifflin, 1956), 49–51.

## Better Poetry through Chemistry

This 2007 essay discusses David Wojahn's *Interrogation Palace: New and Selected Poems* (Pittsburgh: University of Pittsburgh Press, 2006). All quotations cited internally by page number.

1. T. S. Eliot, "Tradition and the Individual Talent," in *Selected Essays of T. S. Eliot* (New York: Harcourt, Brace and World, 1964), 7–8. Subsequent quotations cited internally by page number.

2. John Keats, Letter to Richard Woodhouse, 27 October 1818, in *The Complete Poems,* 3rd ed., ed. John Barnard (London: Penguin Books, 1988), 547.

3. Susanne K. Langer, *Problems of Art* (New York: Charles Scribner's Sons, 1957), 25.

4. Samuel Taylor Coleridge, *Selected Poetry and Prose of Coleridge,* ed. Donald A. Stauffer (New York: Random House/Modern Library, 1951), 62–64.

### Why Poetry Doesn't Count as Song

This 2012 essay uses the techniques of prosodic analysis to set out key distinctions between two art forms that have traditionally been confounded.

1. Ezra Pound, *ABC of Reading* (1934, rpt. New York: New Directions, 1987), 14.

2. Ezra Pound, "A Retrospect" (1918), in *Literary Essays of Ezra Pound* (New York: New Directions, 1968), 3.

3. T. S. Eliot, Letter to Cleanth Brooks, 15 March 1937, in *The Letters of T. S. Eliot,* Vol. 8: *1936–1938,* ed. Valerie Eliot and John Haffenden (London: Faber and Faber, 2019), 537.

4. Walter Pater, "The School of Giorgione," in *The Renaissance: Studies in Art and Poetry, the 1873 Text,* ed. Donald L. Hill (Berkeley, Los Angeles, and London: University of California Press, 1980), 106.

5. William Shakespeare, *The Norton Shakespeare,* gen. ed. Stephen Greenblatt (New York: Norton, 1997), 1957–58.

6. Jon Stallworthy, "Versification," in *The Norton Anthology of Poetry,* 5th ed., ed. Margaret Ferguson, Mary Jo Salter, and Jon Stallworthy (New York: Norton, 2005), 2027. The essay has disappeared from the sixth edition (published 2018).

7. Pater, "The School of Giorgione," 107.

8. John Keats, *The Complete Poems,* 3rd ed., ed. John Barnard (London: Penguin Books, 1988), 344–46.

9. *The Collected Poems of William Carlos Williams,* vol. 1, 1909–1939, ed. A. Walton Litz and Christopher MacGowan (New York: New Directions, 1986), 224.

10. Susanne K. Langer, *Feeling and Form: A Theory of Art* (New York: Charles Scribner's Sons, 1953), 113. Subsequent quotations cited internally by page number.

11. Susanne K. Langer, *Problems of Art* (New York: Charles Scribner's Sons, 1957), 75. Subsequent quotations cited internally by page number.

12. Alex Ross, "Nowhere Bound," *New Yorker,* 4 January 2010, https://www.new yorker.com/magazine/2010/01/04/nowhere-bound

13. *The Variorum Edition of the Poems of W. B. Yeats,* ed. Peter Allt and Russell K. Alspach (New York: Macmillan, 1957), 90.

14. *The Poems of W. B. Yeats: A New Edition,* ed. Richard J. Finneran (New York: Macmillan, 1983), 20.

15. I have scanned all sung texts as I hear them in their musical settings, which, as in scanning poetry, entails occasional subjective judgments. Even where readers might disagree with my ear, our perceptions will not differ so significantly as to negate my argument. In fact, several more musical devices beyond accent, slurring, and melisma can contribute to music's swallowing of poetry, including pitch, tempo, duration, and rests. The accented syllable "Gar" in Britten's "The Salley Gardens," for example, falls

on a half-note, so the singer holds it twice as long as any other pitch in the line. Accounting for all these devices would require offering my examples in musical notation as well as scanning them. I have chosen not to do so because 1) my expertise with written scores is rudimentary, and 2) I am interested in how we experience songs through listening and therefore believe my comparisons will help the general reader most if I apply traditional literary scansion techniques to the identical text as we read it and as we hear it sung.

16. Philip Larkin, *Collected Poems,* ed. Anthony Thwaite (New York: Farrar, Straus and Giroux), 180.

17. *Tennyson's Poetry,* ed. Robert W. Hill, Jr. (New York: W. W. Norton, 1971), 282–83.

18. Algernon Charles Swinburne, "The Higher Pantheism in a Nutshell," *Major Poems and Selected Prose,* ed. Jerome J. McGann and Charles L. Sligh (New Haven, CT, and London: Yale University Press, 2004), 203–4.

19. Gerard Manley Hopkins, "The Windhover," in *A Hopkins Reader,* ed. John Pick (Garden City, NY: Doubleday/Image, 1966), 50.


## Heard and Unheard Melodies

This 1998 discussion of *In Their Own Voices,* an audio anthology of poets reading their work, considers the experience of listening to recordings of poems as opposed to that of reading them on the page.

1. Jon Stallworthy, "Versification," in *The Norton Anthology of Poetry,* 5th ed., ed. Margaret Ferguson, Mary Jo Salter, and Jon Stallworthy (New York: W. W. Norton, 2005), 2027. The essay has disappeared from the sixth edition (published 2018).

2. T. S. Eliot, Letter to Cleanth Brooks, 15 March 1937, in *The Letters of T. S. Eliot,* Vol. 8: *1936-1938,* ed. Valerie Eliot and John Haffenden (London: Faber and Faber, 2019), 537.

3. Susanne K. Langer, *Feeling and Form: A Theory of Art* (New York: Charles Scribner's Sons, 1953), 109.

4. *In Their Own Voices: A Century of Recorded Poetry,* prod. Rebekah Presson and David McLees, with essays by Erica Jong, Al Young, and Rebekah Presson, 1996, Rhino/Word Beat, four compact discs.

5. Rebekah Presson, program note essay, *In Their Own Voices: A Century of Recorded Poetry,* 42.

6. For a variety of persuasive reasons, since the release of *In Their Own Voices* something of a consensus has developed, shared by the staff of the Library of Congress, that the Whitman recording is a fake.

7. Robert Bernard Martin, *Tennyson: The Unquiet Heart* (Oxford: Oxford University Press and Faber and Faber, 1991), 573–74.

8. Some of these omissions, and others I discuss, were rectified by the publication of *Poetry Speaks,* ed. Elise Paschen and Rebekah Presson Mosby (Naperville, IL: Sourcebooks MediaFusion, 2001), a book packaged with a three-compact disc anthology of poets ranging from Tennyson to Sylvia Plath. The book contains the texts of the recorded poems, additional work by each poet, and commentary by contemporary poets. The set begins with Tennyson reciting—hypnotically, as Martin says—from "The Bugle Song" ("The splendor falls on castle walls") and "The Charge of the Light Brigade," and Robert Browning from "How They Brought the Good News from Ghent to Aix" (ending with the poet leading his listeners in three cheers), followed by the supposed Whitman recording, whose authenticity Galway Kinnell debates in his commentary.

9. Included on *Poetry Speaks,* disc 1, track 10.

10. Rebekah Presson, program note essay, *In Their Own Voices,* 35.

# Index

poetry and music (*continued*)
vs. poetic rhythm, 192; music
"swallows" poetry, 189–201; rhythmic
distortion, 190–201; slurring, 190,
191–92, 197–98, 200; syncopation,
196; traditionally equated, 185–86;
triplets, 195
Pound, Ezra, 2, 157, 186, 203; *ABC
of Reading*, 185; Canto 45, 59;
*Cantos, The*, 59; in David Wojahn's
"Pentecost," 172–73; economic
ideas, 54–56, 58–61; *Hugh Selwyn
Mauberley*, 203; influence on
*Paterson*, 54–55; letters in *Paterson*,
54–64; on poetry and music, 185, 201;
"Retrospect, A," 185
Presley, Elvis, 174
Presson, Rebekah, 205, 208
Provençal poetry, 137
Pulitzer Prize, 101, 130

Ravel, Maurice, 84
Ray, David: "Greatest Poem in the
World, The," 208
*Rebel Without a Cause* (Ray), 173
Reed, Lou, 173, 207; *Berlin*, 193, 196;
"Caroline Says," 196; "Sad Song," 193
response theory, 30–31
rhyme. *See under* sound in poetry
Rich, Adrienne, 209
Ricks, Christopher: on Edward
Thomas, 106; rediscovery of James
Henry, 112–13, 114, 116; *Reviewery*, 106
Rilke, Rainer Maria, 178
Roethke, Theodore: "I Knew a
Woman," 204
Rogoff, Jay: *Art of Gravity, The*, 85–86;
"Breathless," 84; "Cain's Gift," 14–16;
Christianity in the poetry of, 82;
"Come Away, Death," 86; "Curtain

Call," 79, 86; *Danses Macabres*, 4,
76–86; "Death and the 7-Year Old
Pilot," 80, 84; "Death at Midnight,"
83; "Death Goes to a Party," 81, 83;
"Death in Disguise," 83; "Death in
the Woods," 79, 84; "Death Makes
the Man," 79; "Death's Animation,"
84; "Death's Deal," 82–83, 84; "Death
Sings Lieder," 83; "Death's Love," 78,
79, 84; "Death's Sentence," 80, 84;
"Death the Dietician," 82; "Folding
the Flag," 16–20; "Horoscope,"
84; "Invocation," 86; "La Valse,"
84; "Light, The," 11–13; *Long Fault,
The*, 5, 17, 24, 85; *Loving in Truth*, 5;
"Matter of Death," 86; "Mennonites
by the Sea," 23–25; sonnets of, 76–86;
"Sweet Decorum," 83–84; *Twenty
Danses Macabres*, 85–86; *Venera*, 76
Rolling Stones, The: "Paint It, Black,"
197, 198
Roosevelt, Franklin D., 61
Rosenberg, Isaac, 106
Rosenthal, M. L., 25, 40, 54, 130, 212–13n2
Ross, Alex, 189–90
Rossetti, Dante Gabriel, 27;
"Woodspurge, The," 107
Rukeyser, Muriel, 120–21; "Ballad of
Orange and Grape, The," 208
Ryan, Kay, 151, 152–56, 157, 162, 169;
"After Xeno," 153–54; "Apology,"
155; "Attention," 153; "Bestiary," 155;
*Best of It, The*, 152–56; "Bitter Pill,
152–53; "Blandeur," 154; compared
with Dickinson, 154; compared with
Stevie Smith, 155; compared with
Wendy Cope, 155; "Doubt," 155;
"Felix Crow," 156; *Flamingo Watching*,
152; "Great Thoughts," 155; influence
of Bishop, 154; influence of Hopkins,

Printed in the USA
CPSIA information can be obtained
at www.ICGtesting.com
LVHW052308270124
770066LV00002B/76